GENRE
FUSION

Purdue Studies in Romance Literatures

Editorial Board

Íñigo Sánchez Llama, Series Editor
Brett Bowles
Elena Coda
Paul B. Dixon

Patricia Hart
Gwen Kirkpatrick
Allen G. Wood

Howard Mancing, Consulting Editor
Floyd Merrell, Consulting Editor
Susan Y. Clawson, Production Editor

Associate Editors

French
Jeanette Beer
Paul Benhamou
Willard Bohn
Gerard J. Brault
Thomas Broden
Mary Ann Caws
Glyn P. Norton
Allan H. Pasco
Gerald Prince
Roseann Runte
Ursula Tidd

Italian
Fiora A. Bassanese
Peter Carravetta
Benjamin Lawton
Franco Masciandaro
Anthony Julian Tamburri

Luso-Brazilian
Fred M. Clark
Marta Peixoto
Ricardo da Silveira Lobo Sternberg

Spanish and Spanish American
Maryellen Bieder
Catherine Connor
Ivy A. Corfis
Frederick A. de Armas
Edward Friedman
Charles Ganelin
David T. Gies
Roberto González Echevarría
David K. Herzberger
Emily Hicks
Djelal Kadir
Amy Kaminsky
Lucille Kerr
Howard Mancing
Floyd Merrell
Alberto Moreiras
Randolph D. Pope
Francisco Ruiz Ramón
Elżbieta Skłodowska
Marcia Stephenson
Mario Valdés

 volume 60

GENRE FUSION

A New Approach to
History, Fiction, and Memory
in Contemporary Spain

Sara J. Brenneis

Purdue University Press
West Lafayette, Indiana

Copyright ©2014 by Purdue University. All rights reserved.

∞ The paper used in this book meets the minimum requirements of American National Standard for Information Sciences—Permanence of Paper for Printed Library Materials, ANSI Z39.48-1992.

Printed in the United States of America
Template for interior design by Anita Noble
Template for cover by Heidi Branham
Cover photo: Courtesy of Sara J. Brenneis

Library of Congress Cataloging-in-Publication Data

Brenneis, Sara J.
  Genre fusion : a new approach to history, fiction, and memory in contemporary Spain / Sara J. Brenneis.
    pages cm — (Purdue studies in Romance literatures ; 60)
  Includes bibliographical references and index.
    ISBN 978-1-55753-678-5 (pbk. : alk. paper) — ISBN 978-1-61249-323-7 (epdf) — ISBN 978-1-61249-324-4 (epub) 1. Historical fiction, Spanish—History and criticism. 2. Spanish fiction—20th century—History and criticism. 3. Literature and history—Spain. 4. Collective memory in literature. 5. Spain—Historiography. I. Title.
  PQ6147.H5B84 2014
  863'.08109—dc23   2013030935

Contents

vii **Acknowledgments**

1 **Chapter One**

Introduction: Origins of Genre Fusion in Spain
- 1 Preface
- 4 Postwar, Transition, and Democracy: History and Literature at the Margins
- 9 A Decade of Historical Memory and Literary Studies
- 18 History, Fiction, Narrative, and Genre Fusion
- 22 The Fiction/History Debate beyond Spain
- 32 Divergent Experiences, Converging Genres

39 **Chapter Two**

Montserrat Roig: Testimony of the Marginalized Catalan
- 39 Testimonial Literature in Spain
- 47 Novelist, Journalist, and Obsessive Reality
- 52 *Els catalans als camps nazis*: Individual Testimony to a Collective Nightmare
- 69 *L'hora violeta*: A Fictional Framing of Historiography

87 **Chapter Three**

Carmen Martín Gaite: Rewriting Spain's Memory
- 87 Spanish Society after Franco: Balancing Revisionist History and Collective Memory
- 96 Martín Gaite and the Uses of History
- 102 *El cuarto de atrás:* A Fantastic Interruption of History
- 115 *Usos amorosos de la postguerra española:* Postwar Society Reinterpreted

131 **Chapter Four**

Carlos Blanco Aguinaga: The Spanish Other in Mexico
- 131 Theorizing Exile Identity: Fluid Borders and Genres
- 140 Total mexicanización or refugiados españoles?
- 153 *Carretera de Cuernavaca:* A Generation Adrift

171 **Chapter Five**

Javier Marías: Genre Fusion in the New Millennium
- 171 The Past in the Present in Twenty-first-century Spain
- 178 Editorializing History: Marías as Witness to a Global Spain
- 185 *Tu rostro mañana:* Facing the Past

205 **Afterword**

Contents

209 Notes
219 Works Cited
235 Index

Acknowledgments

I am grateful to the friends, colleagues, and family who have lent their guidance and support to this project and to me personally over the years. *Genre Fusion* began at the University of California, Berkeley, where many members of the faculty and my Spanish Department cohort were helpful during its formative stages. My deep appreciation goes to Emilie Bergmann in particular for her advice and careful readings, and for her welcome suggestion that Carlos Blanco Aguinaga might fit into my genre fusion model. I'm thankful to Michael Iarocci for the conversations about historiography over early drafts that aided in focusing the manuscript. I'm indebted to the organizers and participants of the 2004–2005 History and Fiction Working Group at Berkeley for helping me develop the theoretical underpinnings of this book. While at Berkeley, I received generous research funding for this project from the Department of Spanish and Portuguese, the Graduate Division, and the Program for Cultural Cooperation between Spain's Ministry of Culture and United States Universities. A special thanks as well to Nicole Altamirano and Julia Farmer, my focus group of two, for helping me develop the term *genre fusion*.

While at Amherst College, I have enjoyed the steadfast encouragement of my colleagues in the Spanish Department and the intellectual stimulation of the campus community. The research support I received from the Amherst College Faculty Research Award Program, as funded by The H. Axel Schupf '57 Fund for Intellectual Life, was timely and generous. I extend an appreciative *arigato* to Timothy Van Compernolle for his mentoring and our collegial conversations over the years. Justin Crumbaugh at Mount Holyoke College has given me unflagging encouragement and advice since our first meeting, which has been enormously helpful. Thanks as well to Zalia Rojas for her meticulous editing during the manuscript's final stages. The enthusiastic exchange with friends, colleagues, and students continues to make the Five Colleges a welcome professional home for me.

I would like to thank the anonymous readers of my manuscript at Purdue University Press for their detailed editorial comments and wise suggestions for further reading. I'm appreciative as well to Patricia Hart and Susan Clawson at Purdue Studies in Romance Literatures for their guidance and dedication to this project.

Acknowledgments

My parents, ever my cheering squad, have supported this and every endeavor I have undertaken. I simply could not have done this without them.

And to Eric, for his love, unwavering encouragement, and copyedits, I am grateful and amazed every passing day.

* * *

Portions of Chapter 2 were previously published as "Montserrat Roig and the Thread of Historiography: From *Els catalans als camps nazis* to *L'hora violeta*," in the *Bulletin of Hispanic Studies*, No. 86 (2009): 659–73. I would like to thank the editors of this journal for their permission in allowing me to reprint sections of this article.

Chapter One

Introduction
Origins of Genre Fusion in Spain

> *Instead of writing history, we*
> *are always beating our brains*
> *to discover how history ought to be written.*
> Georg Wilhelm Friedrich Hegel
> *Philosophy of History*

> *Fiction must stick to facts,*
> *and the truer the facts*
> *the better the fiction—so we are told.*
> Virginia Woolf
> *A Room of One's Own*

Preface

Aristotle theorized the relationship between history and fiction in the fourth century BC by writing that although the historian and the poet may use the same narrative tools, their "true difference is that one relates what has happened, the other what may happen" (68). By that token, the Greek philosopher wrote, "poetry tends to express the universal, history the particular" (68). Yet Aristotle foresaw the central issue that would stymie narratologists and historians in the coming centuries: What happens when the poet writes about history? According to Aristotle, he remains a poet, not a historian: "for there is no reason why some events that have actually happened should not conform to the law of the probable and possible, and in virtue of that quality in them he is their poet or maker" (69). The poet can play with history, while implicitly the historian cannot play with poetry.

Aristotle's poet is today's novelist and short story author; his historian is today's historiographer. Nevertheless, Aristotle's central tenet, that "Dramatic Unity can be attained only by the observance of Poetic as distinct from Historic Truth" (46), is no longer an absolute. Authors of contemporary literature are constantly mixing their fiction with history. Meanwhile, present-day historians have taken to telling the stories behind the events, using the fiction writer's toolkit. The truth and imagination contained in fiction and history are not at odds. Still, the products of these acts of genre transgression are as apt to stir up controversy as they are to become best sellers.[1] Clearly, the boundaries Aristotle theorized are outdated, but what has taken their place?

Many scholars have applied themselves to the task of bridging the divide between history and fiction. Theorists use a multifaceted terminology to describe how they straddle these genres. Jonathan Culler imagines a "*non-genre literature*" located in the "interstices of genres" (258; emphasis in the original) that defies the reader's expectations. Tzvetan Todorov identifies a "frontier of two genres [between] the marvelous and the uncanny" (41) where the fantastic is found. Frank Ankersmit sees "a common ground between the novel and the historical text" (34), but a lack of critical awareness of these commonalities and their relationship to truth. Linda Hutcheon calls history and fiction "porous genres" and notices "overlappings of concern and even mutual influences between the two" (106). Alan Robinson devotes a pair of chapters to "The Narrative Turn in History" and "The Historical Turn in Fiction" to underline their convergences when they narrate the past. Hayden White's "metahistory" (*Tropics* 52), "fictions of factual representation" (*Tropics* 121), and "parahistorical representation" (*Figural Realism* 67) all address, in one form or another, fiction's invasion of history. Mario Vargas Llosa removes any ambiguity that what is at stake is the intersection of what is true and what is false when he refers to "la verdad de las mentiras" in his essay on the coexistence of history and fiction (15–33). Of course, these examples are but a small sampling of the forty-year discussion about the two overlapping genres.

Despite the ongoing debates and attempts to question the dichotomy, the separation of history and fiction remains entrenched in contemporary literary scholarship. Examples of the two genres, particularly by a single author, continue to be studied separately, and thus the divide remains intact. What I call "genre fusion" is a new theoretical approach that addresses this critical absence. It is not simply a way to describe the confluence of history and fiction but rather a critical lens for rethinking narrations of the past. Genre fusion promotes the consideration of history and fiction in conjunction, as two sides of the same story, drawing new insight from the juxtaposition of examples from each category. An application of genre fusion requires at least two texts written by one author. While both texts are concerned with the same historical period or moment, one text must be broadly conceived by the reader and author as "historical"; the other as "fictional." Under these parameters, I argue that considering the author's fictional text alongside its historiographic counterpart produces a polyphonic and thorough telling of the past. Moreover, this approach reveals that a single author oftentimes blends the two genres intentionally, producing a self-conscious combination of history and fiction that can only be achieved by an individual author.

Genre fusion recognizes the taxonomy of these two traditional genre categories but works to break down the barrier between them. To be able to approach literature through genre fusion, author and reader make a pact to put aside the distinction between a factual text and an imaginary text in the interest of communicating a story about the past, which is the ultimate goal of both historical fiction and historiography. Each text is read in light of the other, illuminating interpretive possibilities that are only available when the story of history is given prominence over the text's genre classification. Concerns about the accuracy of the historical story are less important than whether the narrative lives up to the reader's standards of truthfulness. Through the genre fusion approach to literature, historical depth is more critical than historical truth.

Genre fusion gives previously unheard experiences and accounts recognition through equalization. Traditionally, history has consisted of a hegemonic interpretation of the past, while fiction captures a more popular account of the everyday. Yet when one looks to fiction for accounts of the past and to history for storytelling, a new dynamic emerges. Seeking a historical voice in works of fiction to complement a narrative voice in works of historiography results in the emergence of previously ignored or marginalized tales of the past. Our understanding of the historical past is thus greatly expanded beyond dominant discourse when genre fusion is applied to paired texts. Together, the story of history and the story behind history produce a more well-rounded representation of the past; in isolation, either one would be incomplete.

Chapter One

In the interest of examining how this new theory functions in practice, I focus on one country as a uniquely appropriate case study for genre fusion. Spain is undergoing a memory renaissance. The country's historical and cultural currents in the last forty years have produced a host of literature trained on the recent past. Many Spanish authors feel unconstrained by professional distinctions, publishing works of historical fiction and historiography in turn. These texts frequently incorporate an autobiographical component that brings personal and collective memory to the forefront of the author's narratives about history. Spain's particular political situation over the course of the twentieth century has resulted in a perceived absence of texts dealing with subordinate populations. As such, the literature from Spain under examination in this study demonstrates the need to invite previously unaccepted experiences of underrepresented groups to form part of an overarching and representational history of the country.

The politics of memory and history have been playing out on a public stage since Spain's transition to democracy. Fiction and historiography published in Spain in the last forty years reflect the country's growing concern over how its past is remembered and recorded. The four Spanish authors whose work I approach through genre fusion—Montserrat Roig, Carmen Martín Gaite, Carlos Blanco Aguinaga, and Javier Marías—are by no means the only Spanish authors to combine fiction and history. Through this group, however, I demonstrate the varied ways the theory of genre fusion can be put into practice to present a multidimensional past. Although these authors publish distinct works of fiction and nonfiction, they blur them with intention. The advantage of using genre fusion to analyze contemporary Spanish letters is that it respects the autonomy of genre while arguing for the more inclusive and fuller representation of history that is evident when historiography and fiction collide.

Postwar, Transition, and Democracy: History and Literature at the Margins

After a short period of democracy under the Second Republic (1931–36), Spain erupted in a three-year Civil War (1936–39). The country was left divided between the Nationalist victors, represented and supported by Spain's traditionalist institutions of the church, the military, and a political oligarchy; and the vanquished Republicans, who had advanced a program of political reform, the secularization of society, and progressive civil rights. Francisco Franco's dictatorship during the postwar years (1939–75) institutionalized the Nationalist aims, erecting strict legislation and social controls designed to regulate virtually every aspect of Spanish life: conservative modes of dress, gender-segregated schools with an ecclesiastic educational curriculum, censored films, severe limits on linguistic and cultural expression in the Basque Country and Catalonia, the enforced dominance of husbands and fathers over wives and daughters, and the illegality of trade unions coupled with the promotion of state-organized political gatherings, to name only a few. Censorship—both official and self-imposed—restricted topics and viewpoints about which authors could write: the war, exile, and social controls could be hinted at but not addressed directly during much of the postwar. For those authors interested in comprehending a full picture of Spain's past, a project of historical reexamination would have to wait.

Franco's death in 1975 ushered in swift cultural, social, and political reforms during the Transition (1975–82),[2] including free elections and the drafting of Spain's current constitution. Despite an attempted military coup in 1981, the transformations brought about by Spain's return to democracy (1982–present) paved the way for a period of modernization unthinkable during the lean and oppressed years of the dictatorship. Post-Franco Spain promulgated equal rights for women, measured autonomy for regional communities, unmitigated freedom of the press, an economic restructuring, and a cultural explosion manifested most strikingly by the uncensored artistic endeavors and unrestrained social interaction known as the *destape*. The country's eventful twentieth-century timeline, coupled with newfound democratic freedoms and a liberty of expression unavailable during the dictatorship, provided ample inspiration and motivation for authors eager to delve into Spain's past. Further integration into a global economy and information age in the last decade of the twentieth century and first decade of the twenty-first has catalyzed the country's interest in historical reexamination.

Franco's invasive programs of political, cultural, and social control curtailed the interests and input of certain populations during the dictatorship. Women, Basques and Catalans, expatriates, and the politically liberal, including those who were counted among the defeated in the Spanish Civil War, were at best consistently ignored and at worst summarily rejected in arenas of public discourse and governmental representation.[3] The dictator's exclusionary agenda extended throughout Spanish culture and society: from the legislative denial of women's civil rights to the removal of regional languages from street signs and newspapers. While Franco was in power, the experiences and perspectives of those on the periphery were largely absent from Spain's official history. The story of Spain told until the period of the Transition was essentially that of the victors of the Spanish Civil War.

Although authors from the margins of society were able to write and publish in dictatorship Spain, the subject matter on which they focused was limited. Representations of the vanquished in public discourse were still strictly controlled by Franco, and authors of fiction tended to write about Spain's second-class citizens obliquely, if at all. Uninhibited by censorship after Franco's death, however, authors portrayed past as well as current personal and collective experiences of the marginalized sectors of Spanish society more faithfully. As a more complete understanding of Spain's modern history began to enter the public consciousness after 1975, so, too, did the plights of women, exiles, political dissidents, and the populations of Spain's regional communities such as Catalonia and the Basque Country.

Teresa Vilarós argues that the novel had a profound effect on this process of inclusion during the Spanish Transition. Literature stepped in to mediate between the outdated notion of Spain as "different," an idea drawn to a certain extent from the dictator's resistance to economic and political modernization, and Spain as "the same," or as assimilating to a new unified European modernity that openly embraces cultural differences. The novel "offered itself as a smooth cultural artifact of mediation: one that could work as an interface between the symbolic and the economic, between the local and the global, between past and present; and, at the end, between the modern and the post-modern" (Vilarós, "The Novel" 253). Vilarós aptly describes the interest many prose authors from marginalized populations took in Spain's recent history, and her observations extend to the novel as a force for reconciliation between historiography and fiction. The dual-genre movement that eventually emerged would find a corollary in the paired forces Vilarós enumerates, demonstrating a point of contact between the historically interested yet postmodern trend in literature during the Transition, and the transformation of Spain in political, economic, and social terms from a ruled land to a self-governed nation. Stories and histories from the marginalized populations of postwar Spanish society are now central to Spain's literature.

* * *

The starting point to understanding how fiction and history combine and in the process recuperate and reimagine historical memory in contemporary Spanish literature begins with the Spanish Civil War. Attempts at historical understanding through narrative interpretation occupied writers the moment the first bomb fell. However, authors who began to blur fiction and history during the Spanish transition to democracy had the benefit of peace, hindsight, political stability, liberty of expression and, above all, an unquenched desire to delve into their own past. For some, assembling the pieces of the puzzle of historical memory revolved around a dual role as historiographer and writer of fiction, tackling this subject through a body of work that can be solved through genre fusion.

Roig, Martín Gaite, Blanco Aguinaga, and Marías achieve a careful balance between the historical and the fictional in published texts categorized as either fiction or nonfiction. In their effort to craft this delicate equilibrium, they illustrate the theory of genre fusion in contemporary Spanish literature. Three published during the Transition, while one demonstrates the way genre fusion has evolved to consider literature released during Spain's historically charged twenty-first century. All four present a marginalized view of history—that is, one that is at odds with the country's official historical record, especially during the dictatorship—and approximate a personal and collective understanding of Spain's past through the converging genres of fiction and history. These four authors anticipated a movement of historical recuperation in Spanish society, and have proven themselves astute observers and recorders of history as their country began removing its official veil of silence.

Roig, Martín Gaite, Blanco Aguinaga, and Marías are not, strictly speaking, marginalized individuals, having attained varying degrees of critical and popular success through their bodies of work. However, there is a difference between the notoriety they have garnered as authors and their social origins. Our conceptualization of what Homi Bhabha terms "racial/cultural/historical otherness" lies in a "range of differences and discriminations that inform the discursive and political practices of racial and cultural hierarchization" (96–97). Although in terms of race, class, and gender these four authors may belong to a dominant power structure, within the Francoist hierarchy they were relegated to the outskirts of society. Each is a member of a marginalized group who held no place in Franco's "official" history of Spain, and who lacked a literary voice with which to remedy this omission during the dictatorship. Roig and Martín Gaite are women, and Roig is also Catalan; Blanco Aguinaga is a Basque exile; and Marías is a member of a family that suffered for its leftist political alliances after the Civil War. They raise the collective voices of women, exiles, Catalans, Basques, and political enemies of Franco in their writing. All are primarily fiction writers who feel compelled to incorporate history, in a variety of forms, into their novels or short stories. After Franco's death, however, Roig, Martín Gaite, and Blanco Aguinaga became historiographers as well, writing nonfiction texts about Spain's recent history as a vibrant, multilayered period that stands in contrast to the monochromatic Spain portrayed during the dictatorship. Marías is of a different generation and has moved entirely beyond the marginalization his family encountered during the dictatorship. Nevertheless, his development as a historically engaged novelist and essayist confronting the ills suffered by the losers of the Civil War provides a contemporary connection to Roig, Martín Gaite, and Blanco Aguinaga.

Thus, elements of these authors' fiction intermingle with elements of their historiography around a common theme: the experiences of those on the margins of Spanish society during the postwar and dictatorship. They, and others like them, forge a new approach to fiction and history, one that blurs the two fields, demonstrating how history influences fiction and how fiction influences history in post-Franco Spain. These authors bring the stories and experiences of previously marginalized Spanish populations to light during a period of social, political, and literary transition through fictional and historiographic texts. Genre fusion reveals that their disparate texts are two halves of the same story. As I will demonstrate, when the literature of an author such as the four in the present study is examined through the lens of genre fusion, the reader of both texts attains a richer comprehension of the lived experience of Spanish history.

A Decade of Historical Memory and Literary Studies

Commonly considered to be a society's examination of its past, historical memory encompasses the attempts to order and understand the threads of a community's history through the recollections of its individual members. As these individual memories are gathered, they form the collective memory of the entire society. Although Maurice Halbwachs differentiated between historical and collective memory in his clarifying posthumous work, *The Collective Memory*, he placed a decided value on the role of experiential history in collective memory. A "living history that perpetuates and renews itself through time and permits the recovery of many old currents that have seemingly disappeared" (64), in Halbwachs's opinion, opposes a monolithic history or historical memory, which focuses on past events and "the most notable facts" (78).

In the atmosphere of post–Civil War Spain, however, collective memory and historical memory have joined forces. In their work on Spain, Paloma Aguilar and Jo Labanyi both argue that in contemporary practice, these two forms of memory are equivalents. Collective memory, according to Aguilar, "consists of the memory that a community possesses of its own history," although individual members of that community will contribute distinct autobiographical memories to the whole (1). Aguilar defines historical memory, meanwhile, as "an abstraction and simplification of the plurality of memories that exists within any given society" (6). "[G]iven that we presuppose the global nature of this memory (social or collective) and its historical content (it is the memory which a community has of its own history)," equating the two provides a way to connect the present to the past in studies of Spanish memory (Aguilar 6). Labanyi concurs, calling collective memory "a bridge providing a continuum between personal memories and what happened in the past" ("Politics of Memory" 121). Both Aguilar and Labanyi agree that Spain's prolonged contemporary introspection has become a model illustrating Halbwachs's observation that "memory truly rests not on learned history but on lived history" (Halbwachs 57). In Spain, memory looks back at the past without forgetting the present moment.

In the last decade, concrete evidence of the popular interest in historical memory has proliferated in Spain. A glance through one Sunday edition of the widely read Spanish daily newspaper *El País* at the end of the first decade of the twenty-first century illustrates the extent to which the country is still publicly grappling with its memories of the Spanish Civil War and postwar dictatorship some seventy years later. Four separate articles from a July 2008 edition of *El País* illustrate the country's ongoing negotiations with a historical past that does not seem as distant as it first appears. In an interview, Carme Chacón, Spain's then–Minister of Defense, describes how the Defense Department is complying with the Spanish government's Law of Historical Memory, passed in 2007 to oversee the country's tangible interactions with its recent history. By first reviewing and cataloging monuments and plaques, the Department then decides which cultural markers are considered Francoist propaganda and should be removed, and which should remain in place because they are considered architecturally or artistically valuable. Chacón pointedly emphasizes, moreover, that "la ley nos obliga a todos" to comply, including the Defense Department, which was where General Francisco Franco began his long military and political reign and the unrest that propagated the Civil War originated (González 17).

In another section of the paper, a book review recounts the existence of Canadians, virtually unknown relative to their American counterparts, who fought in the Spanish Civil War under their own International Brigade. The Canadian journalist Michael Petrou discovered a trove of declassified archives in the Soviet Union that allowed him to examine the role of Canadians in the war (Fanjul 20). An excerpt of Evelyn Mesquida's memoirs published elsewhere in the paper remembers Spaniards who fought with the French in World War II. Having only just fled Spain after fighting in the Civil War, many weary Spanish soldiers joined the armed forces to escape the miserable conditions of the French internment camps. Their stories continue to emerge.

Finally, Javier Marías's column in the paper's weekly magazine, *El País Semanal*, takes as its inspiration the American television series "Mad Men," set in the 1960s. Marías contemplates the Spain of that era, recalling the unglamorous and unappreciated

Introduction

work of mothers and homemakers subjugated under the Franco dictatorship. These women were so removed from the outside world that once their children grew up they were trapped in a domestic cultural and social isolation. Marías's hope is that no woman today would choose such marginalization ("Siglos de desperdicio"). These articles revisit the country's history from the Civil War, through World War II, to the Franco dictatorship. One edition of *El País*, like much of Spain's conversations about its past, contextualizes history with the benefit of hindsight, exposing a contemporary interest in rethinking the past from the vantage point of an informed present.

But Spain's attention to its historical memory has not been confined to the pages of the Spanish press: it is a trend that has been gaining momentum since the end of the twentieth century. After decades of imposed restraint, when the government curbed public and private discussions of the figures and events that constituted Spain's polemic past, the silence has lifted. A rapid succession of defining moments in the recovery of Spain's historical memory at the turn of the century began to bring the previous seventy years into focus. The Socialist government's enaction of the Law of Historical Memory in 2007 officially regulated the ways Spain would interact with the scars and reminders of its Civil War and postwar dictatorship.[4] During the same decade, authors, filmmakers, photographers, and artists have contributed their own products of cultural memory, forming an integral and visible part of the historical memory movement.

As the relatives of Federico García Lorca—who was shot weeks after the Civil War began in 1936—considered whether to exhume the iconoclastic poet from his mass grave outside of Granada, Miguel Hermoso's film *La luz prodigiosa* (2003) imagined what would have happened had Lorca survived his execution and come to live in Granada in the 1980s. As the Law of Historical Memory ordered the removal of statues of Franco and street signs honoring Falangist luminaries, Francesc Torres presented a video and photography exposition in New York entitled *Dark Is the Room Where We Sleep*. The exhibit contained vivid images of wartime and postwar conflicts in Spain, including a moving photograph of a skeletal hand still adorned with a wedding ring, found during the exhumation of the Villamayor de los Montes mass grave of victims of the Civil War. While in 1999 the Grupo de Estudios

Chapter One

del Exilio Literario organized over a dozen academic conferences commemorating the sixtieth anniversary of the mass 1939 exile of thousands of Spaniards at the end of the Civil War, Pedro Carvajal's documentary *Exilio* (2002) tracked down Spaniards now living in Belgium, England, and the former Soviet Union who were displaced by the war as children. As adults, they all display raw emotions on screen as they consider the conflict of identity that has kept them in limbo between their adopted nationality and their Spanish homeland. And while in 2008 the Spanish national courts agreed to hear complaints of genocide and human rights violations against Nazi guards in concentration camps where Spaniards were imprisoned and killed during World War II (Yoldi 12), the Catalan author Joanna María Melenchón i Xamena published *Mauthausen des de l'oblit*, a fictionalized account of a woman investigating her uncle's imprisonment in a Nazi camp. These events, publications, images, and collective movements only scratch the surface of a decade-long public display of Spain's historical memory. Taken as a whole, these examples—and countless others like them—have transformed the first decade of the twenty-first century in Spain into a collective reflection on the historical significance of the previous seven decades.

The dialogue over if, why, and how to return to memories of Spain's past has raged both inside and outside the country's borders. Even the terminology itself enters into the debate. Figuring into the name of the Asociación para la Recuperación de la Memoria Histórica,[5] a decidedly anti-Francoist organization, as well as into partisan disagreements over the legal and cultural treatment of the country's past, *recuperate* and *recovery* are loaded words in contemporary Spain. Labanyi argues that the term *recovered* positions memory as a "slice of the past waiting hidden," instead of the conscientious action of examining the past from a present vantage point ("Testimonies of Repression" 196). Meanwhile, Ofelia Ferrán expresses a similar opinion that memory is not simply being "recovered" in Spain, but "produced within competing discourses in the present" (44). In essence, however, these terms signify the return to something lost or silenced and connote an improvement in health. The "recovery" or "recuperation" of Spain's historical memory suggests the revival of previously excluded or banned memories in the interest of regaining the social and historical health a more complete understanding of past events provides. But the contention extends beyond terminology.

Introduction

Whether to break the Franco-imposed silence about Spain's divided past was a central political issue after the dictator's death. In 1977, a coalition of political groups enacted the Amnesty Law, aimed at achieving the democratization of Spain without entering into reexaminations and recriminations over the Civil War and dictatorship. The law and its aura of self-censorship came to be known as the Pact of Silence. Debates about the utility of the Pact of Silence have occupied historians, scholars, and Spanish citizens since the accord's apparent rupture at the turn of the twenty-first century. Some, like the historian Santos Juliá, identify the futility of a process of "voluntarily forgetting" when one must first remember what it is he has decided to forget ("Echar al olvido"). This kind of determined forgetting leads to a new memory that must stand in for what is absent, which is what the influential theorist Paul Ricoeur calls "the prime danger": an official history limited to an "authorized, imposed, celebrated, commemorated history" (*Memory, History, Forgetting* 448). Others, like the historian Stanley Payne, argue that the Pact of Silence never existed, and that there has been no forgetting, given that Spain's history has been a topic of conversation both publicly and privately since the war ended. The political scientist Omar Encarnación identifies the utility of the Amnesty Law and the Pact of Silence in solidifying Spain's fragile democracy, while Ferrán counters that a generation of memory was lost when "[a]mnesty became amnesia" (23).

What remains clear is that narratives of the Civil War and Franco's dictatorship positioned on either side of the political divide have recently renewed historical interest in Spain while fanning the flames of contention about what constitutes the country's "true" past. Although the 1977 Amnesty Law has not been repealed, the 2007 Law of Historical Memory modified the Amnesty Law and recognized those who "sufrieron las consequencias de la guerra civil y del régimen dictatorial que la sucedió" ("LEY 52/2007"). The Law of Historical Memory thus signaled an official end to the Pact of Silence, though the Pact's influence had already begun to wane years earlier. The end of this era of silence is a watershed moment in Spanish letters, as critics, novelists, historians, filmmakers, and artists have been making varied contributions to an ever-expanding catalogue of historically minded cultural material ever since. Although Alberto Medina Domínguez argues that a number of filmmakers and authors performed "exorcismo[s] de los fantasmas de la memoria" (21) in their creative works during the Spanish Transition, even more "memory exorcisms" have taken place in the last decade. Sebastiaan Faber discusses the Pact's end as an explanation for the recent surge in books and films with historical overtones in Spain. Carlos Jerez-Farrán and Samuel Amago also see the end of the Pact as the beginning of a wave of historical examination in journalism, science, and politics.[6]

Some of these new objects of historical memory—like Miguel Hermoso's cinematic resurrection of García Lorca in the streets of Granada—are set squarely in the realm of imagination, feeding on history to inform what is otherwise a fictional enterprise. Others—the meticulous excavation and documentation of the mass graves of individuals from both sides killed during and after the Civil War, for instance—are roundly, though often controversially, considered historical documents, given their political connections to a Spain divided by war and dictatorship. Both types of objects add to the growing archive of material on the Spanish Civil War and the Franco dictatorship, topics that until relatively recently were inaccessible to the Spanish public in any real detail. Yet a third category of objects of historical memory skirts the boundary between fiction and history, influenced by both genres to display the nuance of historical reexamination through a fictional lens. Melenchón i Xamena's imagined account of the actual experiences of Spaniards in the Nazi concentration camp Mauthausen is an example of this third, mixed-genre category.

Melenchón i Xamena's effort, like much of the flood of reexaminations of Spaniards in Nazi concentration camps in memoirs, films, and historical accounts in the last two decades, finds its antecedent in Montserrat Roig's 1977 study, *Els catalans als camps nazi*. Roig, a Catalan journalist and novelist, mined her own personalized historiographic study for material that she incorporated into one of her most influential novels, *L'hora violeta*. Roig's two books demonstrate not only the attraction between fiction and history in contemporary Spanish literature, but also the mutual influence one has on the other. Along with other authors of historical fiction and historiography, Roig anticipates the contemporary trend of intermingled genres. She lays the groundwork for authors such as Melenchón i Xamena, demonstrating that historiography and historical fiction, when combined around a common subject matter, promote a more nuanced, detailed, and personalized view of Spanish history than each does in isolation.

Yet, given this argument, why is it that when Spanish society encounters history and fiction, reality and invention, documentaries, films, novels, and historiographies based on real events juxtaposed at every turn, it has left the techniques of writers such as Roig who work between fiction and history virtually unexplored? Why is a single author who operates as both historian and novelist, borrowing techniques from two distinct genres, so difficult to categorize? What is it about fiction and history that makes them prevalent in Spanish bookstores, movie theaters, and in the pages of newspapers, but makes them challenging to understand together?

One answer is the elusive nature of the categories of history and fiction. While there is a basic independent understanding of these two genres, their moments of overlap are much more difficult to define. A number of Hispanists inside and outside of Spain have theorized how history and fiction converge around memory in Spanish literature. Although their work is fundamental to understanding the combined force of historical memory and literature, none of these scholars applies a practice equivalent to genre fusion to contemporary authors and texts.

David Herzberger discusses the postmodern "collapse [of] the traditional generic boundaries" (5) of fiction and history in *Narrating the Past*, offering the postwar Spanish author Juan Benet as one example. For Benet, Herzberger writes, "history… is not one thing and fiction another, but… both share certain temporal explorations and intentions within the frame of narrative discourse" (98). Benet's overlapping essays and novels fit the criteria I have defined for texts to be considered through genre fusion, but Herzberger mainly focuses on the influence of history on fiction, while genre fusion also theorizes fiction's influence on history. Nevertheless, writing in 1995, Herzberger foresees the path of history through post-Franco Spanish fiction that the present study will explore.

José F. Colmeiro expands the theoretical basis from which discussions of the convergences of history, historical and collective memory, and representation can emerge in *Memoria histórica e identidad cultural*. Colmeiro places Spain's historical memory in the context of monuments, films, songs, and novels, concluding that the country is experiencing a memory crisis. While Colmeiro argues that Spanish collective memory has shifted away from the past, the recuperation of historical memory possible during the Transition constitutes a clear reconsideration of the past and a continuation of a collective memory whitewashed by the Franco regime. Colmeiro's informative topographic reading of Spanish memory, will, nevertheless, inform my application of genre fusion to contemporary Spanish texts.

Numerous Hispanists have identified relationships among texts that resemble, but do not arrive at, the parameters needed to apply genre fusion. Labanyi's "historical pastiche," Samuel Amago's "postmodern metafiction," Ferrán's "meta-memory texts," and Manuel Alberca's "pacto ambiguo" approach the genres of history and fiction in Spain as reflections of the country's ongoing engagement with its politics of memory. Each scholar identifies a trend in contemporary Spanish literature that harmonizes with genre fusion without capturing the theory's essential practice of examining overlapping historiographic and fictional texts by the same author.

In a theoretical article, Labanyi discusses a "historical pastiche" and "hybrid cultural practices" in contemporary Spain as "represent[ing] culture as a 'recycling' process in which nothing is lost but returns in new hybridized forms adapting to changed circumstances" (*Constructing Identity* 8–12). History is dynamic in this recycling of cultural production, comparable to the fusion of fiction and history during the Spanish Transition. Labanyi encourages scholars to apply her cultural model to other arenas: "given that culture is by definition a process of hybridization, the study of culture has to be interdisciplinary" (*Constructing Identity* 12). Genre fusion answers Labanyi's call by filtering paired historical and fictional texts through a lens of hybridity.

Amago defines the self-referentiality of postmodern Spanish fiction as "a celebration of literary difference and subjectivity, an important critical reassessment of the historiographical enterprise, and, above all, a useful reevaluation of the role that narrative plays in the understanding of human consciousness" (14). Particularly in his examination of Javier Cercas's *Soldados de Salamina*, Amago recognizes the historiographer's task of compiling and interpreting history implicitly present in the novel (157). Although he "situates his historical account within a self-conscious narrative frame that calls attention to the problems implicit in historiographic representation" (Amago 164), Cercas has not published a historiographic text that follows the same historical period as his novel, and therefore cannot be read through genre fusion as I have defined it. Although I agree with Amago's identification of the key role of the reader in actualizing "historical truth and narrative truth" (144) in contemporary Spanish literature, the author's focus remains solely on the fictional side of genre fusion.

Ferrán coins the term "meta-memory texts" (15) to refer to self-reflexive novels that thematically foreground memory and representation. She argues that the self-conscious quality of these novels allows them to "develop a much-needed culture of memory in Spain," while also representing "a culture of countermemory" by "recover[ing] historical perspectives marginalized by official versions of the past" (15). Although she is concerned with the cultural, political, and social transformations in Spain since the Transition that have contributed to the recuperation of historical memory from the margins of society, Ferrán's theoretical model and genre fusion are different. Ferrán focuses on literature and narrative in her study of "meta-memory texts," whereas the mutual influence of fiction and historiography is central to genre fusion. Nevertheless, Ferrán's work opens an important avenue of inquiry into memory in post-Franco Spanish literature. Genre fusion will fill the gap of "understand[ing] how these literary texts function within broader practices of political and social legislation, civic activism, and historical investigation, all of which are absolutely essential if a country is to work through a past of war and repression that continues to haunt the present" (Ferrán 61).

Manuel Alberca's "ambiguous pact," is another approach to the intermingling of fact and fiction that shares some qualities with genre fusion. Alberca examines what he terms "autoficción" as part-autobiography and part-novel located in an intermediate space the author identifies as "la línea de intersección entre lo ficticio y lo real" (*El pacto ambiguo* 48). This intersection is also the realm of genre fusion, which, like "autofiction," depends on the reader, who may be confused by the text while also providing the key to its interpretation. According to Alberca, the more the reader knows about the author's biography, the more he or she is going to capture certain autobiographical references (*El pacto ambiguo* 62). In works read through genre fusion, the same dynamic also applies to the reader's knowledge of and ability to understand historical referents. Paired texts from Spain under investigation through the lens of genre fusion in this study include autobiographical components that align them with Alberca's theoretical model. Genre fusion, however, compares two or more texts by the same author along self-referential as well as historiographic and narrative lines.

In a similar vein, a number of essay collections on the cultural legacy of the Franco dictatorship have contributed to the body of scholarship on Spain's historical memory. Joan Ramon Resina and Ulrich Winter, Jerez-Farrán and Amago, and Eloy E. Merino and H. Rosi Song have published edited volumes examining representations of historical memory in the cultural production of post-Franco Spain in theoretical and practical terms. Although all of these volumes contain important studies of both fictional and nonfictional cultural touchstones of historical memory, they exclude the overlap between historiography and fiction as a subject of inquiry. Recent monographs by Carmen Moreno-Nuño, Antonio Gómez López-Quiñones, and Kathryn Everly (*History, Violence, and the Hyperreal*) have also framed the debate on memory and Spain's past, though they are focused on one half of genre fusion's target: the presence of history in works of fiction. Genre fusion interprets historiographic texts in contemporary Spain alongside their interactions with historical fiction, thus bringing a new perspective to contemporary Hispanism.

History, Fiction, Narrative, and Genre Fusion

The ability to understand the contributions authors who work between genres have made to Spain's historical memory has been stymied by the lack of a clearly defined terminology with which to guide readers and critics. As a starting point to theorizing genre fusion, the terms central to a discussion of the convergence of fiction and history—a subject referred to in general as the "fiction/history debate"—must be clarified. These working definitions remain, nevertheless, interpreted designations embroiled in a continuous process of redefinition by theorists and audiences alike. To assert that the following definitions are forever fixed would be disingenuous; yet without them, our analysis of the practice of genre fusion would exist only in the abstract.

Fiction is prose in which imagined characters, places, and events predominate. This definition must necessarily encompass both referential and nonreferential discourse, in that under this broad category heading, the subcategory of historical fiction also appears. *Historical fiction* is fiction contextualized and dependent on particular and actual historical events, personages, places, or time periods.[7] Thus, there are two fundamental planes of meaning operating in fiction that will serve as guideposts: the categorization of fiction through its external or internal referential frame, and the discursive style and literary qualities associated with the genre that may not be adequately described in more formal definitions.[8] A clear narrative arc—with a beginning, middle, and end—to the story, narrative voice, character development, and plot are all features important to the discursive or "way of telling" plane of fiction. Meanwhile, the real-world referents that populate a fictional text along its content plane do not need to be entirely accurate; they have the freedom to mingle in the space between the external, actual world of history and the internal, imaginary world of fiction. The author of fiction, whether or not he or she dares to represent the real, does not answer to an overriding authority of "truth," as historiography does. Instead, fiction is allowed the liberty to weave actual and imaginary events in any proportion it desires, because it remains, ultimately, a creative interpretation. Ricoeur, in his extensive theoretical work on time and narrative, describes this playful intermediary process: "Fiction alone, because it remains fiction even when it projects and depicts experience, can allow itself a little inebriation" (*Time and Narrative* 3: 137). Historical fiction, then, despite its foundation in historical reality, is also held to a looser standard of accuracy than historiography: it, too, can intermingle the actual and the imaginary as it pleases.

The term *history* broadly refers to the past and events in the past, while *historiography* signals the representation of the past, most commonly in written form.[9] A key difference between history and historiography arises in the concept of witnessing. An understanding of history, if one is not a direct witness to a past event, emerges most often from written discourse. Indeed, the term *historiography* is widely used to indicate the written record of history. The witness, on the other hand, produces a written or oral testimony of his experiences. This testimony, as it is used by both historians and writers of fiction, is the evidence on which representations of history stand.[10] Witness testimony, however, raises the fundamental problem that plagues historiography and, to a certain extent, historical fiction as well: namely, how does one

Chapter One

determine its accuracy? The "truth value" of testimony, history, and memory must be decided, ultimately, on a case-by-case basis, factoring in the author's and reader's subjective evaluations.

The connective tissue that binds fiction and historiography together, bridging the gap between the imaginary and the representative, is *narrative*. *Narrative* is the written embodiment of events or facts, independent of their fictive or nonfictive status. Therefore, both fiction and nonfiction texts must rely on narrative in the process of recounting events, with the ultimate goal of communicating this confluence of events as a whole, rather than an incomplete, entity.

While fiction, history, historiography, and narrative exist as independent concepts, they also enjoy moments of overlap. Historiography encompasses writing from the annal to the chronicle to the testimonial: all legitimate methods of recording historical events. But the annal and the chronicle, as chronological records of historical events that may assume the form of a timeline or a list of dates and major events, lack the narrative coherence of a testimony. A reader does not sit down to immerse himself in the captivating narrative of a chronicle, nor does an annal necessarily seek to assemble a whole, interconnected entity from the sum of its parts. But the author of a "narrative historiography" places emphasis on the fashioning of a complete historical story, relying on elements of fiction such as narrative voice and arc, plot structure, and characterization. It can be argued that the majority of historiography is narrative historiography, however, and that the addition of "narrative" is redundant. Yet, when examining the intermingling of fiction and historiography, narrative comes to the forefront: it is the means by which both genres concoct a unified story out of the scattered dates, characters, events, and facts that make up their ingredients. Narrative historiography depends on narrative to compose a story from history.[11]

The goal of employing genre fusion to study literature is also to bring history to life. By intermingling narrative historiography with historical fiction, the literary and narratological qualities of historiography and the historicized and representational qualities of fiction are self-consciously fused into one story. In the multiple texts that benefit from the application of genre fusion, historiography is layered with elements more commonly associated with fiction, such as a distinct narrative voice, the incorporation of individual perception, characterization, and plot. Meanwhile, fiction assimilates elements more commonly associated with historiography, such as representations of the real, historical documentation, first-person testimony, and an accurate adherence to historical events. These individual texts still retain their essential qualities, however: the fundamental division between historiography's perception as real and fiction's perception as imaginary remains the ultimate dividing line between the two genres.

Even beyond purely literary notions, the markers dividing genre encompass such factors as the text's marketing as "fiction" or "nonfiction"; the reader's personal assessment of the author as "novelist," "journalist," or "historian"; and the subjective manner that a text's central topic resonates with the public's conception of history versus fiction. It is the struggle against predeterminations that distinguishes these texts and proves them worthy of further examination. Explored using genre fusion, they are revealed as extraordinary forays into a new space of literature where traditional conceptions of genre are granted moments of porosity.

As we will see, theorists across the literary and historical spectrum have grappled with definitions in line with those posed here, yet, in the field of Spanish literature, critical inquiry has only scratched the surface of the fiction/history debate. The texts by Roig, Martín Gaite, Blanco Aguinaga, and Marías examined in depth in the chapters to follow couple the use of narrative elements that straddle genres with a consistent thematic preoccupation in both fictional and historiographic texts. In other words, they address identical historical topics via fictional and historiographic methods, permitting a locus of comparison across genre. Although these authors bring their own personal interpretation to their narrative techniques, looking at them through genre fusion allows us to arrive at an identical conclusion: Two genres combined to tell the personal stories contained in the collective memory deliver a unified, forceful, and compelling narrative voice that activates Spanish history like no isolated text can. At the same time, these dual genres inherently doubt the necessity of traditional generic boundaries dividing fact from fiction.

Genre fusion questions the primacy of historiography over historical fiction in the quest for a comprehensive portrayal of history. Interdisciplinary at its core, genre fusion brings to light how authors set aside rigid genre distinctions in the composition of a text with the goal of serving the ultimate authority: the story. Although these genre divisions have all but broken down in the contemporary literary world, they continue to hold sway in the cultural consciousness. Many authors still write works of fiction and works of nonfiction that adhere to the conventional rules and practices that separate them. Others resist genre categorization entirely, though examples abound of authors who must answer to a reading public demanding to know where the line between truth and fiction is drawn. Applying genre fusion sidesteps these demands. An author who writes a work of fiction and a work of nonfiction, retaining their ultimate generic division yet composing them such that together they confuse the boundaries between truth and imagination, has found a route to explore a single theme from two angles. Indeed, these authors are self-conscious and unequivocal about their methods. Yet the praxis of genre fusion still must defend its assertion that fiction can adequately represent history, and raises critical questions about the adaptability of genre, the capability of author and reader to judge accuracy, and whether this theory offers anything new, or is simply a rehashing of generations of literary reconfigurations.

The Fiction/History Debate beyond Spain

Genre fusion answers theoretical discussions on the relationship between fiction and history with a concrete methodology. The debate on the division or convergence of fiction and history is wide-ranging, ongoing, and truly interdisciplinary. While numerous international theorists and practitioners of fiction and historiography across discipline and genre have lent their voices, a few key thinkers have provided a useful means of introduction and orientation to the debate.[12] Although these scholars and theorists most commonly emerge from outside the purview of Hispanism, their thoughts are especially relevant in the context of contemporary Spanish literature and genre fusion.

Arguably stirring the discussion of the function of narrative across genre most publicly, the historian Hayden White asks: "What kind of insight does narrative give into the nature of real events? What kind of blindness with respect to reality does narrativity dispell [sic]?" (*Content* 5). These questions illuminate the central debate of the fiction/history dialectic: how does fiction interact with "real events," that is, with history, and how does the use of narrative enable the historian to represent these real events with a critical eye? The underlying process at work in White's theory is a hybridization of fiction and history that creates a narrativized historiography and a historicized fiction. These terms have been adopted by scholars such as Ricoeur and Linda Hutcheon in order to differentiate a theoretically "pure" genre, which Gérard Genette notes is "only to be found in the poetician's test tube" (772), from a blended genre.

White also argues for the ideological nature of narrative, which extends to the ways narrative coaxes substance from the text: "It is the success of narrative in revealing the meaning, coherence, or significance of events that attests to the legitimacy of its practice in historiography. And it is the success of historiography in narrativizing sets of historical events that attests to the 'realism' of narrative itself" (*Content* 54). The power White attributes to the author of historical discourse to order the strands of history is captured by his term *emplotment*: historiography's answer to plot structure in fiction. White's argument that history does not already inherently contain such a narrative structure and it therefore must be imposed by the historian has drawn criticism from historians, in particular.[13] White has become renowned for equating the narrative strategies utilized in both fiction and historiography, declaring that "history is no less a form of fiction than the novel is a form of historical representation" (*Tropics* 122). This is an argument that combines the two genres in such a way that their unique and separate nuances are, depending on one's interpretation, either closely identified and reshaped or carelessly conflated.

Dorrit Cohn balks at the postmodern melding promoted by White. She argues for a basic and firm division between the two fields, in which fiction is essentially a "nonreferential narrative" (9) located either strictly within the boundaries of historical accuracy or fully in the realm of fantasy and imagination. Cohn seeks to solidify the genre barriers made fluid by White by excluding historically accurate representation in fiction. She argues that if complete historical precision cannot be proven (and it cannot if one character or a certain setting is invented, for instance), then the text is categorically fictional, and must be excluded from any sense of historical truth.

Neither Cohn's argument for strict boundaries separating history from fiction nor White's argument virtually conflating the two genres describes the interpretive process at work when genre

Chapter One

fusion is employed to illuminate how authors blend fiction and historiography while simultaneously retaining the elements of both forms. White's and Cohn's paradigms limit the scope of fiction and historiography by excluding a middle ground, a point on which Ricoeur elaborates:

> [W]e have to combat the prejudice that the historian's language can be made entirely transparent, to the point of allowing the things themselves to speak… [b]ut we cannot combat this initial prejudice without also struggling against a second one, which holds that the literature of imagination, because it always makes use of fiction, can have no hold on reality. (*Time and Narrative* 3: 154–55)

Out of the legions of scholars working on this topic, Ricoeur has been the most successful in theorizing the moments when these genres converge, the need to guard their unique identities, and the struggle between these two poles. He contends that an accurate representation of reality is possible within the pages of fiction. Ricoeur not only identifies the crux of the contentious fiction/history debate, but also develops terminology that is central to a new generic outlook. The "borrowings" between fictional and historical narratives, Ricoeur argues:

> … lie in the fact that historical intentionality only becomes effective by incorporating into its intended object the resources of fictionalization stemming from the narrative form of imagination, while the intentionality of fiction produces its effects of detecting and transforming acting and suffering only by symmetrically assuming the resources of historicization presented it by attempts to reconstruct the actual past. (*Time and Narrative* 3: 101–02)

Ricoeur's insistence on the "intentionality" inherent in historical fiction and narrative historiography underscores the decision made by authors of both genres: their texts do not spontaneously emerge in a space of blended genre. Instead, these authors are systematic about their "borrowings" from parallel genres, and the texts themselves betray the self-conscious nature of the author's overlapping genres.

The interactions between history and fiction, according to Ricoeur, produce a form of narrative that is central to how humans express their existence: "From these intimate exchanges between the historicization of the fictional narrative and the fictionalization of the historical narrative is born what we will call human time, which is nothing other than narrated time" (*Time and Narrative* 3: 102). Ricoeur's description of this exchange of genre elements as "human time" or "narrated time" demonstrates the centrality of history and fiction to how we understand ourselves and our past. The authors themselves "show how the refiguration of time by history and fiction becomes concrete" (Ricoeur, *Time and Narrative* 3: 101), in order to approximate history via both works of historiography and works of fiction. When genre fusion is utilized, these texts combine, becoming the point at which "human time," "narrated time," personal and collective experience all converge.

Ricoeur also contends that history, in its combination with other disciplines and discourses, allows "ordinary people, often denied the right to speak by the dominant form of discourse, [to] regain their voice" (*Time and Narrative* 1: 110). This argument coincides with John Beverley's definition of testimony as the expression of those who would otherwise be denied a voice in the representation of their individual experience. Ricoeur's description of what he deems the "interweavings of history and fiction" (*Time and Narrative* 3: 101) and his assertion that history applied across discipline allows the heretofore voiceless a means of expression model a point of departure for the blended elements of history and fiction in the works of Spanish writers that genre fusion activates.

This revaluation of the marginalized voice in both historiography and fiction is a crucial aspect of the theory of genre fusion arising from the fiction/history debate. It is an approach that the New Historicists, among others, have vehemently defended, as they argue for the inclusion of both literary and nonliterary texts, such as oral histories and socio-cultural constructions, in the assembly of a new historical model. At its outset, the New Historicism project was eager to study these "counterhistories that make apparent the slippages, cracks, fault lines, and surprising absences in the monumental structures that dominated a more traditional historicism" (Gallagher and Greenblatt 17). These are the omissions that affect "people without history," as Kerwin Klein identifies them, who have been unjustly denied a stake in both traditional historiography and the literary canon ("In Search of Narrative Mastery" 276). Although the New Historicist project privileges the nonliterary "text"—which may or may not be in written form—in its examination of the relationship and power balance between text and context, it is fundamentally interested in a more inclusive view of stories "worth telling." These stories contained in a text or a nontext represent the historical and social consciousness of a culture. What becomes evident, along this line of reasoning, is that an exclusionary course is no longer valid in modern cultural studies, literary analysis, nor historiography. The tales at the margins must be invited to center stage for a rounded interpretation of modernity.[14]

For the historian Pierre Nora, this movement away from the center and toward the periphery is akin to a movement away from history and toward memory. History is undergoing a democratization in which "[m]inority memories" are the product of the "decolonization" of a once-hegemonic past ("Upsurge in Memory" 439). Memory, Nora argues, now has such a broad meaning that it substitutes and encompasses history. The historian must share the task of "manufacturing the past" ("Upsurge in Memory" 441) with individual and collective memory. Not unlike Nora's foundational concept of sites of memory, or *lieux de mémorie*, this shift from history to memory is a popular movement that has also spawned the gradual breakdown of the border between the historical and the literary. The "new kind of history" (Nora, "Between Memory and History" 24) that is born at the intersection of memory and literature is genre fusion, although Nora focuses exclusively on historiography in his theorization.

Hutcheon also approaches the overriding concept of genre fusion in her discussion of "historiographic metafiction," yet she, unlike Nora, stops just short of including historiography in her paradigm. According to Hutcheon, historiographic metafiction refers to a fictional text that utilizes techniques of historiography, a reliance on the "real" or representations of reality, and a self-consciously metatextual narration. Focusing her analysis on determining the discursive practices of postmodernism, Hutcheon poses that the intertextuality inherent in historiographic metafiction and the postmodern novel in general could be better understood as an "interdiscursivity" drawing from a plethora of genres and fields (130). She explains that once the center of these historical and fictional narratives is scattered, "[m]argins and edges gain new value" (Hutcheon 130). This pinpoints the postmodern movement not only toward genre-blurring, but also toward a recuperation of the experiences of marginalized subjects. In many ways, including in her emphasis on the metafictional and self-conscious qualities of these blurred texts, Hutcheon's historiographic metafiction captures the idea of genre fusion. Yet Hutcheon declines to include the nonfiction novel or historiography in her definition of historiographic metafiction. The time has come to renew Hutcheon and Nora's theoretical models not only to encompass the literature of Spain, but also to theorize both fictional and historiographic texts in their natural habitat: together.

* * *

The truth value of historiography and historical fiction, and the underlying history that informs both, constitutes perhaps the central polemical issue in the fiction/history debate. "Truth value" can be interpreted both as a completely objective, scientific evaluation of the precision of historical representation and as the reader's subjective perception of historical accuracy, derived from personal experience and/or previously held notions of history. The scientific evaluation of historical truth largely eludes the abilities and interests of the literary scholar, but leads to the centrality of the reader in interpreting and categorizing the text.

Cohn, straying from her defense of the separation of history from fiction, defends the role of the reader in both determining the historical accuracy of a novel and forming judgments based on this perceived allegiance to or defiance of historical truth (157–59). White agrees to this truthful fluidity, asserting that "[o]ne can produce an imaginary discourse about real events that may not be less 'true' for being imaginary" (*Content* 57). Hutcheon, meanwhile, takes a judicious approach when she writes that "[t]he real exists (and existed), but our understanding of it is always conditioned by discourses, by our different ways of talking about it" (157). According to Andrew P. Norman, "[t]he fact that a narrative is the product of a creative process… does not by itself compromise its truth" (135). Norman's no-nonsense approach to the evaluation of truth in a historical narrative seems to be the most practical: assessing accuracy on a case-by-case basis gets us as close as we will ever come to a final answer. Ultimately, it is the reader who provides this assessment.

Chapter One

Certain historical events and moments (the existence of Nazi concentration camps, for example), no matter their place in a novel or a work of historiography, will strike a chord with those who experienced them directly, or will be so powerful in a collective historical consciousness as to allow no doubt about the accuracy of their referentiality. In these circumstances, however, it is not the text itself that imposes meaning, rather it is the reader who determines the historical accuracy of a text, relative to the experience and knowledge he or she possesses. Stanley Fish describes the way meaning "develops in a dynamic relationship with the reader's expectations, projections, conclusions, judgments, and assumptions" (2), giving the reader an authoritative role in interpreting the text. From a similar vantage point, Cohn reasons that "an individual reader's reaction to [alternate versions of official history] is conditioned by the degree to which the historical material concerned touches on his or her values and sensitivities" (159), and personal experiences. If the reader knows, in a way that is personally satisfying, that what he or she is reading in a work of historical fiction is "true" or "accurate," how does this diminish the historical accuracy of the representation, even when it is located in a fictional text? Nora weighs in that in today's memory over history paradigm, "the truth of personal experience and individual memory" is seen as "more 'truthful' than that of history" ("Upsurge in Memory" 440).

The truth value of the historical content of a text is determined on multiple and transitory levels: by the self-identified genre of the text (whether it is offered as a work of fiction or nonfiction); by the reader's own knowledge and perspective; and by the degree of objectivity with which the historical material is presented, which is in and of itself subject to personal interpretation. Therefore, if a historical novel incorporates the events surrounding World War II, for example, into its setting and plot structure, we cannot dismiss out of hand the accuracy of these portrayals simply because they are located in a fictional text. However, we cannot read them as unbiased truths for precisely the same reason. By the same token, the accounts of history that are included in a historiographic work are also adapted and interpreted by the author, the witnesses, the written discourse, and, finally, the reader.

Wolfgang Iser has acknowledged that this type of reader-oriented actualization of a text leaves it unguarded for accusations of subjectivity (23). However, to Iser's mind, the text should be held to an "intersubjective frame of reference" (25) that moves beyond subjective/objective valuations into a realm where the interaction between the text and reader produces meanings that inhabit, arguably, a space above the fray of the limitations to accuracy or truth. Darío Villanueva agrees, stating that even if an author conceives of his texts as fictional, the reader can still read them as true, "because it is solely up to the reader to grant them such status" (69).

The truth value of history, regardless of its textual manifestation, is constantly under question, and falls into a battleground of accuracy that mimics the middle ground between fiction and history itself. The identification of an unmitigated, objective truth in a work of fiction or historiography is illusory, yet when the text is subjected to the reader's interpretation, these spaces of confrontation produce meanings that intertwine the historical and personal experiences of the reader with meanings contained either within the text or within markers of the text's genre (in its categorization as fiction or nonfiction, for example). These interactions reveal a complex process in which the intentions of the author and the expectations of the reader, mitigated by forces seeking to isolate the text according to traditional generic categories, result in countless interpretive readings located between the poles of fiction and history. The reader is integral in the interpretation of paired works through genre fusion not only by judging their truth value, but also by mentally juxtaposing the two texts. Genre fusion may only be put to use on a historical text and a fictional text when they are read or envisioned in tandem, an often-unfulfilled task that falls directly to the reader.

* * *

Although the aforementioned scholars have charted specific routes through which to navigate the uncertainties surrounding the fiction/history debate, the individual authors, readers, and texts themselves are crucial in comprehending how these maps function on the page. A thorough understanding of the interplay between genres, in this case between Spanish historiography and historical fiction, necessitates both a knowledge of theoretical trends and an examination of the resulting products. These written volumes do not exist in a vacuum: they are the literary and cultural products of a specific period in Spain's history and of the authors who examine the cultural zeitgeist of that period. In 1971, the Hispanist Claudio Guillén called on all writers to gain an understanding of these interrelations, offering the author of the first modern novel, *Don Quijote*, as an exemplary case: "Cervantes… confronted most lucidly the generic dynamics of his day, and the fruitful interaction that existed between the written and the unwritten codes," blending traditional literary forms of the moment with "developing popular forms" (127) to arrive at a text that stretches the boundaries of genre. Cervantes demonstrates "the situation and the challenge every writer is obliged to face, namely, the necessity of an active dialogue with the generic models of his time and culture" (Guillén 128). This statement is as relevant to *Don Quijote* as it is to all contemporary authors, whose literary forms are influenced by their historical moment.

During a period in which Spain re-examines its history while transitioning from a dictatorship to a democracy, and then as it plunges into an age of globalization even more rife with historical revision, Roig, Martín Gaite, Blanco Aguinaga, and Marías integrate the popular historical discourse of the day into both their fiction and historiography. They transform genre to adhere to the specific circumstances under which they live. For these authors, such circumstances demand that history be examined through dual genres, while still retaining the narrative qualities of fiction and the historiographic interest in re-examining the past. However, Guillén argued that the modern tendency of critics and historians has been to study genres, texts, or authors in isolation, elaborating that "[i]f by 'atomicism' one sometimes means the attempt to isolate the single parts of a system, to pry the element apart from the field or the mass to which it belongs, then the modern study of literature, in keeping with its Romantic origins, has been generally atomistic" (133). A study of contemporary Spanish fiction and historiography is transformed by observing the interactions of the "atoms" of literature and, moreover, the states they assume upon fusion. To this end, Guillén's criticism extends to the tendency to separate texts from the readers that actualize them, when in fact the confluence of factors surrounding the joining of these two entities highlights one of the fundamental questions about genre: What determines whether a text is fiction or history? The author's intention, the reader's interpretation, the critical analysis, and the cultural and social *milieu* at the moment of writing and the moment of reading, among other elements, lend themselves to a determination of genre. A study of contemporary Spanish literature filtered through genre fusion is a survey of these distinct answers, representing the multitude of interpretations and perspectives gleaned from a deceptively simple question. Readers and critics are left to speculate on the author's way of thinking when weaving historical elements into both fictional and historiographic texts: we can only reach a point of understanding when we read the text in dialogue with our own interpretation of the narrative.

The last decade has seen a surge in critical works trained on genre in Spanish literature that continue to address Guillén's premise, though without fully realizing a "non-atomistic" approach to literature. Beginning in the Transition, fiction in Spain has exploded to include the publication of a wide range of subgenres—from experimental metafiction to detective novels—and critics have risen to the task of categorizing and analyzing these works in the context of Spain's changing political and cultural landscape.[15] Although a number of critics have evoked a New Historicist approach to modern historical narrative in Spain, they have tended to focus exclusively on the historical novel, glossing over the function of narrative historiography in this new movement toward a historicized Spanish writing born of the Transition.[16] Herzberger, Labanyi, and Randolph Pope, among other scholars, have examined the postwar Spanish novel through its methods of dialoguing with Francoist historiography. Pope answers his own question—"¿Hay alguna relación entre la manera en que los historiadores y los novelistas plasmaron sus historias en el período de la posguerra?" (16)—with an emphatic yes, paving the way for critics to ask the same question of Spanish literature during other periods.[17] However, few scholars have looked at the post-Franco novel in similar terms of its interaction with Transition-era or contemporary historiography. Those critics who do approach post-dictatorship historical fiction have not ventured into a discussion of its historiographic counterpart, even given the existence of a number of well-known writers who are the authors of both genres. Still, critics such as Vilarós, Gonzalo Sobejano, and Robert C. Spires have identified and analyzed the place of history in Spanish fiction, contextualizing historical fiction and subdividing it into categories such as the testimonial novel and the novel of memory. These scholars take a critical approach to fiction that informs an examination of similar trends in historiography and the convergence of both genres.[18]

And yet, as we have seen, there is a clear reluctance to delve into the converging genres of history and fiction in practical or theoretical terms in contemporary Spanish literary criticism. My application of genre fusion to four Spanish authors is an attempt to fill this lacuna. Roig, Martín Gaite, Blanco Aguinaga, and Marías are Spanish authors who have authored narrative historiography and historical fiction with constant thematic preoccupations centered on the same historical period. Their texts arise out of an interest in exploring how history and fiction focus on those at the margins of dictatorship society. As a result, these authors paint a dynamic portrait of the cultural, political, and social impulses operating in post-Franco Spain. Genre fusion illustrates the fundamental function of their work: to provide an in-depth, multi-voiced representation of historical experience via source material on both sides of the fiction/history divide.

Divergent Experiences, Converging Genres

In Spain, the narrative synthesis of history and fiction is an emerging trend bound together with the country's growing interest in its own history after Franco's death. By its nature, genre fusion can only be applied to fiction and nonfiction contained in two or more distinct publications by a single author. These texts must intersect via their historical time period and subject matter. This parameter excludes some of the many contemporary Spanish authors such as Javier Cercas, Josefina Aldecoa, and Arturo Pérez-Reverte who have also published fiction and nonfiction. Although both genres may treat historical topics, genre fusion can only be administered when one text compliments the other via a locus of historical similarity. Cercas provides a case in point: *Soldados de Salamina* is a work of historical fiction; *Anatomía de un instante* is a work of historiography. The former focuses on the story of a Nationalist soldier during the Spanish Civil War; the latter on the attempted military coup in the Spanish Parliament on February 23, 1981. With distinct subject matter and historical time periods, these two texts cannot be interpreted through genre fusion.[19]

Other Spanish authors, such as Jorge Semprún, whose fictional and nonfictional works have been studied extensively, could be theorized in terms of genre fusion but have had the fortune of enjoying an abundance of critical inquiry. The four authors under investigation in this study may be well known in the literary field, but are understudied in light of their practice of joining fiction and history together in their literature. Moreover, they coincide and can be compared based on the overriding thematic focus of their oeuvres: an unofficial version of twentieth-century Spanish cultural history from the vantage point of a population underrepresented during the dictatorship of which they themselves are members. The study of the narrative techniques illustrated by these four authors traces the development and variation embodied by the theory of genre fusion.

At first glance, however, Roig, Martín Gaite, Blanco Aguinaga, and Marías are four very different authors who employ distinct writing styles and subject matter. Although born in Spain, they have followed divergent paths and lived through dissimilar contexts. Yet their unique backgrounds serve to underline the fact that there were many different populations on the fringe of dictatorship society in Franco's Spain. These collectives have countless stories to tell and ways to tell them. Montserrat Roig was a Catalan woman born into a demoralized Barcelona during the dictatorship. Carmen Martín Gaite lived through the Spanish Civil War and came of age at odds with pervasive national attitudes in Salamanca during the postwar. Carlos Blanco Aguinaga was a Basque man exiled to Mexico for most of his life. Javier Marías is a native son of Madrid growing up under the shadow of his father's vehement opposition to the dictatorship. The differences among these four writers highlight their common reliance on the merged genres of history and fiction to tell their own and their collective's version of Spanish history. Genre fusion demonstrates where their professional and personal stories converge.

Blanco Aguinaga and Martín Gaite were children during the Spanish Civil War, an event that drove the former into exile and caused the conservative shift in culture and society that the latter experienced as an adolescent. Roig and Marías are not children of the war, but rather were born into the stifling postwar era. All four absorbed the postwar from the margins of a Spanish society heavy with governmentally enforced scorn for the vanquished and praise for the victors. Roig and Martín Gaite suffered as women, subject to the legislative controls and cultural and social constraints imposed on them by the Franco dictatorship, including the obligatory classes on domesticity for girls, an ingrained lack of career opportunities and professional respect for women, and the pervasive notion of women as subordinate to and/or dominated by men. Roig, as a Catalan, was also one among millions whose language, cultural expressions, and political influence were outlawed by the Franco regime. Blanco Aguinaga, as an exile and a Basque, and thus subject to the same cultural and linguistic restrictions as the Catalans, was wholly excluded emotionally and physically from Spanish society during the postwar, despite a conflicting identification with his peers on the Iberian Peninsula. While Roig, Martín Gaite, and Blanco Aguinaga were professionally active before Franco's death, a look at their publishing history reveals a stark split in terms of subject matter after 1975. Roig published an investigative study of Catalans in Nazi concentration camps in 1977 that would have doubtlessly been censored or prohibited during the dictatorship. Martín Gaite took a critical and ruminating look at Franco's death and her postwar adolescence in her 1978 novel *El cuarto de atrás*. Blanco Aguinaga shifted from literary criticism to novels and essays interested in a Spanish/Mexican exile identity crisis in the early-1980s. These authors experienced their own transitions, closely matched to Spain's political and cultural Transition, in their developing bodies of work. Once confronted with the liberty to publish freely and a collective gravitational pull toward re-examining Spain's past, which clearly even had a remote effect on Blanco Aguinaga in Mexico, they began to chip away at Spain's postwar history, integrating it into their fiction and their works of historiography.

Javier Marías began his career as a writer early, publishing his first novel in 1971 at the age of 19. Marías unabashedly admits that his father's postwar ordeal as a prominent scholar and philosopher in Spain who was marked as an enemy of the Franco state, falsely accused, and imprisoned, had a profound effect on his own writing. This effect is especially visible when Marías picks up the mantle of historical re-examination in the novels and newspaper columns he has published since the turn of the twenty-first century. Although chronology sets Marías apart from Roig, Martín Gaite, and Blanco Aguinaga, the way he incorporates a personal experience on the margins of postwar society into his historical and fictional representations aligns him with his predecessors and foretells how genre fusion can be used to analyze twenty-first century Spanish literature.

Introduction

While the historical writing of all four authors falls under the broad category of historiography, it is here that their textual commonalities and divergent paths are made plain. Given the broadest interpretation of historiography as the written record of history, Roig, Martín Gaite, Blanco Aguinaga, and Marías are historians as well as authors of fiction. However, their approaches to history are uniquely influenced by their professional and personal interests, as well as their particular life experiences. In a traditional historiography, the author's own experiences do not factor into a disinterested telling of history. However, the narrative historiography under examination in this study is undeniably tinged by autobiographic tendencies, drawing history and personal experience together to highlight a characteristic made plain when works of Spanish literature are read through genre fusion. "The task of remembering makes everyone his own historian" ("Between Memory and History" 15), writes Nora. Indeed, this pressing need to extend the boundaries of the historian's profession toward the margins has encouraged these Spanish fiction writers to enter the historiographic fray.

Roig's study of Catalans in Nazi camps comes the closest to a more traditional narrative historiographic text, in her seamless unification of survivor testimony and historical evidence. Nevertheless, she is an overt presence in her text. Martín Gaite writes a socio-historiographic study in her examination of postwar adolescent culture and its effect on love customs, incorporating her own personal memories with archival cultural documents. Blanco Aguinaga authors essays that mingle aspects of historiographic documentation of the experience of second-generation Spanish exiles with intimate and literary reflections on the exile identity of Spaniards transplanted to Mexico after the war. Marías incorporates overarching views of Spanish history as it relates to current events in his columns—part opinion pieces, part historiographic cultural sketches—for the Spanish newspaper *El País*. Despite their distinctions, these texts all fall under a broad definition of narrative historiography: they saturate historical writing with narratological elements closely associated with fiction, resulting in a personalized historical record infused with storytelling qualities.

These authors join their own lives with the postwar experiences of other members of the same marginalized population in both their history and fiction. Only Roig's historical work does not directly include her own experiences, in that the author was not yet born during World War II. Instead, Roig acts as a narrator and mediator between Catalan witnesses of history and the ways their stories are recounted and understood in modern-day Catalan society. The author is, however, self-referential in her novel. Martín Gaite, Blanco Aguinaga, and Marías, on the other hand, blend their own experiences into those of the collective in both genres. These autobiographical tendencies lend an added layer of meaning to each writer's historiographic and fictional texts as both authors and subjects of their introspective historiographies and historical fictions. The inclusion of the author's personal experiences and memories relates to the truth value of his or her writing as judged by readers. These authors have experienced many of the historical forces included in their studies and their works of fiction. They are readers of their own texts and interpreters of the historical events they cover, providing a response to their own work informed by individual and collective experience and knowledge. For this reason, their personal sentiments about the accuracy of the historical record influence whether the text is read as fact or fiction. The voices of Roig, Martín Gaite, Blanco Aguinaga, and Marías provide corroborating evidence that in effect supports the accuracy of their historical narratives. As readers themselves, their interpretations of the events are as valid as any other; as witnesses to history, their testimony is as forceful as the evidence provided by their peers. Roland Barthes's poststructuralist assertion that "the birth of the reader must be at the cost of the death of the Author" (148) does not apply here. The author's overt presence in the narration imposes meaning on the text, at once actualized or ignored by the reader's own interpretation. The self-referentiality in these historically trained texts provides another point of thematic contact between the authors' narrative historiography and historical fiction, underscoring the self-consciousness characteristic in a genre fusion reading. All four authors incorporate their own experiences into their works of fiction and history in part as a means of acknowledging the proximity one genre has to another. Although their publications are not autobiographies, the personal elements these authors weave into their texts fuses them together, encouraging our application of genre fusion.

Introduction

* * *

The four chapters that follow focus on each of these authors in turn, analyzing their body of literature using genre fusion while acknowledging the space both authors and texts occupy in the larger fiction/history debate. In order to locate the practice of genre fusion within the ongoing critical discussions of Spanish fiction and historiography, each chapter also dialogues with contemporary literary and/or historical scholars—which, in the case of Marías, is the author himself—who further contextualize the fiction/history debate in Spain.

The story of the development of overlapping genres in contemporary Spanish narrative begins in Chapter 2 with Montserrat Roig's groundbreaking historiographic work, *Els catalans als camps nazis*. As an early work of historical investigation in post-Franco Spain, Roig's study exposed a period in the country's past that was absent from history books throughout the dictatorship era. In tandem with her historical novel, *L'hora violeta*, Roig's historiographic study emerged from the modern tradition of the testimonial text, which until now has been examined primarily in the context of Latin American literature. Coupled with Roig's professional experience as a journalist and personal experience as a Catalan woman in postwar Barcelona, the author is a starting point from which to begin to see genre fusion's utility when analyzing literature published during the early years of the Spanish Transition.

Chapter 3 turns to Carmen Martín Gaite's seminal novel *El cuarto de atrás* and her socio-historical study of the same postwar period, *Usos amorosos de la postguerra española*. Both texts are read as reactions to the stifling official historiography of the Franco dictatorship. Martín Gaite's profound interest in the social and cultural influences operating during the postwar in her fiction and nonfiction is infectious. Moreover, the author's established place in the Spanish literary canon brings her as-yet critically unexamined intermingling of fiction and historiography during the dictatorship to a wide audience.

Chapter 4 introduces the relatively unknown work of Carlos Blanco Aguinaga, comparing his essays on the identity crises of Spaniards exiled to Mexico with his fictional rendering of this exilic movement in *Carretera de Cuernavaca*, a short story collection. Blanco Aguinaga's representations of exile and its personal reverberations are drawn from a hybrid Spanish/Mexican identity that the author himself acutely experienced. Effectively moving the history/fiction debate in Spanish letters across the Atlantic, Blanco Aguinaga's texts bring the application of genre fusion to overlapping fiction and historiography beyond the confines of the Iberian Peninsula.

Javier Marías's submersion in Spain's past as it weighs on the personal experience of history in his recent novelistic trilogy *Tu rostro mañana* moves the theory of genre fusion toward a twenty-first century ellipsis. In Chapter 5, Marías's novels are read in light of his journalistic considerations of Spain's legacy as the country enters the age of globalization. For Marías, melding genres is a natural outcropping of the author's reexamination of his father's betrayal, and follows in step with Spain's recent attempts to come to terms with the more contentious issues still plaguing its past. A story that begins with Roig's historical aperture in the early years of Spain's Transition comes full circle as genre fusion highlights how twenty-first century Spain publicly wrestles with the ghosts of its past in Marías's writing. This process of historical reconfiguration, it stands to reason, will continue to suit the historical quests of the generations of Spanish writers, filmmakers, and artists to come. To discover how genre fusion will illuminate the literature of the next generation, we must first return to the place where the atoms of this contemporary literary movement of overlapping genres were created.

Chapter Two

Montserrat Roig
Testimony of the Marginalized Catalan

> *Su deportación sólo podrá*
> *terminar el día que los liberemos*
> *de sus recuerdos individuales:*
> *restituyéndolos a la memoria colectiva.*
> Montserrat Roig
> *Noche y niebla*

Testimonial Literature in Spain

Catalan photographer Francesc Boix's filmed deposition at the Nuremberg Trials, in January 1946, illustrates the power of testimony. An unseen interlocutor asks Boix in French, "Does the witness recognize among the defendants anyone who visited the camp of Mauthausen?" Boix looks to his right, rises from the witness stand, and points across the room, responding to the question with one word: "Speer." He proceeds to describe how at Mauthausen he developed photographs of Albert Speer, Hitler's chief architect during World War II, and thus could vouch for Speer's presence at the Austrian work camp in 1943 ("Trial Testimony against Albert Speer"). In a court of law, witness testimony is central to determining innocence or guilt; Speer was convicted and served twenty years in prison for his involvement in Nazi war crimes. Although he died in 1951, Boix would again bear witness thirty years after his testimony at Nuremberg, this time posthumously figuring into Montserrat Roig's stunning rediscovery of Catalans in Nazi concentration camps.

In a literary rather than a legal context, however, testimony—and *testimonio*, its Spanish counterpart—takes on different forms. Subgenres such as testimonial fiction, *la novela testimonial*, and documentary fiction are part of this ample category of testimony.

Chapter Two

Although definitions have been widely addressed and debated in the context of Latin American literature over the last two decades, testimony in contemporary Spanish literature has been studied far less. Given distinct historical circumstances, populations, and literary practices, however, the definition of testimony in Spain cannot simply be appropriated from Latin America. With the aid of scholarly work on the subject from Latin Americanists, however, it can be adapted to a Spanish context.

John Beverley defines testimonial writing in Latin America—which he refers to in general as *testimonio*—as a first-person account by either an illiterate individual or a non-professional writer or narrator who is directly involved in the episode under discussion. This singular author or narrator writes with an urgency to communicate the collective social experience or oppression of a group of people (32–33). Beverley's contemporary in the field, George Yúdice, expands on his idea, stating that:

> testimonial writing may be defined as an authentic narrative, told by a witness who is moved to narrate by the urgency of a situation (e.g., war, oppression, revolution, etc.). Emphasizing popular, oral discourse, the witness portrays his or her own experience as an agent (rather than a representative) of a collective memory and identity. Truth is summoned in the cause of denouncing a present situation of exploitation and oppression or in exorcising and setting aright official history. (44)

Yúdice's interpretation of testimonial writing as narrative situates it within the boundaries of traditional discourse, as opposed to excluding it from the literary field altogether or deeming it a new genre. By highlighting both the motivation behind an individual's decision to author a testimonial text and the drive to expose the truth through this text, Yúdice broaches a contentious issue that arises when testimony meets history and fiction.

Focusing on the testimonial novel, Elzbieta Sklodowska further narrows Beverley's and Yúdice's definitions by asserting that "testimonio has consistently defied the critics by departing from a traditional system of assumptions about truth and falsity, history and fiction, science and literature" (85). In terms of veracity, Beverley emphasizes that "[t]he word *testimonio* in Spanish carries the connotation of an act of truth telling in a religious or legal sense –*dar testimonio* means to testify, to bear truthful witness" (3). In all of these definitions, the issue of truth stands out as a determining factor in testimony, although the extent to which testimony is inherently true is constantly at issue. It is this matter of truth value that prompts René Jara to align testimony with historiography: "Como forma discursiva, el testimonio parece hallarse más cerca de la historiografía que de la literatura en la medida en que apunta hacia hechos que han ocurrido en el pasado y cuya autenticad [sic] puede ser sometida a pruebas de veredicción" (Jara and Vidal 1). The issue of truth in historiography has been debated perhaps as extensively as definitions of *testimonio*. As one of the early voices to question the empirical value of historiography, Hayden White argues that "the dual conviction that truth must be represented in literal statements of fact and explanation must conform to the scientific model or its commonsensical counterpart" ignores the literary qualities in historiography that also present versions of the truth (*Content* 48). Testimonial discourse, like genre fusion itself, challenges the traditional view that historical texts are always accurate and fictional texts always imaginary, and exposes the inadequacy of compartmentalizing a discourse that resides in the contested space between an "absolute" history and an "absolute" fiction.

The question of the veracity of *Me llamo Rigoberta Menchú y así me nació la conciencia* has fueled the debate on testimony in Latin America since its publication in 1983. Menchú's oral testimony was crafted into a narrative by Elisabeth Burgos-Debray, the editor of her autobiography, and translated. Critics questioned whether the final testimonial account was Menchú's voice or Burgos-Debray's interpretation.[1] If the authorial voice of the testimony is not that of the person bearing witness, and consequently that authorial voice may take liberties with what the witness originally presented, can the text be considered an accurate representation of the subject's experience? Moreover, are we to read all testimony as true? Removed from its narrative framework, testimony is rarely a full account. In the context of witnesses of the Holocaust, Shoshana Felman argues that "testimony does not offer… a completed statement, a totalizable account of those events" (Felman and Laub 5). Rather, the author or editor is responsible for constructing a whole narrative out of the fragments of witness memory contained in a testimony. In this sense, testimony is a narrative discourse subject to the same contentious issues of subjectivity and representation as historiography and fiction. In that most testimonial discourse is created by both the witness and the author, both individuals are held accountable for the accuracy of their representation of reality. Like any text that purports to represent reality, however, the reader makes the final determination of truthfulness. Moreover, testimony is molded by the structure of the narrative that captures it, which is characterized by such elements as point of view, discrete beginnings and endings, and direct or indirect discourse. Testimony manifests itself in fiction and nonfiction, weaving together imagination and reality, and thus allowing for the genre fusion of two testimonial texts on either side of the fiction and history divide.

A testimonial novel, it follows, is testimonial discourse appropriated by literature, in which the testimony is reworked or reimagined in a literary form. The Cuban writer Miguel Barnet's definition of the testimonial novel, as Sklodowska has pointed out, does not differ significantly from his definition of testimony itself. Barnet emphasizes the importance of objectivity in the testimonial novel: "Contribuir al conocimiento de la realidad, imprimirle a ésta un sentido histórico, es otro rasgo indispensable de la novela-testimonio" (289). Following these arguments, it is clear that testimony, when central to the formation of either a work of historiography or a work of fiction, may lend either genre an aura of truth. Still, the impossibility of determining the absolute veracity of testimony does not diminish its ability to represent verifiable historical events, much as I have argued regarding historical fiction. On a spectrum of narrative genres, testimony and the testimonial novel lie at the crossroads of fiction and history.

The aforementioned theorists base their assessments entirely on testimony and the testimonial novel in Latin America. Definitions of testimony in Spain, especially as it relates to the testimonial novel of postwar and Transition Spain, are harder to come by. The importance of testimony in contemporary Spain lies in the pressing need to tell a story of oppression or marginalization; in this way, Spanish and Latin American *testimonio* are the same. However, Spanish testimonial novels are generally authored by literate writers of the middle class who may use the testimonial genre to express a larger social concern, but who just as easily may treat an individual subject or experience that cannot be generalized to include an entire social network. In this way, testimony in Spain can express either an individual or collective voice.

Given this definition, Spanish authors of testimonial novels abound throughout the twentieth century, intersecting with what Hispanists have also grouped into the *novela social*, Neorealism, or New Journalism.² Camilo José Cela, Carmen Laforet, Ramón J. Sender, Miguel Delibes, Josefina Aldecoa, and Antonio Muñoz Molina are but a few names in an extensive list of authors committed to testimonial discourse in their novels. The testimonial techniques these authors use to generalize about a common experience are varied. Delibes's *Los santos inocentes* (1981), for example, gathers the voices of a collective group of poor landless Spaniards kept powerless by the landowning middle and upper classes during the postwar. Aldecoa's *Historia de una maestra* trilogy isolates the testimony of one woman to represent her unique individual trajectory as an educator in Spain, Ecuatorial Guinea, and Mexico during the twentieth century.³ These novels were written by literate members of the middle class and employ the testimonial genre as a tool to portray very different experiences of oppression and marginalization with a singular voice or communal voices.

In describing her methodology, Aldecoa explains how her personal authorial "I" becomes the voice of many in her testimonial discourse: "la narración del testigo partícipe... incrusta su vida en la de los demás y empieza a contar olvidando el yo, aludiendo sólo cuando es imprescindible al anecdotario personal" (*Los niños* 10). As a result, for Aldecoa, the personal becomes collective: "Mi propia vida no interesa, pero sí la vida que me ha tocado vivir, en la medida en que mi vida está integrada en la vida de una generación cronológica" (*Los niños* 10). Although Aldecoa discounts the importance of her individual account, it is in fact the starting point for her testimonial representation of collective memory.

Yúdice's definition of testimonial writing as an "authentic narrative" allows a broader sense of the genre, one that equally applies to Latin American authors and to Montserrat Roig, a Catalan author central to the formation of contemporary testimonial writing in Spain. In his introduction to Roig's 1975 collection of interviews with Spanish writers, *Los hechiceros de la palabra*, J. M. Castellet describes a national atmosphere of repression that leaves an impression on both Roig's journalistic and her fictional writing: "la condición de escritor ha sido, en estos años, la de un *outsider*, ... sin acceso a los medios de comunicación de masa que son los que, en las sociedades culturalmente desarrolladas, crean y ayudan a mantener un cultivo social de la literatura..." (Roig, *Los hechiceros* 10). Without this infrastructure of liberty and inclusiveness, the author must struggle to make her voice heard. Castellet emphasizes an even greater sense of marginalization for authors on the periphery, including Catalans: "¿si así ha sido en el caso de la literatura en lengua castellana, qué no habrá sucedido en las literaturas nacionales periféricas, marginadas ellas mismas en bloque, durante años y años?" (Roig, *Los hechiceros* 10n2).

This peripheral national literature and its marginalized authors are subject to a "present situation of exploitation and oppression," as Yúdice describes their experience, and this drives them to "[set] aright official history" (44). In the case of Spain, this national discourse is sanctioned and espoused by Franco, and categorically excludes the expression of a national identity by the Catalan people. It is during this era of oppression that Roig is moved, as a witness to the Franco dictatorship and its debilitating impact on Catalan identity, to tell the collective story of her people. Roig is a literate middle class writer who does not always narrate in the first person, but who relates the testimony of Catalans like herself who have been denied a voice in the official discourse of Spain. After the death of Franco in 1975, the most immediate forms of censorship are lifted, and Roig is free to express the anger and pride of her generation. While Roig does not present herself as a firsthand witness in most of her texts, she is a testimonial writer in the larger sense that she employs the stories of individuals to communicate collective experiences, overcoming the obstacle of imposed silence. Moreover, she is a member of this larger Catalan collective, and as such, her experiences fall into the collective memory she seeks to gather. She produces testimonial literature that is necessarily molded by a narrative framework to present a totalizing picture of the historical context of her subjects.

In her studies of recent Spanish testimonial texts, Jo Labanyi argues that testimony is not only a legal tool, but, like memory, also a method by which to gain "insight... into emotional attitudes toward the past in the present time of the speaker" ("Testimonies of Repression" 193). In highlighting Spain's lack of a post-dictatorship Truth and Reconciliation Commission, Labanyi draws a distinction between the public place of testimony in late-twentieth-century Latin America and the private or "silence[d]" place of testimony in Spain ("The Languages of Silence" 24–27).

The author's work on Spanish nonfiction testimony places a particular emphasis on the historical veracity of texts published after the new millennium, but recognizes that the whims of "notoriously nonchronological and nonfactual" (Labanyi, "Testimonies of Repression" 196) memory are not always addressed in them. Labanyi's observations are particularly useful in examining Roig's testimonial works, which were published during an earlier period of public and private silencing in Spain. Roig does not shy away from addressing the caprices of memory in testimony. Rather, Roig's subjective approach embodies the "'politics of feeling'" ("Testimonies of Repression" 204) in Spanish testimony that Labanyi proposes as an answer to Beverley's "politics of truth" in Latin American testimony.

Two scholars have made strides in understanding Roig's literary production in terms of Latin American models of testimony. Mercé Picornell Belenguer's objective, in her study of Roig's literary use of testimony, is to update the generic possibilities of testimonial discourse, locating it in a space also inhabited by fiction, history and autobiography (29). The author asserts that Roig "utilitza les tècniques de diversos gèneres per a transmetre els seus relats testimonials,... [i] se'ns mostra com una presència constantment involucrada en els fets que es narren. L'experiència personal de l'autora passa a ser part rellevant de l'elaboració del relat testimonial" ("utilizes the techniques of diverse genres in order to transmit her testimonial narrations,... [and] she shows herself as a constant presence involved in the events that she narrates. The personal experience of the author becomes a relevant part of the elaboration of the testimonial account," Picornell Belenguer 160), melding her own personal experiences with those of the witnesses whose testimony she curates.[4] Indeed, this autobiographical quality is evident throughout the Spanish texts in this study read through genre fusion. The "diverse genres" to which Picornell Belenguer refers are further evidence that Roig fuses her narrative historiography and historical fiction around the common bond of testimony.

In *La voz testimonial en Montserrat Roig*, Christina Dupláa sees testimony as central to the representation of history in Roig's texts. That history is subjective, however, and depends on the author's and the witnesses' perceptions of the past as it is reconstructed through testimony (Dupláa, *La voz testimonial* 21). This subjectivity is especially plain in Roig's work, where the author elicits the

Chapter Two

testimony of others to events she herself did not witness. Both Picornell Belenguer and Dupláa base their ideas on Beverley's definition of *testimonio*, revising it to describe Spanish testimonial literature. Dupláa, however, supplies the caveat that Roig's use of varied narrative perspectives (first, second, and third person) aligns her work more with the *novela testimonial*, as defined by Barnet. Dupláa also proposes that given the flaws in equating history with truth, it is more productive to dismiss this question and move on to other facets of the discussion (*La voz testimonial* 21). However, the reader's expectations of truthfulness or historical accuracy must necessarily enter into the equation, especially in historiographic or testimonial texts. Dupláa argues that the reader is responsible for determining this historical accuracy in the testimonial novel, comparing what is presented in the novel with the historical information that he or she possesses—which will vary from reader to reader, depending on his or her level of historical knowledge—while the author is responsible for the novelistic elements in testimonial fiction. The inclusion of outside documents (photographs, letters, diaries, etc.) contributes to the sense of historical accuracy that has become central to testimony. Dupláa argues that these varied documents—woven into Roig's testimonial texts—"*ayud*[*an*] a la recuperación memorística de *lo real* con elementos que d[an] más historicidad a la narración" (*La voz testimonial* 35; emphasis in the original). As we will see, historical accuracy is central to Roig's testimonial fiction and nonfiction, even though the reader alone determines to his or her own satisfaction whether the author is truthfully representing the past.

Dupláa insists that "lo que humaniza al discurso [testimonial] y le da este sentido esperanzador y reconciliador de cara al futuro es su propia *hibridez*" (*La voz testimonial* 38; emphasis in the original), that is, its intermingling of history and fiction. Although she overlooks the testimonial qualities of Roig's historiography, Dupláa clearly identifies the genre fusion—or hibridity—that can be applied to Roig's testimonial and history fiction. For Roig, the goal of testimonial discourse is not only to represent reality symbolically, but to "*denunciarla* para *transformarla*" (Dupláa, *La voz testimonial* 38; emphasis in the original), connecting the author's goals with those of testimony as defined by Beverley: an urgency to communicate a wrong with the ultimate goal of changing the system that propagates it. These relatively recent definitions of testimony in Spain are integral to two of Roig's texts, and coalesce around their interpretation through genre fusion.

Novelist, Journalist, and Obsessive Reality

In the introduction to her 1975 collection of interviews of Spanish authors, Roig defends what she sees as her dual role as journalist and novelist, underlining her interest in historical reality:

> Como a mí me atrae la novela y el periodismo de creación, dirigí mis intereses hacia esos dos campos y, por lo tanto, ver qué opinaban de su oficio novelistas y prosistas. Si del conjunto se trasluce la obsesión por una realidad histórica muy determinada —y también agobiante— no es culpa de ellos ni mía: es que esa realidad obsesiona. (*Los hechiceros* 14)

Roig's attraction to the captivating nature of historical examination foreshadows a curious role-reversal yet to come. In her 1980 novel *L'hora violeta* the author explores, through characters and intertext, her own complex attraction to the historiography that emerged from her journalistic examination of Catalans in Nazi concentration camps. Five years earlier, she formulated her thoughts on the reverberations of historical reality in her fiction as such:

> Quizá también se encuentre por parte mía una defensa pertinaz del realismo como fórmula válida en literatura. ... Pido en ello mis excusas: el realismo en literatura es la fórmula que me interesa más porque me parece que la realidad y todas sus zonas, que son inmensas, es de lo más apasionante. (Roig, *Los hechiceros* 15–16)

These statements reveal a passion about realism and history that Roig unabashedly admits influences her fictional work. Curiously, when the author is directly asked about her incorporation of journalism into fictional texts a decade after the experiment in blended genres that characterizes *L'hora violeta*, she responds:

> Distingo mucho entre el periodismo y la ficción; el periodismo es para mí la búsqueda de lo que no entiendo, de una realidad completamente distante de mí. ... Aunque tu visión de la realidad siempre es subjetiva, siendo periodista los datos que utilizas

Chapter Two

> siempre tienen que ser verdaderos. ... He visto realidades distintas en el trabajo periodístico, he ido a mundos distantes, pero no los sabría introducir en el campo de la literatura; quizá porque me afectan poco también. (Nichols 171)

Roig first eagerly touts her formula for incorporating reality into fiction, then distances herself from an intermingling of the two genres. These contradictions demonstrate that the author herself is tied to traditional genre distinctions when speaking about her work, but that these distinctions are not as evident in the work itself. In trying to grasp Roig's shifting opinions on the role of the real in fiction, it is helpful to consider her specific response when she reports on a less "distant" subject matter: Catalan deportees during the post–Civil War period. In this case, Roig combines journalistic and literary elements when writing about a topic we might infer deeply affects her both personally and professionally. In her 1977 study *Els catalans als camps nazis* and in *L'hora violeta*, this interweaving of journalism and literature takes the form not only of overt inclusions of anecdotes and citations from the former into the latter, but also of an intermingling of the very historiographic and narrative techniques that drive Roig's discourse. While the author may make the gesture of separating herself into the discrete entities of journalist and novelist, an analysis of her texts using genre fusion tells a different story.

* * *

The tales of Catalans who fled Spain in 1939 fearing political persecution after the Spanish Civil War create the explicit connection between *Els catalans als camps nazis* and *L'hora violeta*. As a result of Francisco Franco's amicable relationship with Adolf Hitler, many of these Catalan exiles were deported from France to Nazi concentration camps during World War II. Roig, although born in 1946 and thus never directly affected by the conflicts in Spain and Western Europe, shares with the Catalan deportees a common resistance to the Franco regime. Roig and her family struggled against the dictator's oppressive measures in Catalonia. Despite laws expressly forbidding it, the author grew up speaking, reading, and writing in Catalan, a political act hidden in the mundane. Furthermore, Roig maintained an involvement in leftist politics throughout her life, most strikingly in her efforts to keep the Catalan language and culture at the forefront of public discourse during the years after Franco's death and throughout Spain's transition to democracy.[5] Roig has said that "escribir en catalán era como respirar. Incluso no era casi ni un hecho político, sino una identificación muy fuerte con el entorno" (Nichols 153). All the same, publishing in Catalan during the Franco dictatorship and even during the Transition was a political act, in that Roig was conducting public discourse in a currently or formerly illegal language. By virtue of her continued interest in representing the Catalan experience and language in novels and journalism, Roig sought to counterbalance the marginalization of Catalonia and its people during the dictatorship.

Roig's involvement in leftist politics went beyond language and books. She participated in anti-Franco protests while a student at the University of Barcelona; contributed to the Primer Congrès de Cultura Catalana, a 1976 meeting to plan the reintroduction of Catalan culture into mainstream society through the post-Franco era; joined and later broke ties with the Catalan Communist party in the 1970s; and wrote about Catalan authors, politicians, and other public figures in her journalism. In all of these endeavors, she communicated the importance of Catalan culture and autonomy during the years of Spain's transition to democracy to a wide audience.

With Adolfo Suárez's reinstatement of the Catalan Statute of Autonomy in 1977, Catalan politics also began a process of realignment, soon to be followed by the "Llei de Normalització Lingüística" which made the Catalan language official and provided a definition of Catalan identity.[6] Teresa Vilarós describes the period of transition beginning in 1975 as a "spontaneous movement concerned above all with reconstructing and reconfiguring Catalan national identity," and she equates Roig with "the open cultural expression of Catalan identity, ... long denied and repressed under Spanish (Castilian) hegemony in general, and under Franco's dictatorship in particular" ("A Cultural Mapping" 38). Vilarós furthermore calls Roig's contributions a sign of "post-dictatorship optimism," in a desire to unite "cultural (literary representation) and scientific life... and the everyday sphere":

> Montserrat Roig and many other representatives of Catalan culture in the years of political transition saw it as their collective task to bridge this divide. They aimed to end the cultural

and scientific isolation of the Catalan language and culture in both the national and the international context at a moment when democratic freedoms suddenly made this possible. ("A Cultural Mapping" 37–38)

Roig's desire to end Catalonia's isolation takes the form of a renewed engagement with the region's history, a goal Kathryn Crameri has deemed one of the means by which "post-Franco Catalonia has turned to the past in order to find a way forward into the future" (44). Roig was emblematic of this collective drive to restore an interest in Catalonia by merging cultural or literary representation with scientific or historical representation.

Until her death in 1991, Roig was a visible persona in popular journalism, writing for Catalan newspapers, producing television programs, and authoring collections of interviews as well as historically based travelogues and studies.[7] Her equally influential narrative spans short stories, personal essays, and novels about three successive generations of two Catalan families.[8] As a woman in a patriarchal society and a Catalan promoting nationalism at a time of forced Spanish unity, Roig was doubly marginalized, while still firmly establishing her testimonial voice on behalf of both populations. Kathryn Everly sees "[w]omen and Catalans, in a much broader sense, confront[ing] not only political exile but also various forms of social, linguistic, and personal exile that force them into a silent corner" (*Catalan Women Writers* 15). They are consequently afforded the space to "reimagine themselves" (Everly, *Catalan Women Writers* 16) as well as to rewrite Spain's official history from the perspective of a marginalized subject. This state-imposed marginalization and the subsequent metamorphosis of the cultural climate in Spain created a unique atmosphere of historical reexamination during the Transition as "the oppression of the dictatorship followed by the watershed of the post-Franco years … served as a catalyst for women to rewrite and reinterpret an 'official history'" (Everly, *Catalan Women Writers* 25–26), an opportunity of which Roig took full advantage.

Roig has often been studied as an author of the post-Franco generation who confronts issues of feminism, gender, and memory, although her work covers an even broader range of subjects, including history, politics, and autobiography. Critics have been reluctant to delve into these "reality based" topics, however, and as a consequence, Roig's blending of fiction and historiography has rarely been examined. When history does enter into critical examinations of Roig's work, it is often as a footnote to her treatment of gender issues.[9] In many of her texts, especially novels such as *L'hora violeta* in which multiple generations of women give voice to the Catalan feminine experience, Roig does actively subordinate the question of history to the overarching issue of gender.[10] In *Els catalans als camps nazis*, on the other hand, historical discourse is not subordinated to a feminine discourse. While Roig is dedicated to incorporating the marginalized voices of women into her historiographic study, this aspect of the text is only one among its many noteworthy aspects, not the least of which is Roig's uncovering of a previously ignored population of Catalans in Nazi camps. The author has described her view of history as filtered through two distinct perspectives, each a *mirada bòrnia* ("one-eyed glance"): if she closes one eye, history is intertwined with her own personal experience as a woman; if she closes the other eye, history is the reflection of a universal human experience (Roig, *Digues que m'estimes* 105). By focusing exclusively on a gendered interpretation of Roig's writing, scholars effectively minimize the historical presence central to the author's texts. My analysis of Roig's interweaving of fiction and historiography puts this feminist approach to one side to be able to concentrate on the historical approach Roig describes in her second, ungendered glance.

Despite Roig's blending of narrative historiography with historical fiction, made evident by overlapping *Els catalans als camps nazis* with *L'hora violeta*, these texts have rarely been compared in any detail. *Els catalans* is a sprawling and groundbreaking historiographic and testimonial study mentioned mainly in the context of Roig's novels as an example of her journalistic work and autobiographical tendencies; only sporadically is it examined independent of Roig's fiction.[11] *L'hora violeta*, the final novel in Roig's trilogy about the Miralpeix and Ventura-Claret families, has been analyzed from many angles, but the influence of *Els catalans* on the novel is generally centered on references about superficial borrowings from the historiographic study incorporated into the sequence of the novel. By reducing *Els catalans* to a source text for *L'hora violeta*, these studies downplay the independent value of *Els catalans* as a historiographic study, while also failing to capture any but the most overt influences between the two texts.[12] Skimming over the deeper relationship Roig has constructed between

Chapter Two

Els catalans and *L'hora violeta*, scholars who study both texts in conjunction have concluded that Roig's conscious interweaving of fiction and historiography is, at best, a movement toward new journalistic trends and, at worst, an afterthought.

Nevertheless, these two texts not only converge in terms of their testimonial narrative style, but they also approach similar questions of truth, memory, self-representation, and the place of history in everyday life, opening up a new line of inquiry into historical and collective memory in postwar Spain. Additionally, their structures, inclusion of fictional and nonfictional archival material, incorporation of historical data, and thematic juxtapositions expose the author's self-conscious melding. Roig's authorial hand steadily guides the two texts together, resulting in a breaching of genre barriers and a depth of historical expression. By incorporating testimony's "politics of truth" and "politics of feeling" into a single unified narrative, examining Roig's works through genre fusion provides a seldom-seen portrait of a marginalized population during a decisive period in Spain's past.

Els catalans als camps nazis: Individual Testimony to a Collective Nightmare

Soon after their arrival in the camps, the deportees introduced in *Els catalans als camps nazis* begin to comprehend what their lives will degrade to in the weeks, months, and years to come. One survivor recounts a scene as he entered Mauthausen:

> [E]ns van portar de seguida a les dutxes i ens van fer despullar. Vam quedar tal com vam néixer, amb un fred que pelava. Va venir un intèrpret alemany que s'havia apuntat per a lluitar voluntari amb en Franco. Aquell home ens va engegar un discurs:
>
> —Sabeu on heu entrat? Això és un camp de tercera categoria. Sabeu què vol dir? Us vull donar un consell d'amic, perquè jo he estat a Espanya i us tinc certa simpatia. Si no voleu morir de qualsevol manera d'aquí a tres mesos, mireu cap allà.
>
> Els focus van il·luminar els filferrats. Hi havia tot d'homes atrapats, enxampats als fils, recargolats.
>
> —Us ho dic de debò —va continuar l'intèrpret—. Suïcideu-vos, és el millor que podeu fer. Si no, morireu d'una altra manera, com els que hi ha per terra.

Aleshores vaig adonar-me que allò que trepitjava i que em pensava que era humitat era sang… (Roig, *Els catalans* 146–47)

[They took us immediately to the showers and made us undress. We were naked as the day we were born, bitterly cold. A German interpreter who had enlisted voluntarily to fight with Franco came up. He started lecturing us:
"Do you know where you are? This is a category three camp. Do you know what that means? I want to give you some friendly advice, because I was in Spain and I feel a certain kindness towards you. If you don't want to die in any old manner three months from now, look over there."
The lights illuminated the barbed wire fence. They were full of twisted bodies, caught on the electric wires.
"I'm giving it to you straight," the interpreter continued, "Kill yourselves, it's the best thing you can do. If not, you're going to die some other way, like the ones on the ground."
Then I realized that what I was stepping on and what I had thought was dampness was blood…]

The initial shock is worn thin by the daily repetition of the same dehumanizing routine: hours of back-breaking work, minute breaks for scant amounts of food, beatings earned by minimal infractions, and the constant presence of death. At the end of the day, another deportee explains: "'Tornàvem al camp cap al tard i aleshores a formar, sovint tres o quatre hores, a l'*Appellplatz*, per veure els qui havien mort. Els qui no podien resistir queien allà i ningú no els podia tocar'" ("'We returned to camp in the evening and then on to the formations, usually for three or four hours, at the *Appellplatz*, to see who had died. Those who couldn't tolerate it stayed there and no one could touch them,'" Roig, *Els catalans* 152). These deeply disturbing stories are clearly valuable as historical documentation, but in terms of Roig's wider narrative, they gain added significance because they are all included, verbatim, in *L'hora violeta*.

In his introduction to *Els catalans*, Artur London, a former International Brigadist in the Spanish Civil War and a concentration camp survivor,[13] summarized Roig's work as such: "Montserrat em va explicar que estava escrivint un llibre sobre el destí dels seus compatriotes catalans que, després de la desfeta de la República espanyola, havien estat enduts per la tempesta de la Segona Guerra Mundial i sobre els quals el franquisme havia intentat de fer caure el vel de l'oblit" ("Montserrat explained to me that she was writing a book about the destiny of her Catalan compatriots who, after the defeat of the Spanish Republic, had been carried away by the tempest of the Second World War and over whom Francoism had tried to make the veil of oblivion fall," Roig, *Els catalans* 5). This deceptively simple outline includes two details that will become tropes in this text and later in *L'hora violeta*: first, the inclusive description of the Spanish exiles as "Catalan compatriots," associating them not only with the rest of the Catalan people, but with Roig herself; second, the threat of oblivion that hangs over the entire history, one that Roig and the subjects of her study will constantly labor to defuse. These threads are apparent in Roig's intention with the text, as told to London: "'La nostra tasca, la dels periodistes, del escriptors, dels artistes, és aclarir les zones fosques de la memòria col·lectiva dels nostres pobles...'" ("'Our task, that of journalists, writers, artists, is to shed light on the dark zones of the collective memory of our people...'" Roig, *Els catalans* 5). Roig dedicates herself to the recuperation of a Catalan identity lost during the silence imposed by the Franco regime. She is driven to compile the testimony of those who lived the experience of deportation to and existence in Nazi concentration camps in an attempt to recover a facet of the collective memory of the Catalan people. As compiler, observer, and author, she is an integral part of this testimony and the construction of a collective memory. Her project never strays from the goal of revising Franco's official history to include the voices of those at the margins. Roig not only self-consciously splices her two texts together, but is wholly aware that this narrative synthesis is positioned to revise Spain's historical memory.

Roig published *Els catalans* in 1977,[14] during the period of unparalleled transition in Catalonia inaugurated by Franco's death. The text is a public acknowledgment of a story that was, until this time, rarely told and officially denied. Roig's study not only appeals to a sense of Catalan nationalism, a pride in the struggles and accomplishments made by its people, but it also presents Catalonia on a world stage, as an integral participant in European history. Beyond the historiographic impulses in the text, Roig's retelling maintains an emotional appeal that, like the political and cultural advances made in the years after Franco's death, announces Catalonia as different from the rest of Spain, and, moreover, worthy of a place in the official history of the country. *Els catalans* arrives at a crucial moment. It will influence the way the history of those on the margins is communicated in post-Franco Spain as well as how Roig will thread historiography through her subsequent work of fiction.

Although Dupláa asserts that "[n]o one wrote about the history of Catalans and other Spanish Republicans who died in Nazi concentration camps" ("Essay, Memory, and Testimony" 216) before Roig, in actuality the author came across the topic by reading a collection of letters detailing Pere Vives i Clavé's experience of deportation and his eventual death in Mauthausen, published posthumously five years earlier. This Catalan man's death in the camp inspired Roig to see him as "una mica el símbol de la innocència sacrificada per l'irracionalisme sistematitzat a través d'un ordre polític" ("something of a symbol of innocence sacrificed for irrationality systematized through a political order," Roig, *Els catalans* 12). The trope of an individual representing a collective disorder would firmly take hold in Roig's study. Additional accounts of Spaniards in Nazi camps were available by the time Roig began writing,[15] many first person testimonials or testimonial novels.[16]

Although Roig was not the first scholar to uncover the presence of Catalans in Nazi concentration camps, her approach to the subject is a unique combination of personal memoir and a strictly historical account of the era. Roig makes the text her own by employing a combination of historiography, testimony, and storytelling to her study of the Catalan deportees. Via the first-person accounts of survivors and Roig's third-person narration, the 547-page volume includes a narrative chronology of the experiences of the deportees starting with their initial exile in France from 1939 to 1940, through the liberation of the German camps in 1945, to the survivors' lives well into the 1960s and 1970s, when Roig contacts many of them. *Els catalans* clearly labors, following Yúdice's definition of testimony, to "[set] aright official history" (44). The agent of collective memory is not a witness to the events but rather Roig herself, who collects, orders, and narrates survivor testimony, contextualized within the historical events of the period. What gives *Els catalans* qualities of the Spanish *testimonio*, furthermore, are the literary elements with which Roig imbues the text. She weaves lengthy quotations from concentration camp survivors with a narration that purposely calls attention to itself. After one survivor describes an aspect of the extermination process, Roig responds with a one-sentence paragraph: "Les seleccions per a morir eren arbitràries" ("The selection of who was to die was arbitrary," *Els catalans* 186). Roig's intervention reveals an attention to narrative detail more commonly associated with works of literature: alternating long and short paragraphs or sentences, and a statement that, while obvious from the context, shocks the reader in a manner suggestive of oral storytelling. Roig deftly incorporates her voice into the voices of the survivors she interviews, creating an added layer of first-person authority and highlighting her role as the storyteller who augments suspense, provides characterization, and develops a plot, all within the boundaries of historiography.

Roig's role as intermediary between the testimony of the survivors and the composition of the story is evident throughout the text. In one instance, she discusses a deportee whose job was to record the cause of death and inventory prisoners at the camp, writing: "En Joan de Diego no vol parlar d'ell mateix, però nosaltres sabem que va fer molta feina al camp" ("Joan de Diego did not want to talk about himself, but we know that he did a lot of work in the camp," Roig, *Els catalans* 189). Roig's hand guides the narration here, first creating a pact between herself and the reader—even obliquely counting herself among the witnesses—then providing the personal details that are central to any story, but that often fall outside the scope of a traditional historiography. In the case of de Diego, he later confesses to Roig: "'Després acompanyava els morts fins al crematori. Jo anava al seu darrera, tot portant el llibre de registres sota el braç. Ho feia més que res pensant en els seus familiars, a fi que aquell mort no se sentís tan sol'" ("'Afterwards I accompanied the dead to the crematorium. I went behind them, with the registry book underneath my arm. More than anything, I did this thinking about their families, so that the dead person didn't feel so alone,'" *Els catalans* 196). This exchange presents a memorable and emotionally charged scene to the reader: Roig records de Diego's inner thoughts alongside the more practical matters of his task counting the dead. These profoundly personal moments serve to temper the historiographic impulses of the text with the emotion, suspense, and omniscient narration of a work of literature. Armed with an arsenal of narratological strategies, Roig and the deportees are storytellers, building on the literary qualities of a text in which the readers are directly invited, by Roig's first-person narration, to participate. The result is a work of narrative historiography, made unique by its dependence on these literary elements. The reader is drafted to defend the legitimacy of this marginalized historical moment, making his or her participation a political act by accepting a collective history that contradicts Franco's official history.

The text compiles individual testimonies in which the survivors who recount episodes of horror recur throughout the text as though they were characters in a novel. Roig focuses on the experiences of a number of deportees in particular who gradually become the protagonists of *Els catalans*. Their harrowing tales of survival form the cornerstone of her historiography, drawing out the development of the personas of individual deportees, allowing personal narrative to speak for a collective experience, and accentuating the volume's storytelling quality. This turn toward a more literary-minded discourse is no coincidence: Roig will extract these stories from *Els catalans* and weave them into *L'hora violeta*. She manipulates the value of these tales as true episodes while coveting them both for their captivating literariness and for the historical contextualization they lend her fictional text. The anecdotes themselves—a word that cannot aptly describe these reports, which are horrifying yet by all accounts accurate[17]—constitute the bulk of Roig's study, filling in her chronological framework with the occurrences that bind historical events to the people who lived them. An examination of a number of the specific experiences relayed to Roig by two survivors who will figure prominently in *L'hora violeta* underscores the historiographical emplotment and true-life character development that openly structures the novel. This character development is not inherent in the experiences of the deportees themselves, however. Their transformation from autonomous individuals to numbers becomes apparent as the narration progresses: "A poc a poc, els nostres deportats han de deixar d'ésser homes. Comencen a ésser menys que els animals, un número i prou, comencen a ésser no res" ("Little by little, our deportees have to stop being men. They begin to be less than animals, a number and that's it, they begin to be nothing at all," Roig, *Els catalans* 145). Roig juxtaposes the human reactions to cruelty contained in the survivor's testimony with their subhuman treatment in the camps; the progression between these two extremes constitutes another method of examining the deportees as individuals who represent a collective agony.

In the first chapter on the "Origen i destí dels deportats" ("Origin and Destiny of the Deportees"), Roig relates Casimir Climent i Sarrion's experience at the age of six when his father obliged him to look at anarchists executed against a wall. His father told the young Climent: "'mira'ls bé, t'ha de quedar gravat a la memòria, perquè tu no siguis com ells'" ("'take a good look at them, they should be recorded in your memory, so you won't wind up like them,'" *Els catalans* 30–31). This early exposure to the violence that would lead to the Spanish Civil War would prove to be only a precursor to what Climent would witness as a Catalan prisoner inside Mauthausen. His memory will become the cornerstone of a new Spanish historical memory. His motivation to record what he sees spares him from the fates of his fellow prisoners and allows their stories to join a revised historical record.

From his privileged post inside the offices of Mauthausen, Climent secretly kept duplicate lists of the Spaniards who entered the camp and those who survived. His lists, which appear in the hundred pages of appendices to *Els catalans*, would prove invaluable for the later study of the camps. His personal intervention led to Roig's encounters with survivors of the camps. Furthermore, his testimony illuminates the inner mechanisms of the Mauthausen machine from the perspective of a prisoner who is both witness to and victim of the torture propagated by the SS and the *Kapos* at the camps. Climent describes boxing matches that took place on Sundays between deportees, while the howling of prisoners confined to their cells and slowly starving to death was hauntingly audible: "'Udolaven de fam i de set i de por. S'estaven a les fosques i no els donaven res per a menjar i per a beure. Al cap de deu dies encara en quedaven de vius que s'enterraven entre els morts per tal d'escalfar-se'" ("'They howled from hunger and thirst and fear. They were in the dark and they didn't give them anything to eat or drink. After ten days those that were still alive buried themselves between the dead ones to stay warm,'" Roig, *Els catalans* 156). Climent died in 1978, after submitting himself for annual treatments in a mental institution, not unlike many of his fellow deportees. His individual testimony to the deaths of countless prisoners—not just Catalans—becomes the collective memory of the survivors, all of whom witnessed the cruel slaughter of their fellow prisoners. Those who survived the camps suffered lasting personal repercussions from their nightmarish experiences.

Roig's acquaintance with the deportee Joaquim Amat-Piniella is difficult but ultimately enlightening. She meets him in 1972, after reading his quasi-fictional autobiography, and his experiences in the Nazi camps come to have a profound effect on her, as she explains: "He conegut molts ex-deportats catalans, hi he vist reaccions i actituds diverses davant de la deportació nazi i les seves romanalles, però foren els ulls terriblement cansats de l'Amat-Piniella allò que més coses em van saber dir del què havia significat l'infern nazi" ("I've known many Catalan ex-deportees, I've seen different reactions and attitudes toward the Nazi deportation and its waste, but it was the terribly tired eyes of Amat-Piniella that told me the most about what the Nazi hell meant," Roig, *Els catalans* 12–13). Amat-Piniella's eyes reflect his arduous struggle to survive in Mauthausen. He seems to revive somewhat when he learns that Roig is planning to tell the story of the Catalans in the camps, playfully telling her that "'Els ex-deportats estem tots tocats'" ("'The ex-deportees are all crazy'") and repeating "amb un somriure una mica irònic, que la veritat, la veritat, no la sabria mai" ("with a slightly ironic smile, that the truth, you'll never know the truth," Roig, *Els catalans* 13). These references to the compromised memory of the survivors and the truthfulness of their stories force Roig and the reader to doubt the historical veracity of the deportees' accounts. This doubt imbues *Els catalans* with a fictional element: the reader does not always know with confidence where the line between reality and imagination is drawn.

Amat-Piniella's death is imminent, and Roig posits that "fou precisament el seu deler per ésser objectiu, equilibrat, per trobar l'harmonia entre la memòria malalta i la comprensió d'un món trasbalsat, el que matà per segona vegada en Joaquim Amat-Piniella, l'estiu de 1974" ("it was precisely his eagerness to be objective, balanced, to find the harmony between evil memory and the comprehension of a disturbed world, that killed Joaquim Amat-Piniella for the second time, in the summer of 1974," *Els catalans* 12). His first death was the demise of his spirit in the camps; his second, his physical death years later. Amat-Piniella, like Roig and the protagonists in *L'hora violeta*, agonizes over the

Chapter Two

traps laid by a degrading memory and a powerfully subjective bond to history. Roig posits that the historical objectivity he seeks is impossible in the pages of a testimonial historiography: only Amat-Piniella, the witness, knows the truth.

The associations Roig cultivates while writing *Els catalans* yield myriad first-hand accounts of the camps. The reader observes the characters and personalities of these survivors develop throughout their imprisonment and over the course of their lives after the camps, as their reactions and scars continue to evolve. Roig's personal relationships with Climent and Amat-Piniella, among other deportees, color her historiography, incorporating a subjectivity and a wider, more personal context of the historical moment into the text that is generally not supplied in a strictly historiographic study. These literary traits—Roig's interaction with the text and the deportees, their detailed accounts of everyday life in the camps, and the narrative structure she builds with these characters and stories—are balanced by and seamlessly blended into the historiographic qualities of the volume. They are the elements that allow us to analyze this text and her next novel through the lens of genre fusion.

Roig maintains a constant authoritative presence throughout *Els catalans*, outlining her approach to the project in the introduction, as we will see, while laboring to make herself both heard and ignored in the body of the text at different moments. As the narrator, she weaves quotes from the deportees themselves, collected from her own personal interviews and correspondence with survivors, with accounts she has composed from her research. Dupláa has even argued that Roig's voice is more forceful than the first-person testimonies she quotes due to Roig's staunch defense of marginalized voices from her own culture (*La voz testimonial* 59). The reader is reminded at intervals that Roig is the intellect behind this study, and that her investigations drive the text's historicity. She writes, for instance: "Quina mena de gent són aquests deportats? Al llarg de les meves entrevistes he pogut comprovar que provenen de la classe treballadora, alguns de capes mitjanes o de la pagesia" ("What kind of people are these deportees? Throughout my interviews I have been able to verify that they come from the working class, a few closer to the middle class or to the peasant class," *Els catalans* 26). Roig is firm about her place as interlocutor for the deportees, her role in verifying their accounts, and her ability to broaden what they tell her into generalizations about this historical period. She cites Climent's final number of Spanish Republican deportees who survived the camps as 2,183. In a footnote, however, she also cites the number of survivors determined by another historian—2,191—commenting that "[l]a xifra d'en Climent sembla, doncs, força exacta" ("Climent's figure seems, then, rather exact," *Els catalans* 131n22). This glossing highlights Roig's function in the text both as narrator, returning to the figure of Climent for his assessment of the survivors, and historian, comparing Climent's number with another historian's in order to corroborate Climent's calculation. Roig's intervention not only underlines her goal of historical veracity, it momentarily ruptures her storytelling rhythm, and, as such, establishes this intermingling of literature and historiography as a central feature of the text. Ultimately, though, these two competing numbers of survivors prove that historical truth is only determined by the author and reader's interpretations.

Nevertheless, Roig reminds the reader that she controls the story: "Encara que alguns testimonis em van dir el nom dels qui no aguantaren el dolor, he preferit «oblidar-los». El culpable, a la llarga, no és el qui parla sota les tortures, sinó qui les hi infligeix" ("Although some witnesses told me the names of those who couldn't tolerate the pain, I have preferred to 'forget them.' The guilty party, in the long run, is not the one who informs under torture, rather it is the one who inflicts the torture," *Els catalans* 83). Roig's disgust and condemnation of the actions of the Nazis is clear even though she constructs the text as an objective historiography. That objectivity is compromised when Roig intentionally omits details, yet she incorporates herself into the text with these asides, a presence that is characteristic of genre fusion. In maintaining a personal and subjective connection to her work, the survivors she interviews become "[e]ls nostres deportats" ("our deportees," Roig, *Els catalans* 15, and elsewhere in the text) who have made a lasting impression on the author. "Un ampli i profund ventall psicològic es va desplegar al meu davant mentre recollia dades i testimonis per a aquest llibre" ("A large and profound psychological range opened up around me while I recalled facts and testimony for this book," *Els catalans* 18), Roig recalls. Dori Laub writes that a listener such as Roig "by definition partakes of the struggle of the victim with the memories and residues of his or her traumatic past" (Felman and Laub 58), another sign that the author has become so intimately involved with her testimonial text that it has psychologically affected her.

The personal effect Roig describes goes beyond the impact of the deportees on Roig to include their impact on collective Catalan society. The text's essential testimonial quality functions both as a means of righting an unjust omission and as a preventative measure historically, illustrating Beverley's and Yúdice's definitions of the purpose of textimonial discourse. Roig's multiple roles as narrator, investigator, editor, and historian guide the text toward the desire for change in which the testimony of a few becomes a collective story of the oppressed: "el que compta és això: que el seu record ens serveixi a nosaltres, en la lluita particular i col·lectiva, en els nostres desigs per fer possible un món que ells somiaren que seria real a la nostra època" ("what counts is this: that their memory helps us, in the individual and collective fight, in our wishes to make possible a world about which they only dreamt and that could be real in our time," *Els catalans* 18). While delving in great detail into the past, Roig maintains a vision for the future with *Els catalans*: that Spain's official discourse will never again exclude those at the margins, and, by the same token, that tragedies such as the Holocaust will never be repeated. Her historiography is thus both a personal and political statement.

In Dupláa's estimation, the theme of Roig's text coagulates around a central history—the presence of Catalans in Nazi concentration camps—filtered through not only the testimony of survivors, but also through Roig's narration. The "fictional" aspect of the text is derived from the author's mediating and subjective voice. Roig's agency in the delivery of the survivors' testimony positions her as the moralizing storyteller. Furthermore, Dupláa argues that both faces of the text, the literary and the historiographic, are subjective in their own right, inasmuch as history is also filtered through the author's narration:

> Para problematizar el discurso testimonial, calificado de género híbrido por estar lindando los límites del análisis histórico y del literario, propongo, de nuevo, que aceptemos el compromiso de que en el testimonio hay historia —lo que se pretende es recuperar la memoria histórica dando voz al silencio— y hay ficción. Por decirlo en otras palabras: *histórico* es el tema que se propone y *ficticia* es la aproximación a él. (*La voz testimonial* 53; emphasis in the original)

However, the "historical" and "fictional" qualities of Roig's text are not so easily divided into theme and approach. While history is clearly the central theme of *Els catalans*, the narratological strategies Roig uses fall into two categories: the literary, guided by a narrative approach influenced by fiction-writing; and the historical, given that Roig's text recounts actual historical events and treats questions of historiography.[18] In an exploration of these two basic categories, it becomes evident that *Els catalans* can be read through the lens of genre fusion, in which history and historiography intermingle with literary elements through a testimonial discourse. When paired with *L'hora violeta*, the text completes a detailed and personalized history of marginalized Catalans during the postwar.

The wealth of documentation Roig provides is perhaps the most striking of the historiographic elements of *Els catalans*, and lends another personal touch to the narrative. Spaced throughout the text are photos of Mauthausen, Catalan prisoners, the dead, and the SS officers, many of which were taken and saved by Francesc Boix. Boix later used these photographs to incriminate Nazi officers during his riveting testimony at the Nuremberg trials, demonstrating the concrete utility of these nontextual elements in a legal context. In addition, Roig includes maps of the interior layout of Mauthausen, some of which are hand-drawn by the deportees. She reproduces drawings, postcards, and letters written by Catalan prisoners, some attesting to the aid Climent provided in saving others. Roig inserts into the text official documents, letters, and certificates pertaining to medical experiments, proof of internment, and permission granted to the prisoners to communicate with family members. Meticulous lists of Catalans who died at Mauthausen and their origins, taken in large part from the lists Climent assembled while in the camp as well as lists of Catalans at other Nazi camps, at Nazi "sanatoriums," in transports from one camp to another, and of Catalan teenagers imprisoned in the camps fill the volume's appendices.[19] The sheer abundance and variety of information contained in Roig's study distinguishes the work as not only highly historical and well documented, but also as an immensely personal means of recovering Catalan collective memory for both the author and her subjects, many of whom contributed to the volume with their own saved documents, photos, and letters.[20] These materials add to the collective drive to rewrite history shared by all of the survivors who participated in *Els catalans*.

Roig is not a Mauthausen survivor, but she positions herself as a member of a larger forgotten collective. In the prologue, she writes: "Els qui vam néixer després de 1939 hem hagut d'anar desbrossant el nostre passat recent, un passat que ens ha deixat massa tares per a poder restituir del tot la nostra salut històrica" ("Those of us who were born after 1939 have had to clear-cut our recent past, a past that has left us too defect-ridden to be able to completely restore our historical health," *Els catalans* 11). Roig asserts the need to reincorporate these marginalized stories into Spain's official history in order to restore her generation's and her own "historical health," a goal shared by those who seek the "recovery" or "recuperation" of Spain's historical memory twenty-five years later. She goes on to emphasize her personal identification with history:

> A banda l'atracció que sento pel món de la ficció, sempre m'he sentit atreta per la història del meu país. El silenci que han fet planar per damunt d'els catalans, dels republicans, dels vençuts de la guerra, m'ha semblat, tot sovint, que era un silenci que volien fer planar per damunt dels meus i de mi mateixa. Veia que si no retornàvem la paraula als qui l'havien de tenir quan els pertocava, nosaltres no la tindríem mai en la seva totalitat. (Roig, *Els catalans* 11)
>
> [Setting aside my attraction for the fictional world, I have always felt a strong attraction for the history of my country. The silence imposed upon the Catalans, the Republicans, those defeated in the war, has frequently appeared to me to be a silence that they wanted to impose on my people and me personally. I saw that if we did not give back the right of speech to those who needed to have it when it was their turn to use it, we would never have it in its totality. (Translated in Dupláa, "Essay, Memory, and Testimony" 217)]

Roig equates breaking the silence of the Catalan prisoners with breaking her own silence, and the silence imposed on all of "her country," Catalonia. *Els catalans* is Roig's opportunity to claim a unified voice for marginalized Catalans like herself in the future of Spanish public discourse. Published the same year the Spanish government enacted the Amnesty Law, Roig's volume sounds one of the first alarms against this official Pact of Silence.

Yet despite Roig's desire to regain a sense of Catalan history for the benefit of the collective memory of her generation and herself personally, notions of what constitutes historiography seem to be elusive for the author. After she introduces some of the deportees who inspired her to relate their experiences, she takes a broader look at the volume she has composed:

> En realitat, aquest llibre no és més que la coordinació de totes aquestes veus: totes elles formen una convincent presència col·lectiva. De tota manera, cal dir que és un llibre obert, una obra que haurà de ser continuada, revisada i ampliada. Em consideraria prou satisfeta si algun historiador s'hi engresqués, després de la lectura, i en fes el llibre decisiu des del punt de vista historiogràfic. (Roig, *Els catalans* 13)

> [In reality, this book is nothing more than a coordination of all of these voices: all of them form a convincing collective presence. In any case, this must be called an open book, a work that should be continued, revised, and amplified. I would consider myself satisfied if a historian motivated himself, after reading this, to write the decisive book from the historiographic point of view.]

Historiography—the writing of history—is created by the materials Roig has amassed here: testimony, third-person description, historical background, documents, chronology. By calling for a historiographic revision of her work, Roig suggests that the perspective she has used is not, in fact, historiographic, although she does not define it otherwise. Perhaps this genre ambiguity lies in the nagging question of historical accuracy or truth; in the demand to know the "real events." This is a question Hayden White has explored, and one that continues to arise in reference to the Holocaust.[21] Moving beyond the debate over truth, which cannot ever be fully resolved with regard to testimony,[22] it is clear that Roig has, in fact, written a historiographic narrative.

Other historians have taken up Roig's challenge to write a "decisive book from the historiographic point of view" focused on Spaniards in Nazi concentration camps. The drive to tell the history of Catalans and Spaniards in Nazi camps has expanded in recent years to include documentaries on regional Catalan television, a host of new testimonial accounts, and an interdisciplinary textbook for high school students with a focus on Mauthausen, among many other texts and films.[23] In his 2004 volume, *Spaniards in the Holocaust: Mauthausen, the Horror on the Danube*,

Chapter Two

David Wingeate Pike presents Roig as a fellow historian. Pike's work follows Roig's form and content almost identically: he cites survivor interviews and published memoirs, focuses on everyday life in the camp, and follows a chronological progression from deportation to liberation. His text is not as saturated with documentary material as Roig's, lacks the storytelling quality of *Els catalans*, and places greater emphasis on SS officers and non-Catalan Spaniards than Roig does. Pike cites *Els catalans* numerous times and indexes the author as "Roig, Montserrat (Sp. Historian)" (438). Clearly, although Roig may identify herself as a journalist and novelist, with *Els catalans* she legitimately rises to the task of a historian with a wide-reaching influence. Despite Roig's definitive authorial presence within the text, her authority to define the text is undermined by her difficulty in pinpointing the historiographic nature of her volume, further proving that *Els catalans* is not easily separated into either a "historiographic narrative" or a "testimony": it is both.

* * *

The survivor testimony Roig uses to uncover the daily occurrences in the camps thirty years after the end of World War II reveals that history is also complicated by the memories of the deportees themselves, who at times remember conflicting accounts of the same event. Still, these slight lapses in memory seem inconsequential when compared with the Nazis's wholesale denial of the existence of the camps at the Nuremberg trials or the discredited politicians and historians who publicly air denials of the Holocaust even today. Any historiographic text must necessarily grapple with questions of veracity, and Roig's study is no exception. Despite its ample use of literary techniques, *Els catalans* is not fiction: it is a human account of history. Notwithstanding Roig's insistence that *Els catalans* is not a decisive historiographic text—and no historiographic text can be "decisive"—the author understands the underlying doubt a reliance on survivor memory and testimony places on her study's relationship to reality:

> Aquest llibre, doncs, no intenta cap altra cosa que aproximar-se a una realitat. És un conjunt de veritats viscudes per homes i dones distints, amb un *background* divers, homes i dones que no han rebut els embats del nazisme de la mateixa manera i que

no ho han recordat després des d'idèntiques circumstàncies.
(*Els catalans* 18)

[This book, then, tries to do nothing less than approximate a reality. It is a collection of truths lived by different men and women, with diverse backgrounds, men and women who have not refuted the onslaught of Nazism in the same way and have not remembered it from identical circumstances afterwards.]

In using the plural "truths," Roig acknowledges the multivaried nature of history and testimony. Francoist historiography recognized only one truth; Roig's post-Franco historiography recognizes many. Although the details of the survivors' memories may not coincide, the larger historical question of the text, the one that Roig is asked countless times when writing it—"'Ah! Però és que hi va haver catalans als camps nazis?'" ("'Oh! So there were Catalans in the Nazi camps?'" *Els catalans* 11)—cannot be argued, and, furthermore, is the foundational historical fact on which the text is based. Roig reveals an urgency in her volume to restore the experiences of the marginalized Catalan deportees to Spain's "official" History. "Hay que devolver a los vivos su lugar en la vida y a los muertos su lugar en la Historia" (*Noche y niebla* 349), she writes in her introduction to the Castilian edition. She utilizes the dialectic between lowercase history and uppercase History to differentiate between the objective retelling of events, in which history is ostensibly written for its own sake, and the metanarrative construct of a monolithic History, in which history becomes self-serving of a particular ideology.[24] Catalans in Nazi camps have never been invited to join this Francoist History.

The deportees themselves are unable to forget their experiences. To them, history is fused with the torture and hardships they underwent in the camps. One survivor whose testimony is integral to Roig's work writes to her as the project begins with a caveat: "'tinc moltes dificultats a recordar detalls lligats als actes que he viscut [...] Però el que diré serà cert, indiscutible. Diré la veritat, el que no vol pas dir TOTA la veritat, ja que no "inventaré" res'" ("'I have a lot of difficulty remembering details related to the acts I've seen [...] But what I will say will be true, indisputable. I will tell the truth, which means I won't tell ALL of the truth, but that I won't "invent" anything,'" Roig, *Els catalans* 18). Memory, as Roig will explore more fully in *L'hora violeta*, is not only accountable to reality but also to a witness's need to remember: for many deportees, it is the desire to forget what has happened to them that controls their memories of this era. Another deportee is fully skeptical about the information that Roig will be able to collect about a decades-old event based on memories that are fluid (*Els catalans* 19). But how else to reconstruct a world and a time that few saw firsthand other than by memory? Roig counters that "[n]omés la memòria humana, la voluntat de memòria i el record viu dels qui ho patiren, pot reconstruir tot un món que sembla inversemblant" ("only human memory, the will of memory and recollection seen from those who suffered it, can reconstruct a whole world that appears improbable," *Els catalans* 132). It seems that the most convincing way to dispute the notion that the deportees' memories are fallible is the public and collective recognition of their struggle, offered as proof in the pages of *Els catalans*.

This public recognition comes again to the Catalan prisoners in Mauthausen in the guise of King Juan Carlos I's visit to the camp in January 1978. Until the Spanish King's tour of Mauthausen, which in an instant recorded the experience of Spaniards in Nazi camps in Spain's official history, memory was the only method of proving this historical moment had existed. Roig's epilogue to the Castilian edition of *Els catalans* describes that, as a result, "[e]l Rey, pues, ha recordado oficialmente que han existido deportados españoles en los camps de exterminio nazis," something that Franco never publicly acknowledged. Consequently, "[e]s la primera vez en nuestra historia que se reconoce este hecho" (*Noche y niebla* 349). Roig sees this as a step forward, albeit a small and ceremonial one, for the recuperation of a Catalan collective memory lost for decades. Still, even Roig's ironic depiction of this watershed moment betrays a lingering sense of injustice. This subject of great historical importance is only "officially" recorded when the King of Spain sets foot at Mauthausen—witnessing the existence of the camp firsthand—not when, a year earlier, Roig published *Els catalans*, much less thirty-five years before that, when the Catalan deportees were still imprisoned in Mauthausen. The legitimacy of testimony, it seems, resides in the relative and public legitimacy of the witness. Juan Carlos I is the ultimate authority to dispel a Spanish history created by the dictatorship, a bitter consolation to the thousands of deportees in Mauthausen whose stories remain untold. Roig's next task would be to test the legitimacy of testimony within a work of fiction.

In *Els catalans* Roig presents the reader with a historiographical text that not only provides a thematic, contextual, and historical inspiration for a work of fiction, but also lends this historical novel its specific plot and character development. Insofar as Roig is the author of both texts, *L'hora violeta* does not borrow from *Els catalans* so much as intentionally continue her project of recuperating a Catalan historical identity. *L'hora violeta* extends Roig's research on Catalans in Nazi camps into even more personal and contentious historical territory. An analysis through genre fusion of the novel overlaid on its historiographic partner demonstrates the theory's impact on the recuperation of Spain's historical memory.

L'hora violeta: A Fictional Framing of Historiography

When Norma, the writer-protagonist of *L'hora violeta*, asks herself why she writes, her answer delves into the unresolved details of a life story: "Descriure els colors, els matisos que se'ns escapen dins del present real, la llum que ens meravella" ("To describe the colors, the details that escape us during the actual present moment, the light that leaves us perplexed," Roig, *L'hora violeta* 215). These nuances fill in the gaps around the action of the story, rounding out an otherwise flat narration. They are also the details that transform historiography into narrative historiography, a transformation that Roig achieves in *Els catalans als camps nazis* and that Norma achieves in her retelling of the deportees' life stories in *L'hora violeta*. Published three years after *Els catalans*, *L'hora violeta* is a fictional exploration of a Catalan family and its social network during the postwar and post-Franco years. The novel noticeably engages many of the same issues Roig grapples with in her historiographical work, to the point of overt and intentional overlap, though it traces characters and chronology in a self-consciously fragmented manner, unlike the ordered chronology of *Els catalans*. Genre fusion reveals Roig's explicit blending of *L'hora violeta* and *Els catalans*, bonding her two texts through their common themes of memory and testimony, an identical postwar historical time period, and episodes shared by both works. Examined in conjunction through genre fusion, the two texts delve into individual stories that renovate our understanding of postwar Catalan historical memory, while at the same time demonstrating how the historian goes about this renovation.

In the opening exchange between Natàlia and Norma in the "Primavera de 1979," Natàlia has gathered her mother Judit's diary and letters. She asks Norma to use these materials as the basis of a narrative about her mother and Kati, who were intimate friends during the Spanish Civil War. Natàlia and her family have served as the inspiration for Norma's last two novels, although Natàlia criticizes Norma for having let herself be "sedui[da] per la història externa" ("seduced by external history," Roig, *L'hora violeta* 20) in previous novels, and advises her on the interactions between literature and history:

> "Em sembla que no som capaços de valorar la realitat fins que aquesta no es converteix en record. Com si així volguéssim tornar a viure. Per això crec que la literatura encara té un sentit. La literatura no és història. La literatura s'inventa el passat a partir d'uns quants detalls que han estat reals, encara que sigui a la nostra ment." (Roig, *L'hora violeta* 13)

> ["It seems to me that we're not capable of valuing reality until it's converted into memory. As though in this way we wanted to live again. Because of this I still believe that literature makes sense. Literature is not history. Literature invents the past basing itself on a few details that were real, although they were only real in our minds."]

Although we have seen the power of memory in resurrecting Spain's past in Roig's previous text, Natàlia's assertion that accurate and thorough representations of history have no place in literature will be disproved not only by Norma's treatment of Judit and Kati but by *L'hora violeta* itself. In the novel, historiography in the guise of *Els catalans als camps nazis* haunts the passages of literature and breaches the boundaries of genre. Natàlia and Norma's ongoing debates over memory and history reflect Roig's own self-conscious questioning of the interactions between these two fields in *Els catalans*. The characters in *L'hora violeta* add fiction to their subjects of discussion, allowing Roig to theorize many of the same questions that genre fusion raises within the pages of the novel itself.

Norma is first established as a double of Montserrat Roig on the opening page of the novel, directly referencing one of Roig's previous texts by recalling:

Montserrat Roig

> Jo havia enllestit un llarg llibre sobre els catalans als camps nazis i la veritat és que no m'havien quedat ganes de remoure el passat. La història de la deportació m'havia deixat mig malalta i escèptica. I la Natàlia volia que em fiqués dins l'univers de dues dones que no havia conegut, encara que n'havia escrit alguna cosa a les novel·les anteriors. (Roig, *L'hora violeta* 11)
>
> [I had finished a long book about Catalans in Nazi camps and the truth is that I didn't have any desire left to stir up the past. The history of the deportation left me somewhat sick and skeptical. And Natalia wanted me to stick myself into the universe of two women whom I had never met, although I wrote something about them in the previous novels.]

These references to *Els catalans als camps nazis*, *Ramona, adéu*, and *El temps de les cireres* identify Norma directly with Roig.[25] Moreover, this passage also inaugurates Roig's reliance on testimonial discourse in the novel, as characters assume the roles of witnesses to their lives and interactions with history. Finally, Norma's statement introduces an ongoing metatextual discussion about historiography and the historian's personal reactions to her project that will thread its way through the novel just as it rose to the surface for Roig as the historian investigating *Els catalans*.

The second section of the novel, "L'hora perduda" ("The Lost Hour"), flashes back to 1975, just before Franco's death. Here, Natàlia's conversations with Norma revolve around the haunting problems that arise when reality and imagination collide. Natàlia describes Norma's continued struggle to comprehend the horrors about which she is writing:

> La Norma passà moltes nits d'insomni, no suportava els relats sobre les obsessions dels ex-deportats, visions de cambres de gas, crematoris, filferrades elèctriques, cossos que ballaven a la forca… Durant moltes nits, la Norma havia tingut la mateix somni: una llarga carretera plena de manyocs de carn ensagnada, mutilada. Cossos torturats, fets a trossos. I la Norma caminava descalça per la carretera tot procurant no trepitjar els membres destrossats. De tant en tant, però, la Norma relliscava, la sang encara no s'hi havia assecat i era humida, gelatinosa. Com a rerafons, en una ombra, s'alçava la xemeneia del crematori, que semblava esperar-la per devorar-la. (Roig, *L'hora violeta* 67)
>
> [Norma spent many nights of insomnia, she couldn't tolerate the stories about the ex-deportees' obsessions, visions of gas

chambers, crematoriums, electric barbed-wire fences, bodies that danced on the gallows... During many nights, Norma had the same dream: a long road full of mountains of bloodied, mutilated flesh. Tortured bodies, broken into pieces. And Norma walked barefoot over the road trying not to trip over destroyed body parts. Still, Norma slipped once in awhile, the blood hadn't dried, it was wet, gelatinous. Like a background, in shadow, the chimney of the crematorium rose, appearing to wait in order to devour her.]

Norma's dreams directly paraphrase the scene witnessed by one of the concentration camp survivors upon entering Mauthausen in a previously cited passage from *Els catalans*. However, beyond the literal connections with Roig's historiography, this passage also explores Norma's personal absorption in history. The horrific images of the Nazi camps invade her subconscious as she imagines herself integrated into a scene she never witnessed. Even in the pages of a novel, though, Laub's identification of the residual effects of witness testimony is valid. Natàlia is clearly also affected thirdhand by Norma's historical forays, testifying in great detail to her friend's nightmares. Both women personalize history, making it tactically real and horrifyingly engrossing, just as the deportees experienced it and Roig recorded it in her historiographic account. Natàlia explains that she and Norma are both fated to live with "la llosa de la història carregada al damunt" ("the tombstone of history carried on their backs," Roig, *L'hora violeta* 67), betraying the mournful weight of history borne by those who choose to remember and record it. This is the weight that Roig herself carries after delving into the horrific experiences of concentration camp prisoners in her historiography. The author's self-analysis through Norma's dream explores the agonizing consequences of Roig's project to recuperate Spain's historical memory. Roig and Norma's identification with their subjects places them squarely into the historiography they write: in Norma's case, she becomes one of the Mauthausen prisoners in her dream. This is the deeply personal side of Roig's historical research, only fully explored when we read her two texts side-by-side using genre fusion.

Natàlia continues to question the capability of literature to represent history, especially when she sees history as a function of an untrustworthy memory. Much like the deportee in *Els catalans* who doubts the memories of his compatriots, Natàlia asserts:

> Car el temps dins de la memòria no té res a veure amb el temps de la història.... tot és fet a base de retalls fraccionats que a poc a poc formen una narració íntima, la del record. L'ordre que prenen els records dins de la memòria personal no són mai ni cronològics ni coherents. Si ho encertes, de vegades les paraules t'ajuden a lligar-los per a formar-ne una "història." (Roig, *L'hora violeta* 89)

> [Because time within memory doesn't have anything to do with historical time.... everything is made based on fractured remnants that little by little form an intimate narration, that of memory. The order that the recollections follow within personal memory are never chronological nor coherent. If you choose correctly, sometimes the words help you to tie them together to form a "story" with them.]

Natàlia's train of thought brings her closer to the realization that, in fact, history is composed of fragments of memory, like Norma's nightmare. While *Els catalans* is ordered chronologically and "coherently," in *L'hora violeta* Roig takes a less linear approach to the representation of history, constructing her fragmented narrative out of the equally fragmented memory and testimony of her characters. While the novel includes many of the same elements as her historiographic study—documents, testimony, foundational historical events—the task of reassembling the pieces into a clear and unified historical narrative is left to the reader. In *Els catalans*, Roig reordered the fragmented memories of her subjects, while in the novel, the reader must complete a mental reordering to be able to understand the story. We are apprentice historians, given the hands-on task of assembling a cohesive historical novel out of these disparate parts. Roig thus involves the reader in a tangible demonstration of the proximity between history and fiction.

But Natàlia disagrees, separating fiction and history into two discrete entities: "L'ordre de la imaginació s'escapa a totes les dades, a tots els fets. Aquesta és la revenja de la literatura contra la Història" ("The order of imagination escapes all dates, all facts. This is the revenge of literature against History," Roig, *L'hora violeta* 89). In *L'hora violeta*, where even a dream faithfully represents the past, Natàlia's observation is not true. History strikes back, perhaps not against literature so much as in conjunction with it, to assert its rightful place in the novel, and its rightful place in an authoritative History. While an element of doubt may creep into

Chapter Two

the reader's assessment of the historical accuracy of the novel's narration, in truth all historical writing is subject to interpretation and manipulation. As White has declared: "'History is a text,'" so that "every approach to the study of the past presupposes or entails some version of a textualist theory of historical reality of some kind," demanding interpretation, as all texts do ("New Historicism" 297). This fact does not discourage historians from the task of recording and understanding history, nor should it dissuade from reading *L'hora violeta* as a reinterpretation of historical events and a metatextual analysis of the presence of history in literature, all through a fictional narrative. Norma and Natàlia, as fictional counterparts to Roig and the deportees, in essence channel the experience of historians and their professional challenges as they move among the emotional forces of skepticism, incredulity, acceptance, and belief in their quest to compose a coherent narrative of the past.

* * *

In the central novel-within-a-novel, "La novel·la de l'hora violeta" ("The Novel of the Violet Hour"), history is explicit but nonlinear. A nonchronological collection of diaries, letters, and oral testimony spanning the years 1936 to 1964 document Judit's life and relationships. As the narration makes temporal shifts through the decades, a pattern of connections between characters and historical moments emerges. The reader is an active participant in the reordering of Judit's life, and must filter the events through individual testimony and the whims of Judit's memory. This bestows on the reader the historian's task, while also asking for the reader's judgment of the historical veracity of the story. As in any analysis through genre fusion, the reader's assessment of accuracy depends in part on his or her familiarity with the historical period and events.

An omniscient narrator—perhaps Norma, the author of a retelling of Judit's life—recounts the years 1936 to 1938 and introduces Kati, who has a profound impact on Judit. Kati is a modern, fashionable woman, scandalous for the era, while Judit is a traditional Spanish wife and mother. At the outset of the Civil War, Kati and Judit begin an intense friendship. They are abandoned in a city dominated by women, since the men have left for the front. Under these unusual circumstances, Kati and Judit discuss ambitions that run counter to the traditional role of women, including Kati's assertion that "'[l]a guerra és de tots… no solament és cosa dels homes'" ("The war is for everyone… it's not just something for men," Roig, *L'hora violeta* 122). Kati is active in the war effort and conscious of the effects of this historical moment on her surroundings. Although she assures Judit that she will never follow the social expectations of the era and fall in love, she eventually finds love with Patrick, an Irishman fighting with the International Brigades. Despite her feminist beliefs about the war and, by extension, her embodiment of the transformative role of women in the Civil War, Kati is entranced by Patrick's ahistorical conversation: "S'enamorà d'això, que no parlessin de la guerra, ni dels desastres del front, ni dels enfrontaments entre comunistes i anarquistes, ni del futur" ("She fell in love with that, that they didn't talk about the war, or the disasters at the front, or the confrontations between Communists and Anarchists, or the future," Roig, *L'hora violeta* 140). Kati's alternating fascination and repulsion with the war mirrors the way the novel itself experiments in the space between history and fiction. Although Kati escapes the war while she is with Patrick, the novel's overarching message is that Spanish history is always a part of the daily lives of its citizens.

When Patrick dies at the front, Kati can no longer avoid the reality of war. She begs Judit to flee with her, afraid of how a Nationalist victory will disrupt her life and the lives of women: "'Però, no t'imagines com serà la nostra vida si els feixistes entren? Que no sents el que diuen?'" ("'But, can't you imagine what our life will be like if the Fascists enter? Are you not hearing what they say?'" Roig, *L'hora violeta* 143). Yet the war has taken a different toll on Judit: she must wait for her husband Joan to return from the concentration camp. In her desperation, Kati commits suicide and Judit is left alone to carry the weight of a once-shared history. The story of Kati and Judit, although fictional, lays bare the roles of women in wartime Barcelona and how their lives intertwine with the historical moment. Their drama illustrates the effect of the war on a silent population at the rearguard, experiences that are integral to a thorough revaluation of Spain's historical memory.

In diary entries dated September 20, 1942 through September 15, 1948, a specificity that highlights Roig's commitment to the chronology of historiography even within fiction, Judit recounts the immediate postwar years in which she and Joan struggle to function as a family. Joan returns from a Francoist concentration camp after almost four years and Judit prepares for a changed man: "He d'estar preparada per a tot, per a trobar un home més vell, amb els ulls potser impermeables. ... Tots tornen de la mateixa manera, sense esma per a viure" ("I need to be prepared for everything, to encounter an older man, maybe with impermeable eyes. ... They all return the same way, without the will to live," Roig, *L'hora violeta* 98). Judit anticipates a collective identity of the concentration camp victim, one that is already common knowledge in Barcelona, and steels herself with details of the physical transformation of the camp survivors. Joan returns a broken man from the Galician camp of Betanzos in 1943 and cautions Judit that she "no sa[p] com era, allò" ("[doesn't] know how it was," Roig, *L'hora violeta* 99). But Judit has also been demoralized, in her case by the traumas she experienced at home: the war and Kati's suicide. The misery Joan and Judit faced have a direct effect on their national identity, according to Judit: "Aquest país no és el meu i, a en Joan, no li queden forces per estimar-lo. ... Tots els seus amics han desaparegut. I jo, sense la Kati. Em sento buida" ("This isn't my country and, as for Joan, he doesn't have the strength to love it. ... All of his friends have disappeared. And me, without Kati. I feel empty," Roig, *L'hora violeta* 99). Roig dedicates various chapters in *Els catalans* to the return of concentration camp survivors to their families, abandoned by friends and distrustful of Spain and Catalonia after having been defeated and deported to the camps. But in the novel she focuses less on the Brigadist Patrick and the camp survivor Joan than on those they left behind. Instead of a recapitulation of the testimony of Republican soldiers and concentration camp survivors, Roig writes an intimate portrayal of the invisible experiences of the actors gathered backstage from the primary historical drama in the novel. Thus, Roig provides a level of historical detail untapped by traditional historiography that works in conjunction with the background she has provided in *Els catalans*.

Joan and Judit struggle to return to a sense of normalcy during the immediate postwar years. The juxtaposition of Judit's happiness with Kati during the war and her anguish with Joan after it ends again shows an alternating view of history. The novel's historical backdrop is either embraced as an oddly positive influence, as when Natàlia writes to Norma that "'ens calgui una guerra per a saber estimar'" ("we need a war to know how to love," Roig, *L'hora violeta* 18) and Kati and Judit enjoy their wartime freedom, or that backdrop is viewed in terms of its collective negative impact, causing Kati's suicide and Joan's ruin. This emphasis on history as a controlling force in everyday life and individual emotions continues with the birth of Joan and Judit's third child, Pere, born with Down syndrome in 1943. Kati and Pere become strongly identified in Judit's diary. Whereas Judit finds little solace in her husband and two other children, she continues to write of the delight she felt with Kati during an otherwise bleak period: "M'enyoro dels dies passats a la guerra, amb la Kati. No sé per què penso que vaig ser tan feliç, durant la guerra. És estrany: va ser l'època en què vaig veure més mort i més tristesa i, tot i això, vaig ser feliç" ("I miss the days of the war, spent with Kati. I don't know why I think I was so happy during the war. It's strange: it was a time when I saw more death and sadness and, despite all of that, I was happy," Roig, *L'hora violeta* 104). The contentedness Judit finds with Pere, her "fill de la guerra" ("child of the war," Roig, *L'hora violeta* 101), mirrors the happiness she felt with Kati, her wartime friend, and establishes the theme of history repeating itself through successive characters and across generations in *L'hora violeta*. These intimate diary entries pull the reader into Judit's innermost self, where historical events have not only shaped her life, but have influenced how she categorizes the people around her.

Judit falls into a depression at the death of Pere in 1948, as she did when Kati committed suicide, and begins a slow withdrawal from the world around her. Ten years later, a fragmented third-person narration recounts the monotony of Judit's life. She actively dislikes her son and his wife, she and her daughter Natàlia do not communicate, she is still obsessed with thoughts of Kati and Pere, and her husband remains unchanged from the concentration camp. Judit's sister-in-law Patrícia witnessed how Judit's contentment dissipated with Kati's death and the end of the war, and provides her own interpretation of these past events in a monologue dated 1964. Although Patrícia is apolitical, craving the end of the war more than the triumph of one side or the other, history is still a relevant force in her memories of the era. The birth of Judit's daughter, in Patrícia's mind, is directly connected with historical events: "'La Natàlia va néixer pel març de 1938, ho recordo bé perquè era el mes de les bombes fortes, les bombes que van fer tan de mal a la ciutat'" ("'Natàlia was born in March of 1938, I remember it well because it was the month of the forceful bombings, the bombing that did so much damage to the city,'" Roig, *L'hora violeta* 120). Natàlia's wartime birth and her rebellious nature makes Patrícia equate her with Kati, another example of the way Roig organizes disparate personal stories around an overarching interest in history throughout the novel. The collected diary entries and Patrícia's monologue form the collective memory of an isolated segment of the Spanish population in Barcelona during the postwar. These voices, like the concentration camp survivors interviewed in *Els catalans*, provide testimony that Roig compiles into a microcosmic representation of the postwar Catalan experience.

* * *

"L'hora dispersa (Ells i la Norma)" ("The Disperse Hour [Them and Norma]") returns to the present, focusing on Norma's life. Here, Roig's narration shifts to an imprecise chronology. Without specific historical references, Norma's memory establishes the historical context of this section, again drawing a parallel between the ordering functions of memory and historiography. Norma's memory alternates among her present life after leaving her husband Ferran and beginning an affair with Alfred, the story of Judit and Kati she is writing at Natàlia's request, and her work on Catalans in Nazi concentration camps, published three years earlier. Norma, like Roig, is committed to writing literature based on reality. She fictionalizes events and people such as Kati and Judit, and integrates her subjects' lives into her own in the case of the Catalan deportees. Roig achieves the same result as her implied author one frame removed by weaving *Els catalans* into the narrative thread of *L'hora violeta*. The reader is privy to Norma's digressions as she composes the novel of Kati and Judit, pondering her own life while making connections among her subjects. Norma's thoughts about Alfred, whom she feels has betrayed her by refusing to leave his wife for her, lead her to decide how she will compose the dynamic between Kati and Judit in her book: "Va ser aleshores quan decidí que la Kati se suïcidaria per castigarse, perquè tenia por de continuar vivint després de la mort d'en Patrick. ... I va entendre la Judit, va entendre que se sentís traïda després del suïcidi de la Kati" ("It was then that she decided that Kati would commit suicide to punish herself, because she was afraid of continuing to live after Patrick's death. ... And she understood Judit, she understood that she felt betrayed after Kati's suicide," Roig, *L'hora violeta* 182). Norma shows that literature's interpretation of reality can be faithful or may be invented. Kati's motivation for her suicide was a facet of her life that was not recorded in the letters and diary entries Natàlia provided to Norma. Norma's freedom to rewrite Kati's suicide distinguishes *L'hora violeta*, as historical fiction, from Roig's narrative historiography, and demonstrates the liberty of the author to create and play within the framework of an historical context. The reader may have read Kati's suicide as part of the novel's premise in the previous section, but Norma's overt manipulation of the story shows that truth in the pages of historical fiction is left entirely to the reader's judgement.

Sparked by Alfred's question, "'Com era un dia en un camp d'extermini?'" ("'What was a day in an extermination camp like?'" Roig, *L'hora violeta* 185), Norma's thoughts return to her study of Catalans in Nazi camps. Norma's answer is interspersed with direct quotations from *Els catalans*: she narrates the story of the German interpreter who points out the electrocuted deportees on the barbed wire fence, explains how the dead were left in the *Appellplatz* after formations, and recounts the Sunday boxing matches, accompanied by the howls of prisoners confined to their cells (Roig, *L'hora violeta* 185–86). Roig recycles all of these episodes from her historiographic text. Some are even highlighted by unexplained quotation marks, yet lack footnotes to guide the reader to the original source material.[26] These intercalated stories constitute the most literal way Roig weaves *Els catalans* into *L'hora violeta*, but their significance complicates the interplay between fiction and historiography. Roig does not acknowledge her sources in *L'hora violeta*, as she does in her highly documented historiographic text, raising questions about the author's intention in writing her historical study into the pages of her novel. Is Roig reluctant to interrupt the flow of her fictional narration by directly citing this survivor testimony? Or is this a subtle method of drawing the reader's attention to the metatextual discussion and overlapping genres evidenced in the novel? While these queries are left unanswered, the blending of fiction and historiography is ultimately an example of how, even at a structural level, combining

Chapter Two

these two genres is not as simple as inviting history into fiction, or vice-versa, a warning that Natàlia continues to sound to Norma. Still, Helen Wing's assertion that Roig "does everything possible to keep the reader within the realm of fiction and fully conscious of the text as text" (91) does not describe the author's intention in the novel. Roig pointedly brings the historiography of *Els catalans* to bear on *L'hora violeta,* producing what Ofelia Ferrán calls "a productive 'dislocation' of the fine line between historical and fictional writing" (210). These forays into historiography are tempered by Norma's personal stake in the stories told and her relationship to the tellers, much like Roig's active authorial presence in *Els catalans* and her relationships with the survivors she interviewed.

Norma's memory of her conversation with Alfred about the camps inspires a foray into forgetting in the story she is writing about Kati and Judit, tinged with her desire to erase the images of the past that continue to haunt her:

> Escriure sobre l'oblit. Sobre l'oblit de l'escrivent de tot allò que no ha viscut, que no ha presenciat, però que ha sentit ben endins. Cal oblidar els camps nazis, cal oblidar l'amor. ... I voldria escriure sobre l'oblit, integrar l'oblit a la vida quotidiana. La Kati se suïcidà perquè no volia aprendre a oblidar. La Judit va sobreviure perquè en va saber. ... Mauthausen, Ravensbrück, la guerra civil, els bombardeigs, tot aquest passat que no havia viscut però que li havien fet sentir com a seu. No les idees, sinó les persones que havia conegut i que serien fantasmes que sempre hauria d'arrossegar amb ella. La por dels anys joves, sota el franquisme... Capacitat d'oblit, tot un mestratge. Però, era just l'oblit? (Roig, *L'hora violeta* 186–87)

> [Writing about forgetting. Forgetting everything the chronicler hasn't lived, hasn't witnessed, but that she has felt deep inside. One has to forget the Nazi camps, one has to forget love. ... And she wanted to write about forgetting, integrate forgetting into everyday life. Kati committed suicide because she didn't want to learn how to forget. Judit lived because she learned how to do it. ... Mauthausen, Ravensbrück, the Civil War, the bombardments, all of this past that she hadn't lived but that she had felt as though it were her own. Not the ideas, rather the people she had met and who would be ghosts that she would always have to drag around with her. The fear of those early years, under Francoism... The capacity to forget, a whole train of thought. But, was forgetting just?]

Norma conflates a lifetime of forgetting in her fears of confrontation, confusing a confluence of images in the process. Survivors she knows fade into ghosts she imagines. Deportees' memories of the Nazi camps are analogous to her memories of Francoism. The desire to forget is complicated by the guilt to remember. Norma's stream-of-consciousness digression reveals the personal connection and emotional response she has to history, even a history she has not witnessed: it is manifest in the people she knows and the scenes that populate her dreams. This merging of past and present, of personal experience and the imagined experience of others, of forgetting and remembering, finds its counterpart in Roig's personal reactions to the deportees in *Els catalans* who lived through a historical moment the author never experienced. It is also Roig's decisive way of combatting Spain's recent history of "forgetting" its past through her strategic interweaving of historiography and fiction.

Roig invites survivors whom she interviewed for *Els catalans* into her novel as anonymous deportees. Utilizing genre fusion, this intermingling becomes even more obvious. A reader who has closely read both texts would be able to identify this convergence of characters, but with no help from the author herself. Roig attempts to keep her character-splicing unobtrusive, omitting footnotes and the actual names of the deportees. Norma contacts a deportee whose book based on his concentration camp experience deeply affected her. When, during the course of their long conversation, Norma calls the deportee "l'home que havia decidit morir-se per segona vegada" ("the man who had decided to die for a second time," Roig, *L'hora violeta* 188), it is clear that this nameless character is a double for Joaquim Amat-Piniella. Amat-Piniella died "per segona vegada" ("for the second time," *Els catalans* 12) in 1974, while Roig was writing *Els catalans*. This connection is even more solid when Norma repeatedly emphasizes the deportee's eyes—the "ulls terriblement cansats" ("terribly tired eyes," *Els catalans* 13)—as a window into his inner pain as he describes daily life in Mauthausen. Genre fusion reveals how Roig weaves together real and invented characters in her novel, demonstrating the descriptive nature common to both her narrative historiography and historical fiction. Roig makes a self-conscious choice to share narrative material between her two volumes; genre fusion actualizes this intentionality.

Chapter Two

After the Amat-Piniella character's death, Norma visits another deportee living in Paris. At a café, he presents her with meticulous lists of Catalans and Spaniards from the camps, containing "el nom, data d'entrada al camp, data de trasllat al camp annex, número de matrícula, data de la mort" ("the name, date of entry into the camp, date of transport to the annexed camp, registration number, date of death"), all of them "[n]oms desconeguts que no existien per a la història" ("unknown names that didn't exist for history," Roig, *L'hora violeta* 192). This deportee, who is possessed by "la mania de la fidelitat històrica… i ho demonstrava en corregir qualsevol dada minúscula d'un altre ex-deportat" ("the mania of historical accuracy… and he demonstrated it by correcting any minimal piece of data from another deportee," Roig, *L'hora violeta* 193), is clearly a representation of Casimir Climent, whose detailed lists fill the last 100 pages of *Els catalans*. He serves to reference Roig's penchant for historical precision in *Els catalans*, and confuses the boundary between fact and fiction in the novel.

The fictional Climent provides Norma with countless documents pertaining to the Catalans in Nazi camps, but repeats the line that, in actuality, Amat-Piniella says to Roig: "'La veritat, no la sabreu mai'" ("The truth, you will never know it," Roig, *L'hora violeta* 193). The "vell deportat" or "l'ex-deportat que s'assemblava a en Louis de Funes" ("old deportee," "the ex-deportee who looked like Louis de Funes," Roig, *L'hora violeta* 191; 193; and elsewhere in the novel), as he is labeled in *L'hora violeta*, describes growing up as the illegitimate and barely acknowledged son of an authoritarian Minister of the Spanish Court who was friendly with the Queen and harbored deep animosity toward anarchists. After an anarchist was killed with his own bomb, the "old deportee" recalls his father telling him "amb la veu plena de ràbia" ("with his voice full of rage") as he pointed out the man's desiccated body incrusted in a wall: "'Veus, guaita, guaita com moren'" ("'Here, look, look at how they die,'" Roig, *L'hora violeta* 195). This character's story is closely matched to what Climent recounted to Roig in *Els catalans*, but gives an the additional backstory and contextualizing details that compliment Climent's original testimony. In the novel, the Climent character reveals other pieces of information that Roig has either invented or chose to exclude from *Els catalans*: he entered a mental institution because his wife stopped sleeping with him after he was released from the camp, he knew deportees whose wives took and married lovers after their husbands' disappearances, and he knew that other survivors who identified their compatriots under torture were subsequently divorced and ostracized. The fictionalized Climent is defensive of the humanizing factors he reveals about the deportees' lives in the camps and afterwards. He does not want Norma to portray the survivors as heroes, nor to idolize them. The novel adds intimate details to the experiences of real-life deportees such as Amat-Piniella and Climent that would have been inappropriate or extraneous to Roig's historiography, where we learned of Climent's treatments in mental institutions, for instance, but not the specific personal tolls exacted on his life after the camps. Yet these facets of the deportees' lives dovetail with *L'hora violeta*'s thematic thread of history made personal. Whether or not these details are imagined or accurate is impossible to prove; Roig leaves that decision up to the reader.

In the end, these two deportee characters are not idolized in the novel. On the contrary, they are depicted frankly, and Norma finds them both fascinating and bothersome. When the deportee based on Climent calls to tell her he is dying and asks that she visit him in Paris, Norma refuses, wanting to forget the unforgettable. The reflection of Climent in *L'hora violeta* serves the same purpose as Climent's testimony in *Els catalans*: it is symbolic of the importance of an inclusive historical memory. Without Climent's lists of the Spaniards in Mauthausen, or without his disquieting stories of the deportees ostracized upon their return to Spain, our knowledge of history is incomplete.

Yet the individuals from *Els catalans* repurposed as characters in *L'hora violeta* underscore the repeated warning that we will never know the truth. The singular historical touchstone of the Nazi concentration camps produces diverse accounts from these Catalan deportees. Roig strives to present their experiences in a well-rounded and unbiased manner in her historiographic study and novel, while infusing both texts with an unavoidable subjectivity as she filters the testimony of the deportees through her personal interactions with them. She describes the Catalans as heroic survivors and providers of aid to others in the camps, while also portraying them as individuals suffering lonely and broken lives after their experiences in the camps. A reading of both Roig's historiographic and fictional texts is necessary to learn the complete, and at times seemingly contradictory, story of the Catalan deportees.

Still, as with any historiographic account, an absolute truth is ephemeral. Norma intertwines her memories of her encounters with the Catalan deportees with her current marital problems and her struggle to write the story of Kati and Judit. Norma imagines Natàlia's criticism of her manner of conflating herself with her characters: "'No ets un personatge de novel·la, maca, ... ets una persona real. Per què t'obstines a convertir-ho tot en literatura?'" ("You're not a character in a novel, honey, ... you're a real person. Why do you persist in making everything into literature?" Roig, *L'hora violeta* 214). But Norma does not see these characters as fiction. To her, they are real and her representations of Kati, Judit, and the deportees are simply a narrative transformation of reality: "sabia que, en definitiva, la vida s'acosta molt més a l'art que no l'art a la vida, com ja ha estat dit una pila de vegades" ("she knew, definitively, that life was so much closer to art than art to life, as has been said so many times," Roig, *L'hora violeta* 215).

Norma's interior battle over what is real and what is not, and her ultimate decision that she is not inventing, but rather that reality can be read as art, is an apt representation of Roig's narrative ambition in these two texts. While *L'hora violeta*'s classification as a fictional text is not open for debate, it is clear that historiography has claimed a stake in the novel. History enters overtly, through a focus on the historical truth of the Catalans in Nazi camps and the inclusion of historically based testimony and figures from this era. The addition of Roig's voice via the character of Norma mirrors the way the author frames the narration of *Els catalans* with her own subjective observations. In addition, Norma and Natàlia raise questions of historical accuracy, memory, and the interplay between history and fiction throughout the novel, in an on-going debate that reflects Roig's contradictory interviews cited at the beginning of this chapter and her denial that *Els catalans* is a definitive historiography. Still, analyzing the author's dual usage of the subject of Catalans in Nazi camps in her historiography and novel through genre fusion demonstrates the primacy, functionality, and fallacies of a testimonial recuperation of collective experience as a means of capturing Spain's unofficial history. Although as readers we cannot know to what extent Roig identifies with the character of Norma beyond the obvious juxtapositions, Norma's personal and professional struggles to come to terms with the deportees and their experiences clearly reflect the uneasy relationship and challenge to objectivity that arises between the writer/historian and her human subject when the topic under investigation is so close to the author's personal experience and knowledge.

Genre fusion joins *Els catalans* and *L'hora violeta* around common questions of the caprices of memory, the reliability of historical documentation and testimony, the role of the historian in communicating and transforming the past, and the examination of history across fictional and nonfictional genres as a means of influencing the ways these topics will be approached in future discourse. The points of overlap between the author's historical investigation and her emotional response to her subject matter apparent through genre fusion signal Roig's overwhelming drive to resurrect the personal and collective aspects of historiography that extend from *Els catalans* to *L'hora violeta*. This reading results in a destabilization of Spain's once-monolithic official history to reflect the Catalan experience at the margins of society.

Genre fusion shows how both texts together explore history through everyday experiences: the routine of the concentration camp; the lives of Catalans during the Spanish Civil War; the political and social shifts of the postwar. In *L'hora violeta* and *Els catalans*, these major historical events serve as background to personal experience, but also facilitate connections between eras, as characters of distinct generations find common ground and a collective voice. Both texts are structured around documentation: in the novel, Judit's diaries, Natàlia's letter to Norma, and Patrícia's oral testimony resemble the letters, lists, and testimony in Roig's historiographic study. To be sure, both texts are bound to testimonial discourse, as *testimonio* or the testimonial novel. They rely on the accounts of marginalized Catalans, be they imprisoned deportees or women who are denied a voice in dictatorship Spain, to testify to a historical period in an attempt to force the incorporation of these voices into mainstream discourse. Finally, both texts engage with the question of truth versus invention in historical accounts. The deportees do not blindly trust memory to represent their experiences, but they—along with Roig herself—fiercely defend their stories in an attempt to argue for their place in Spain's official history. Similarly, Norma questions the accuracy of her interpretation of Kati and Judit's life, but when it comes to her study of Catalans in Nazi camps, she is convinced that the deportees' testimony will fill a gap in the official telling of history.

Chapter Two

The absolute difference between *Els catalans als camps nazis* and *L'hora violeta* is that the former is a historiographic text and the latter is a novel. As such, the traditional distinction between these two genres is clear: one is based on reality and the other on imagination. But in a genre fusion analysis of the convergences of these two texts we have witnessed their moments of escape from their pre-ordained genres. *Els catalans* utilizes a literary narrative structure in order to weave a story about the deportees, while *L'hora violeta* incorporates historiography in order to contextualize its fictional tale. Just as Akiko Tsuchiya has written that "Roig reveals the processes of narrativization and fictionalization to be crucial to the understanding of history" (171) in *Els catalans*, so too does genre fusion show the process of historicization to be integral to the understanding of fiction in *L'hora violeta*. With fluid borders between genres and the author's overlapping interest in both history and fiction, Roig's narrative historiography and historical fiction exemplify the purpose of genre fusion in post-Franco Spanish literature: to expose the stories of those on the margins as central to a drive to recover the personal and collective experiences of history. Genre fusion actualizes the profound historical representation contained in Roig's two texts and forces the country to confront, in the author's words, "the dark zones of its collective memory" through the testimony of those who experienced these traumatic periods of Spain's past.

Chapter Three

Carmen Martín Gaite
Rewriting Spain's Memory

> *El testigo pretencioso se arroga la misión olímpica*
> *de estar contando la Historia, se siente en posesión*
> *de la verdad blanca o de la verdad negra.*
> *El testigo vocacional se limita a contar historias,*
> *sin más, porque le gusta hacerlo, a recordar*
> *lo que vio, porque supo mirar.*
> Carmen Martín Gaite
> *Agua pasada*

Spanish Society after Franco: Balancing Revisionist History and Collective Memory

After nearly three days lying in state at the Palacio de Oriente, during which hundreds of thousands of mourners filed past his open casket, Francisco Franco's flag-draped coffin was transported some 60 kilometers outside Madrid to the Valle de los Caídos. There, it was ceremoniously lowered into a grave marked concisely with a cross and his name. Spaniards across the country were riveted to their television screens on November 23, 1975, watching the somber proceedings unfold. Franco's family, military representatives, and the Chilean dictator Augusto Pinochet, among others, observed from inside the Valley's cavernous mausoleum (Preston 779–80). On that November morning, the novelist and historian Carmen Martín Gaite was watching the funeral proceedings with her daughter in a neighborhood bar. Martín Gaite took notice of the dictator's daughter, Carmen Franco, who appeared inside the Valle de los Caídos with the rest of her family on the television screen. Franco's daughter not only shared a first name with Martín Gaite but was also born less than a year after the author and had lived a portion of her childhood and adolescence in Martín Gaite's hometown of Salamanca. This onscreen image of a particular lesser-known figure of history became an instant catalyst for the writer.

Watching a member of her own generation and gender participate in one of the most symbolic moments in Spain's transition from dictatorship to democracy lit a spark in Martín Gaite. The deceased dictator's placement in the ground, a heavy tombstone carefully eased over his coffin, signaled a definitive end to Franco's reign and turned Martín Gaite away from the kind of monumental history she was witnessing on television. Instead, as she explains in the guise of her fictional counterpart in her novel *El cuarto de atrás*, a historical event became personal both for herself and for Carmen Franco at that moment. This event led her to a different way of envisioning her relationship to the nation's history:

> [M]e parecía emocionante verla [a Carmen] seguir andando hacia el agujero donde iban a meter a aquel señor, que para ella era simplemente su padre, mientras que para el resto de los españoles había sido el motor tramposo y secreto de ese bloque de tiempo… con el fin de que apenas se les sintiera rebullir ni al tiempo ni a él y cayeran como del cielo las insensibles variaciones que habían de irse produciendo, según su ley, en el lenguaje, en el vestido, en la música, en las relaciones humanas, en los espectáculos, en los locales. … Fue cuando me di cuenta de que yo, de esa época, lo sabía todo, subí a casa y me puse a tomar notas en un cuaderno. (Martín Gaite, *El cuarto de atrás* 137–38)

Stripped of its historical significance, the events of that November in 1975 simply involved "that man" in a hole, but the moment has the power to reverberate beyond its spatial and temporal constraints. Spaniards felt Franco's presence in every aspect of their public and private lives, in such a way that it seemed as though the dictator even controlled time during his rule. The notes Martín Gaite begins taking on the morning of the dictator's burial, however, break Franco's grasp on time. The author is finally permitted to cast aside the Francoist mythology lorded over Spanish historical writing for the better part of forty years and recall history the way she sees it.

Her notes draw her to popular publications and her memories of a time that she and Carmen Franco—worlds apart politically—experienced together culturally. In *Usos amorosos de la postguerra*, the historical study that also grew out of the moment when Martín Gaite decided to contemplate the cultural products of her childhood, she explains: "[a] raíz de la muerte del general Franco, empecé a consultar esporádicamente algunos periódicos y revistas de los años cuarenta y cincuenta" (12)· The transformative instant when Martín Gaite spots Carmen Franco onscreen during the dictator's funeral echoes through two of her most historically engaged books—a novel and a work of historiography—empowering the author to take control of the historical memory she had been fed throughout the dictatorship. Martín Gaite is the author of this new form of historical writing, she claims she "knows everything" about a formative era that has had lasting effects on her as an adult, and she is not going to let a detail as trivial as genre come between her and history.

The difference between Martín Gaite's innovative historical writing and its predecessors is stark: written historiographic discourse in postwar, dictatorship Spain, as captured in magazines, history books, and proclamations of the era, was the official history of Francoist Spain. In *Narrating the Past: Fiction and Historiography in Postwar Spain*, David Herzberger describes history during the regime as a tool to buoy the state. In the process the Francoist version of history became equated with truth, and thus assumed a mythical status; dissent was disallowed (16–17). In this way, Herzberger explains, the regime's historiography "serve[d] to diminish history and nullify its vast potential to bear a diversity of meanings" (*Narrating the Past* 22). Regional, feminine, and class-conscious histories were devalued, if not altogether censored. "True" Spain was born during the Catholic reunification of 1492, with King Ferdinand and Queen Isabella serving as models of Spanish righteousness and unceasing faith. This historical timeline jumps from Spain's Golden Age directly to its "second reunification" when the Nationalists won the Spanish Civil War in 1939, bypassing the divisive ages of liberalism, intellectualism, and populism that intervened, threatening to pull Spain off track. Franco's Castilian, Catholic, patriarchal, middle-class history was a fable: a "static entity anchored in all that is permanent and eternal… rooted in the formative strategies of myth" (Herzberger, *Narrating the Past* 33).

Martín Gaite describes the spirit—or dispirit—of prohibition during the early decades of the postwar that quashed any retrospective consideration of the Civil War, even though the war left a

Chapter Three

visibly broken and divided Spain in its wake. Thus the immediate present was ignored in favor of a reality based in a fantastic notion of the truth:

> La guerra había terminado. Se censuraba cualquier comentario que pusiera de manifiesto su huella, de por sí bien evidente, en tantas familias mutiladas, tantos suburbios miserables, pueblos arrasados, prisioneros abarrotando las cárceles, exilio, represalias y economía maltrecha. Una retórica mesiánica y triunfal, empeñada en minimizar las secuelas de aquella catástrofe, entonaba himnos al porvenir. Habían vencido los buenos. Había quedado redimido el país. (Martín Gaite, *Usos amorosos de la postguerra* 13)

Spaniards marginalized during Franco's dictatorship did not fit the mold of this single, unifying truth/myth/history. They were the losers of the war who could not get behind the dictator's unfailing rhetoric of triumphalism. Their experiences and viewpoints can only be explored in alternate histories. But these texts were considered subversive during the dictatorship, and thus were rare. However, they proliferated once Franco's death permitted a diversity of opinion that began to challenge openly the dictator's monolithic historical truth.

Begun just after Franco's death in 1975, Martín Gaite's *El cuarto de atrás* is one of the first of many post-Franco novels to address the omissions of Francoist historiography. Herzberger labels *El cuarto de atrás* a novel of memory, which he explains as "those fictions in which past time is evoked through subjective remembering, most often by means of first-person narration" that delves into a past "largely eschewed or appropriated by historiography under Franco" (*Narrating the Past* 66). This definition accurately describes *El cuarto de atrás*, a novel narrated in the first person that probes aspects of postwar culture that were either willingly ignored or by definition excluded by Francoist historiographers. Martín Gaite's text is a complex amalgamation of literary and historical innovations, bucking trends the author herself was following just a few years before.

Earlier novels—*Entre visillos* (1958), *Ritmo lento* (1963) and *Retahílas* (1974)—placed Martín Gaite among social realists such as Ignacio Aldecoa and Juan Benet in mid-century dictatorship Spain. These writers operated under the constant threat of censorship. As such, they manifested a commitment to history that necessarily obfuscated direct historicity, such as specific mentions of the Spanish Civil War. Instead, the social realists set their stories in the severe poverty and oppression of postwar Spain without drawing attention to the ultimate cause of this misery. They circumvented these limitations by adopting a testimonial quality in their work that aligned them with the task of the narrative historian, dedicated to immediacy in "representing the present not 'as if' they had been there, but specifically as witnessed and lived time" (Herzberger, *Narrating the Past* 54). By infusing their publications with the realities and daily struggles the vast majority of Spaniards suffered during the postwar, the social realists were able to combat, however obliquely, the idealist vision of the postwar propagated by Francoist historians. Their implicit contradictions with Franco's mythical history made their subtle dissent visible: "Rather than the past, the social realists focus on the present; rather than the epic, the mock epic; rather than the individual, the collective; and rather than the heroic, the quotidian" (Herzberger, *Narrating the Past* 64).

When the figurehead of Francoist historiography disappeared, the possibilities of expression greatly expanded. Martín Gaite pulled away from the social realist project, but not from the fearless dedication to history that characterized it. During the Transition, the author remained dedicated to counterbalancing Franco-era historiography by focusing on the everyday existence of women during the postwar and how their experiences affected their present-day lives. In the post-Franco era, Martín Gaite was finally able to draw a direct link from the Republican loss of the Spanish Civil War, to the subsequent social oppression under Spain's dictatorship, to her own experiences as a young woman during this era, and to the ways all of these factors converged to mold her identity as an adult in contemporary, democratic Spain. As a postmodern revision of collective dictatorship society, Martín Gaite's work clearly demonstrates the country-wide shift from a stagnant, monolithic history to a dynamic and unobstructed view of the past that began to emerge once Spanish historical writing no longer had to answer to Franco's limited paradigm.

Martín Gaite does not seek to conquer Spanish history for the post-Franco era, rather her new historical project turns inward: "She does not set out to invent new myths that dispute the old ones, but rather posits a counterdiscourse in which history is awakened to the fragmented and indeterminate essence of the subjective" (Herzberger, *Narrating the Past* 72). Though the stranglehold on literary expression and historiography during the postwar had abated after Franco's death, post-Franco Spanish novelists were not entirely unencumbered by Francoist historiography. Especially during Spain's transition to democracy, these authors continued to meet barriers to recounting history, and some remained marginalized from Spanish society. Martín Gaite, one of the most widely studied Spanish writers of the twentieth century, faced an uphill climb in her quest to counter the official historiographic discourse of the Franco regime. Although her popularity as a novelist grew, Martín Gaite's qualifications as a historian did not provide the entree she needed for scholars to consider both her fiction and nonfiction as seriously historical. José F. Colmeiro's work on historical memory provides some insight into a state of collective history in Spain that has created an atmosphere in which an author like Martín Gaite still struggles for the historical recognition she merits.

In *Memoria histórica e identidad cultural: de la postguerra a la postmodernidad*, Colmeiro argues that twenty-first century Spain still suffers from an identity crisis aggravated not by a lack of collective memory of the Franco regime, but by a flawed historical memory of these years. He defines "collective memory" as a symbolic rather than literal entity that represents the cultural consciousness of a community, taking the form of a "conjunto de tradiciones, creencias, rituales y mitos que poseen los miembros pertenecientes a un determinado grupo social y que determinan su adscripción al mismo" (Colmeiro 15). Although this collective memory becomes a necessary "construcción ideológica para dar un sentido de identidad al grupo, a la comunidad, a la nación" (Colmeiro 17), it is constantly reinvented through the fluctuating memories of the group. "Historical memory," on the other hand, is "una conceptualización crítica de acontecimientos de signo histórico compartidos colectivamente y vivos en el horizonte referencial del grupo" (Colmeiro 18). These historical memories reflect a critical way of thinking about the past and constitute a testimonial record, which is the type of memory Colmeiro believes is in crisis in Spain. The country's "voluntaria amnesia colectiva" (Colmeiro 19) stems from a relatively speedy transition from dictatorship to democracy that left Spaniards eager to disassociate themselves from a contentious past in favor of conforming to new ideologies (Colmeiro 21). Colmeiro's argument, while not suggesting the existence of a wholesale historical amnesia in Spain during and after the Transition, laments the absence of concrete historical materials—monuments and streets dedicated to the Republic, for example—to commemorate and, on an even more basic level, remember Spain's past.

Since the publication of Colmeiro's work in 2005, the landscape for historical memory has changed significantly. Scholars such as Jo Labanyi and Paloma Aguilar see collective and historical memory as more or less the same. In contemporary Spain, these forms of memory consist of "shared (and contested) understandings of the past" (Labanyi, "Politics of Memory" 121) that are substantive as opposed to theoretical. Moreover, a shift in Spain's movement to monumentalize its own history has been afoot for over a decade. The 2007 passage of the Law of Historical Memory and subsequent state-mandated removal of any remaining Francoist iconography from Spain's cultural topography, the publication of obituaries for Republicans killed during the Civil War, plaques commemorating mass grave sites, and the founding of the Centro Documental de la Memoria Histórica in Salamanca all point toward governmental and popular memory movements.[1] Thus a country-wide historical reexamination takes pains to counteract what Colmeiro calls a "fragmentación de la memoria nacional" (34). Given the reunification propaganda of the Franco era, this drive to unite the country around a counter-discourse is an ironic response to the dictator's decades-long stranglehold on history. Colmeiro's overall argument, however, does not take into consideration another significant way Spain has critically memorialized its history: through written texts published during and after the Transition that labor to confront Spain's divisive past. These works can be considered monuments in their own right. Although Colmeiro describes the protagonist of *El cuarto de atrás* as frustrated by the "devaluación cualitativa de la memoria" (32) produced by the flurry of memory texts to emerge after Franco's death, it is clear by Martín Gaite's own example that not all of these memory texts are created equal.

Montserrat Roig's recuperation of the testimony of Catalans in Nazi concentration camps, as we have seen, along with Carlos

Chapter Three

Blanco Aguinaga's analysis of the fate of second generation Spanish exiles in Mexico, and Julian Marías's drive to counteract his father's wartime betrayal, form a body of work composed of individual tangible testaments. Perhaps it is the post-Transition attitude that "la memoria histórica es una mala inversión de capital cultural sin rentabilidad política" (22) to which Colmeiro points that has deflected attention from Roig's and Blanco Aguinaga's texts, encouraged the concentration on Martín Gaite's fictional recuperation of memory as opposed to her socio-historical study of the same material, and limited the analysis of Marías's cross-genre historically engaged texts.[2] These works have been undervalued as symbols of a Spanish desire to understand the past and as concrete examples of the process of reaching into the historical and collective memory of generations of Spaniards. What these texts, and others like them, may lack in political capital, they recuperate as contributions toward filling the memorializing void about which Colmeiro writes.

Although Colmeiro approaches memory in contemporary Spain, he arrives at the conclusion that an official history continues to exist long after the dictator is gone and the country has become a fully assimilated democracy, aided by a static historical memory that is in need of contradiction.[3] Colmeiro cites the back room as a space that, to his mind, represents memory's state of flux in modern Spanish society. He interprets this place as a "form[a] de resistencia viva frente a esta memoria adormecida y encerrada en el archivo de la historia oficial" (Colmeiro 30). Martín Gaite clearly anticipates Colmeiro, in that the back room is the locus for the physical and conceptual recuperation of an unofficial collective Spanish memory in *El cuarto de atrás*. For Colmeiro, Martín Gaite is the ideal writer who utilizes history in order to battle the forgetting evidenced in modern Spain, by putting "pequeños parches al gran agujero histórico del pasado" (Colmeiro 32–33) in her literature and battling Spain's "imperante amnesia histórica generalizada" (Colmeiro 32). From her back room, described as "un archivo del pasado inaccesible que ocasionalmente se puede abrir desde el presente por la acción de un catalizador" (Colmeiro 31), Martín Gaite melds historical data with a sociological study of the past, acting as a catalyst to historical recuperation. She relies on her own memory in the composition of the novel, supplementing it with archival research—the provenance of the historian. By assuming the role of social historian in both *El cuarto de atrás* and *Usos amorosos de la postguerra española*, Martín Gaite confronts the prevailing collective and historical memories of her generation of Spaniards in her dynamic rewriting of postwar historical myth.

Martín Gaite's texts provide a pleasant correction to Colmeiro's assertion that Spain's historical memory is in dire need of revision. She is able to tap into the collective memory of her generation, through common cultural criteria, in order to rewrite a generational history of the postwar years as well as to contextualize these experiences in the present day. Martín Gaite draws a clear line from the Francoist feminine ideals of the postwar to the beginnings of the democratic, feminist movements of the Transition. She uncovers moments of counter-discourse against Franco's dominant historical narrative, emphasizes the importance of fantasy as a means of escape during and after the postwar, and exposes startling details of a hidden collective Spanish past. The author reminds a generation of the popular culture they shared during the regime as adolescents, and enumerates the effects these cultural products had on them as they enter middle age, marked by Spain's parallel entry into democracy. Concurrently, Martín Gaite ponders the question of history in the everyday lives of Spaniards, following Michel de Certeau's assertion that day-to-day life is as central to the historical understanding of a period of time as the "great" historical events that form the spine of a timeline. For Martín Gaite, it is evident that "everyday practices, 'ways of operating' or doing things, no longer appear as merely the obscure background of social activity" (Certeau xi), but come to the foreground of her historical imagination.

While *El cuarto de atrás* has been analyzed countless times since its publication, and continues to be the source of a steady stream of academic debate, the nonfiction text that grew out of Martín Gaite's novel remains almost wholly untouched. Many critics have noted the overt connections between *El cuarto de atrás* and *Usos amorosos de la postguerra española*, but few have examined the texts as two halves of the same story. Examined through the lens of genre fusion, it is clear that both works fall headlong into the fiction/history debate, grappling with the struggle between the fantastic and the real through similar narrative recourses, resulting in texts that are not only enhanced but spellbinding when read together. An analysis of Martín Gaite's works through genre fusion

Chapter Three

proves essential to the recuperation of a revisionist collective and historical memory in post-Franco Spain.

Martín Gaite and the Uses of History

Martín Gaite belongs to a generation of "niños de la guerra,"[4] though her self-conscious involvement with history sets her apart from many of her contemporaries.[5] Born in Salamanca to a left-leaning family in 1925, she was fourteen years old when the Civil War ended. Soon after, she settled in Madrid and began to associate with a group of friends who would later, as writers, come to be known as the Generación de medio siglo. Her marriage and separation from a member of this group, Rafael Sánchez Ferlosio, was later followed by the sudden death of her only adult daughter. Martín Gaite's versatile interest in history, however, has been a constant throughout her life. In 1972, after establishing herself as an influential Spanish novelist, Martín Gaite earned a doctorate in history from the University of Madrid. Until her death in 2000, she continued to write fictional and nonfictional texts that demonstrated an on-going historical engagement.

Josefina Aldecoa, one of Martín Gaite's friends during her early days in Madrid, has written that one of the binding characteristics of their generation is how they filter an intimate history through memory in their literature:

> Porque en la historia lo que más nos interesa, es la gente que hizo esa historia, los personajes que la vivieron y qué sentían, qué pensaban esos personajes. ... [E]s verdad también que la memoria del escritor que conoció de primera mano ese momento, añade o quita detalles a los sucesos vividos. La memoria selecciona, interpreta, suaviza, archiva los recuerdos en un orden que obedece a leyes personales. Esa es la diferencia entre la novela y un ensayo histórico o un libro de texto de Historia que son o deben ser rigurosamente objetivos. ("Nosotros" 15–16)

Martín Gaite's memory and firsthand knowledge of defining periods of Spanish history personalize the majority of her historical accounts. But in the author's early historical texts, she demonstrates the tendency Aldecoa describes of focusing on the lived experiences of history during other time periods: namely, on the Inquisition in *El proceso de Macanaz. Historia de un empapelamiento* (1970), and on the eighteenth century in *Usos amorosos del dieciocho en España* (1972). Martín Gaite describes the thematic connection between *Usos amorosos del dieciocho* and its follow-up, *Usos amorosos de la postguerra*, as the "enfrentamiento de las mujeres con las consignas amorosas que les impone la época en que les ha tocado vivir" (*Usos amorosos del dieciocho* xx–xxi). In *Usos amorosos de la postguerra* these "consignas amorosas" will apply to Martín Gaite herself, a fact the author recognizes even before she has begun to research the book. She writes that if she were to analyze her "modo de pensar, elegir y proceder," she would arrive at the conclusion that these impressions "influirá subrepticia e irremediablemente en todo cuanto diga y escriba" (*Usos amorosos del dieciocho* xix). Martín Gaite recognizes that she will be both author and subject of a volume covering a historical period she has lived through. By examining *El cuarto de atrás* and *Usos amorosos de la postguerra* together through genre fusion, it is clear that the author addresses not only her personal experiences and memories of a particular historical moment, but also the thought processes that lead her to select and organize these strands of her own memory.

Martín Gaite explores her commitment to the lived experience of history in countless nonfiction essays and journalistic articles, touching on topics as wide-ranging as postwar song lyrics, the death of Spanish literary figures (e.g., Ignacio Aldecoa), a consideration of the role of the interlocutor in narrative, and thoughts about the subversive nature of "Puss in Boots," to name only a subset.[6] Presenting her doctoral dissertation in 1972, in an introduction Martín Gaite later published as the essay "De licenciada a doctora," the author describes her constant interplay with history:

> La relación del pasado con el presente, de las historias inventadas con las verdaderas, del lenguaje estereotipado con el que pugna por indicar las angustias y necesidades del individuo, de los comportamientos privados con los públicos eran evidencias inseparables ya de mi capacidad de reflexión y contemplación... (*Agua pasada* 365)

For Martín Gaite, history is a dynamic confluence of public and private lives, truth and fiction, interpreted and influenced by the present-day historian. After considering her transition from the Inquisition, to novel-writing, to eighteenth-century Spanish courtship customs, she asks herself and her dissertation committee: "¿quién iba a declararse filólogo, novelista o historiador sino, en todo caso, una mezcla desbarajustada de las tres cosas?" (Martín Gaite, *Agua pasada* 365). The author is wholly self-aware of the generic intermingling evident in her work. Nevertheless, literary critics have been reluctant to explore her blending of fact and fiction across genre.

Yet Martín Gaite has never suffered from critical oblivion. The exuberant response to her writing, and especially to her novels, began in earnest when she won the Nadal Prize for *Entre visillos*. Critical interest surged again when she received Spain's National Prize for Literature in 1978 for *El cuarto de atrás*, which has since become one of the most studied modern Spanish novels. A number of these critical responses focus on aspects of genre in the novel, although the concept of genre fusion, as I have defined it, is rarely applied.[7] And although Martín Gaite earned more accolades a decade later, winning the Anagrama Essay Prize in 1987 for *Usos amorosos de la postguerra española*, this volume has elicited far fewer critical responses, perhaps with the assumption that the narrative from which a nonfiction historical text is spun is representational, and does not bear interpreting. But Martín Gaite's is not a traditional historiography.

Joan Lipman Brown has analyzed Martín Gaite's writing extensively, and identifies two main questions around which the author's work revolves: "a preoccupation with the relationship between the nonconformist individual and society and an intense interest in the characteristics of narrative art" ("Carmen Martín Gaite" 75). Martín Gaite's interest in collective society and in the properties of narration are clear in *El cuarto de atrás* and *Usos amorosos de la postguerra*. These elements serve in part to focus the author's thoughts on Spanish history as well as to draw a parallel between the two outwardly distinct texts. Colmeiro describes *El cuarto de atrás* as taking place in "un terreno genéricamente inestable y continuamente mutable, metamorfoseándose entre libro de memorias, novela fantástica y metaficcón" (159). Where Colmeiro identifies a generic instability among these seemingly disparate parts, however, genre fusion locates a stability. Robert Spires, meanwhile, sees a metafictional game at work in which "the literary text is integrally woven into the sociohistorical text of the country" (*Beyond the Metafictional Mode* 123). Historiography is yet another genre that Martín Gaite transcends in the fluid, boundaryless movement described by Colmeiro and Spires, and although Colmeiro only alludes to *Usos amorosos de la postguerra*, it, too, undergoes a process of genre metamorphosis.

While critics are inclined to connect *El cuarto de atrás* loosely to the author's other historical texts or more generally to her historically minded approach to narrative,[8] rare is the critical study that provides a direct comparison of the novel to *Usos amorosos de la postguerra*, despite their indisputable points of overlap. Perhaps another barrier to the critical juxtaposition of these two volumes is illustrated by Debra A. Castillo, who interprets the use of the historical in *El cuarto de atrás* as secondary to the fantastic. She states that "[t]he parameters of the playing field of form and force in this novel are designated by the choice of the most recognizably fictive of all fictional genres, the fantastic, radically allied with the 'historical' tale of a 'real' person" (818). Castillo's use of quotes when referring to history and the incarnation of Martín Gaite undermines these elements in *El cuarto de atrás*, revealing Castillo's ultimate assertion that there is only one genre at work in the novel: "it is essential to this novel that both history and fiction be revealed as fantasy; both are equally escapist" (822). This assessment contradicts Martín Gaite's self-identified role as novelist, historian, and linguist, interested in fantasy, history, and language (or narrative, in this case) as equally valuable and conjoined entities. Moreover, it challenges Martín Gaite's own fluid perspective on the dialectic between the real and the fantastic. Responding to the Real Academia Española's definition of a fantastic object or concept as "quimérico, fingido, que no tiene realidad y consiste solo en la imaginación" (*Diccionario*) in her essay "Brechas de la costumbre," Martín Gaite refutes this paradigm on a single point:

> que lo ficticio no tenga realidad. Sería más correcto decir que cobra otro tipo de realidad, no regida por las mismas leyes que tienen vigencia para lo que se ve y se palpa. Lo fantástico, es decir lo inventado, trasciende estas leyes e instala su discurso en otro plano. Pero realidad, ¡vaya si la tiene! Si no la tuviera, no entraría tantas veces en conflicto con la otra, no podría llegar a influir en el individuo—como lo hace—tanto o más que esa otra realidad cotidiana, histórica y comprobable. (*Agua pasada* 157)

The conflict between fiction and history as a battle between the invented and the real extends far and wide, from novelist to

Chapter Three

historian to theorist. Martín Gaite's defense of the fantastic moves beyond the arguments proposed by Hayden White and Paul Ricoeur, who identify the importance of the historical in fiction, to argue that at times the real aspects of the fantastic outshine in magnitude even the real aspects of the real. Although she divides reality into two differently regulated discursive planes, depending on whether it is located in a realistic text or a fantastic text, Martín Gaite claims that both exert an extraordinary influence on the individual. Moreover, her definition of the real is also noteworthy, in that it includes the everyday, the historical, and the verifiable: without a doubt three markers of her own brand of socio-cultural historiography.

In Martín Gaite's historically engaged fiction and nonfiction the fantastic exists in tandem and as a counterweight to reality. To be sure, labeling *El cuarto de atrás* a fantastic novel is a valid conclusion. Yet one must consider the centrality of history, Martín Gaite's own distinctly liberal definition of the fantastic, and the dialogue between the two genres throughout the novel to appreciate just what a uniquely "fantastic" novel it is. Tzvetan Todorov defines the fantastic—in a volume that makes a cameo appearance in the novel—in terms of "a hesitation common to reader and character, who must decide whether or not what they perceive derives from 'reality'" (41). That "hesitation" is also the space of genre fusion, where the reader's role in determining whether what he or she encounters is real is key in deciding whether a text is fictional or historiographic. In this sense, the fantastic and the historical are equally important in *El cuarto de atrás*; in fact, they elicit essentially the same response in the reader.

* * *

Christopher Ortiz has read *El cuarto de atrás* in conjunction with the elements of *Usos amorosos de la postguerra* without arriving at the reductive conclusion that the latter is simply the name of the essay the protagonist of the former is working on during the course of the novel.[9] Ortiz interprets the blending of genres in *El cuarto de atrás* as Martín Gaite's subjective and political value judgments. He indicates that *Usos amorosos de la postguerra* "more systematically" (Ortiz 40) approaches the same historical material as the novel. By limiting his scope to Martín Gaite's approximation of history in her fictional text, however, he does not explicitly reference the practice of genre fusion. Ortiz conjectures that a conflict between autobiography and fiction plays with the reader's preconceived notions of genre: is it true or is it fantasy? Martín Gaite's message, according to Ortiz, is that both history and the reader take an active or operative role "explor[ing] how discursive systems form and shape subjectivity, thus determining women's material and social conditions" (33). The reader's agency in interpreting these historical undercurrents is a central characteristic of genre fusion.

Ortiz argues that the critical desire to see *El cuarto de atrás* as fantastic has obfuscated history's structuring role. While the interplay between fact and fiction in the novel is complex, by its nature the "undecidability and contradiction are what make all narrative compelling and effective and potentially subversive or repressive" (Ortiz 37). Ortiz's observations, while trained on *El cuarto de atrás*, naturally fit *Usos amorosos de la postguerra* as well. History is confusing: it is not presented to the individual as a cohesive, linear narrative. Martín Gaite reflects this inherent complexity in her narrative style through her protagonist's confusion within the novel and the seemingly stream-of-consciousness quality of the nonfiction text. History is a dynamic entity in Martín Gaite's texts, "reveal[ing] that neither history nor its facts are neutral" (Ortiz 49). With this radical valuation, Ortiz implicitly connects Martín Gaite to White's readings of historiography, in which White argues that history is an ideologically charged entity.[10] History is not benign in Martín Gaite's texts, either. The author's historical representations demand the recognition that postwar culture influenced a generation of women in a generally pejorative manner, an assertion that elicits a spectrum of positive and negative responses from historians and readers. However, Ortiz argues that Martín Gaite is constantly "[aware] of the need for another text, another way of representing her social identity" (47–48) and of broadening definitions of genre in order to create a more elaborated representation of herself and her experience of Spanish society. As such, she answers her critics with a more rounded view of history: this "other" text is *Usos amorosos de la postguerra*.

El cuarto de atrás and *Usos amorosos de la postguerra* are based on a shared history, but by using genre fusion, we can see that their connection runs far deeper. Both texts possess an unconventional narrative style, ground-breaking in the context of fiction or historiography. They revolve around the author's lived experience, and provide not only a working model of a historical re-evaluation of the Franco era, but also a theoretical framework behind Martín Gaite's writing of the text itself: a metatheory, included in and applicable to both texts. The blending of historiographic and fictional texts theorized by genre fusion, as we have seen in the previous chapter on Roig, remains almost wholly unexplored in critical studies of modern Spanish literature. Ultimately, the blurring evidenced by genre fusion's application to *El cuarto de atrás* and *Usos amorosos de la postguerra* moves beyond the barriers of genre to uncover a narrative pastiche of postwar fantasies, courtship customs, childhood historical imagination, and adult musings on society that transform our perceptions of postwar Spanish culture.

El cuarto de atrás: A Fantastic Interruption of History

By 1975, Martín Gaite maintained two literary objectives, both "inextricably linked to the cultural and literary developments which had been and still were taking place" during the Transition (Brown, *Secrets* 150). The author wanted to write about the social history of the postwar years, and was also interested in writing a fantastic novel. As the author's alter-ego in *El cuarto de atrás* posits, "¿Y si mezclara las dos promesas en una?" (Martín Gaite, *El cuarto* 128). By combining the two projects, Martín Gaite opened up a space between history and fiction that would make genre fusion's application possible. She also heralded the arrival of a new phase in Spanish literature, once Franco's power over the publishing industry had become a distant memory. Interviewers speaking with Martín Gaite soon after the book's publication are endlessly fascinated by the author's intermingling of fantasy and history in the text, a relatively novel narrative technique. One interviewer asks her if the text is "una novela histórica o… una historia novelada," to which Martín Gaite responds:

> Es una novela basada en datos ciertos. Los que escriben novelas históricas suelen hacer literatura con datos vagos; mi novela, en cambio, es un libro de investigación histórica escrito de una manera poco habitual, ya que resulta mimético. … Comprendo que ese libro me ha empujado a escribir de otra manera. No sé explicarlo, pero sí sé que es así. (Del Villar 11)

The revelation that Martín Gaite envisions *El cuarto de atrás* as a mediator between historiography, because it includes factual historical data, and fiction, because it is in essence still a novel, is central to the text's actualization through genre fusion.

Yet the author still avoids definitively categorizing the novel. The essential "what is it?" debate about the text in these early reviews and interviews allows Martín Gaite to play with her descriptions of genre, just as she plays with genre itself in the novel. In two instances, she enigmatically introduces moments from the novel into the setting of an interview, telling one journalist that the man in black sat "en la misma butaca que ocupas tú ahora" (Lacruz Pardo 16), and pointing out to another "*el bar desde donde me telefoneó* el caballero de negro" (Izquierdo 19; emphasis in the original). The author deliberately confuses the borders between fiction and reality in these interviews, just as she does in the novel itself. When an interviewer asks her which profession she identifies with—poet, novelist, short story writer, or researcher—Martín Gaite responds that she envisions herself easily embodying all of them:

> Creo que no hay tanta diferencia entre los géneros a que aludes, o por lo menos no debiera haberla. ... Para mí lo importante es la forma de narrar, y esta pasión por narrar era la misma cuando me enfrenté con historias del siglo XVII [sic] que la que me lleva a contar otra historia cualquiera inventada o vivida por mí. (Izquierdo 17)

Indeed, the "invented" elements in Martín Gaite's canonical *El cuarto de atrás* have been the focus of the majority of the critical analysis of the novel. But with genre fusion, narration is the great equalizer between fiction and historiography. *El cuarto de atrás* is a prelude to her historical study, *Usos amorosos de la postguerra*, and Martín Gaite treats the novel's fantastic elements as indivisible from its historical discourse. Both fact and fantasy lend a subversive tone to a novel that ruptures the entrenched situation of literature under the dictatorship. Through the lens of genre fusion, *El cuarto de atrás* and *Usos amorosos de la postguerra* together consider fantasy a necessary escape from the mythic status afforded dictatorship culture, but ultimately the fantastic is inseparable from the reality of the postwar era.

Chapter Three

* * *

El cuarto de atrás takes place during a single stormy night. A mysterious man in black appears at "C.'s" door at a late hour, apparently to interview her. Amid fantastic details—C.'s dreamlike states, an anthropomorphic cockroach, a little box of memory pills, a phone call from someone who might be the man's distraught lover, pages at C.'s typewriter that multiply by themselves and seemingly reproduce the novel in the reader's hands—the interviewer draws out a disjointed account of C.'s experience of the Spanish postwar era. The man in black is indulgent of C.'s flights of abstraction and silence. He is the ideal interlocutor who elicits her life story. She recounts formative childhood experiences, cultural touchstones of her adolescence, historical events that affected her, and how all of these moments have manifested themselves in her writing career and the way she envisions her work. Furthermore, C., as both the protagonist and narrator of this novel, challenges the reader's expectation of fiction. Given that C. and Carmen Martín Gaite have identical life experiences and have written the same books,[11] should the novel be read as autobiography? This confusion demands the reader's active interpretation of the novel's historical background and autobiographical elements.

Some critics have been reluctant to identify C. fully with Martín Gaite, arguing that there are aspects of the author's life that have been omitted from the novel, such as her marriage to and separation from Sánchez Ferlosio. They argue that if Martín Gaite wanted her narrator/protagonist to embody a full incarnation of herself, she would have named her "Carmen Martín Gaite" instead of "C." Nevertheless, clearly the narrator/protagonist in *El cuarto de atrás* is a fictional entity whose biography mirrors Martín Gaite's.[12] The author may disguise herself in a fictional creation, but the historical and social material she incorporates into the novel are based on verifiable historical data, culled through Martín Gaite's recollections and the archival research she undertook in the 1970s. She is more forthcoming with this data in *Usos amorosos de la postguerra*, where she explicitly offers herself as the subject of her own investigations. Following Montserrat Roig's use of notation (or lack thereof) to indicate references to documented history in her novel and historiographic study, Martín Gaite makes extensive use of footnotes in *Usos amorosos de la postguerra*, yet relies on undocumented historical material in *El cuarto de atrás*. The transparently autobiographical and historiographic nature of *Usos amorosos de la postguerra* illustrates both discourses' transformations when they are incorporated into fiction. Martín Gaite may manipulate her personal history in *El cuarto de atrás*, but its ultimate truth value is still visible, just below the surface of a fantastic story.

Waking to a disorienting conglomeration of images, *El cuarto de atrás* opens in medias res. C. stumbles over her thoughts on dreaming and wakefulness just as she trips over the chaos of things—shoes, newspapers, books, drawings—littering her apartment floor. The order of a personal historiography emerges from this disorder of objects in her apartment, while the disorder of memory mimics the protagonist's submersion into dream states. C. describes her surroundings as "esa caterva de objetos cuya historia, inherente a su silueta, resuena apagadamente en el recuerdo y araña estratos insospechados del alma, arrancando fechas, frutos podridos. ¡Qué aglomeración de letreros, de fotografías de cachivaches, de libros… !; libros que, para enredar más la cosa, guardan dentro fechas, papelitos, telegramas, dibujos, texto sobre texto…" (Martín Gaite, *El cuarto* 16). Latent in the paraphernalia on her floor are the memories associated with each object that, moreover, record the dates, images, and intertexts activating each object as a relic of history. Unlike Roig and Javier Marías, Martín Gaite does not include tangible reproductions of drawings, photographs, and other realia in the pages of the novel. Nevertheless, these intertexts are the concrete, detailed, and annotated manifestations of the past that the author will use as resources for her social and cultural examination of history in *El cuarto de atrás* and *Usos amorosos de la postguerra*.

One of these many objects, a copy of *Introducción a la literatura fantástica*, turns the protagonist toward the promise she made to Todorov (or his book) to write a fantastic novel, which is clearly this novel. According to C., Todorov is preoccupied with "los desdoblamientos de personalidad, de la ruptura de límites entre tiempo y espacio, de la ambigüedad y la incertidumbre" (Martín Gaite, *El cuarto* 19). Indeed, in his volume Todorov foretells literature "abandoning the division into genres" (7) that characterizes genre fusion and *El cuarto de atrás*. Moreover, Todorov explains the reader's assessment of a fantastic text as "defined by the reader's own ambiguous perception of the events narrated" (31). This process is similar to the one at work when the reader of a historiographic text or a work of historical fiction must assess the events narrated in order to satisfy himself of their truth value. The doubling between C. and Martín Gaite, the rupture between a present and past space, and the uncertainty that C. encounters during a "noche en vela, cuando lo real y lo ficticio se confunden" (Martín Gaite, *El cuarto* 17) are all manifestations of Todorov's fantastic literary vision. Yet these doublings and ruptures are also indications of the history that interrupts Martín Gaite's and C.'s flights of fantasy, all in need of interpretation by the reader.

The man in black's unorthodox and disjointed interview spurs the memories and flashbacks to C.'s adolescence that constitute the historical side of the novel. Asking her about her writing style and her works in progress, the man in black elicits two significant details from C. that make her autobiographical connection with Martín Gaite transparent. First, C. relates the circumstances of her grant to study in Coimbra, Portugal, an experience that matches Martín Gaite's life story exactly:[13]

> Pero hubo que arreglar muchas cosas, la primera mi situación anómala con el Servicio Social, una chica no podía salir al extranjero sin tener cumplido el Servicio Social o, por lo menos, haber dejado suponer, a lo largo de los cursillos iniciados, que tenía madera de futura madre y esposa, digna descendiente de Isabel la Católica. (Martín Gaite, *El cuarto* 42)

C.'s explanation for why she was allowed to leave Spain for Portugal at a time when expectations for adolescent women were focused on the contributions they could make to the nation models Martín Gaite's strategy for her personal exploration of history in the novel. By relating her own individual postwar experience followed by the collective experience of her generation, the author surveys the various social and cultural forces at work in postwar Spain. These individual and collective experiences contradict the Franco regime's conception of postwar society, illustrating how Martín Gaite and other girls like her were marginalized during the dictatorship. C. shows that she and her peers who considered antiquated the idea of preparing themselves for marriage and motherhood through the Social Service requirement found ways to elude the system. Thus, the protagonist/narrator reveals the subversive attitudes that boiled below the surface of authoritarian postwar society. Furthermore, by mentioning Queen Isabel, she ties the state's expectations regarding her personal behavior to the reigning Francoist mythology, which held the Catholic kings as the country's still-relevant archetype. This anecdote connects Martín Gaite and her generation of postwar girls to larger historical and societal questions. As an adult, she re-envisions this time period and how it led her to a career as a writer who calls Francoist historiography into question. Genre fusion's characteristic project of delving into the personal backstory of history contextualizes these autobiographical details and the author's positioning on the margins of Francoist social norms.

The man in black's questions stimulate C.'s flashback to a visit to a spa with her father, an episode from Martín Gaite's life that forms the basis for her first published novel, *El balneario*.[14] Her interlocutor asks:

> —¿Hace mucho que vive en esta casa?
> —Desde el año cincuenta y tres.
> Suspiro. He vuelto a coger el hilo, como siempre que me acuerdo de una fecha. Las fechas son los hitos de la rutina.
> —Precisamente ese año—reanudo—es cuando empecé a escribir mi primera novela, esa que le decía antes que es bastante misteriosa…, cuando no me oyó. (Martín Gaite, *El cuarto* 47)

An exact date jogs the narrator's memory, leading her to relate a precise moment in historical time with that moment's personal and routine significance, a method she will use again in *Usos amorosos de la postguerra*.

C.'s flashback to the spa includes both her recollections of the norms of comportment for "modest" and "decent" girls, as well as the defining historical event of the attempted assassination of Hitler. At the time of *El balneario*'s publication in 1955, the censors would not allow this kind of direct historical reference to Hitler, who had supported the Nationalists during the Spanish Civil War. But as C. recounts the episode in a post-Franco literary space, she can incorporate the event into her memories, realizing it had a profound impact on how she approached history as a girl. C. recalls to herself:

> [Y]o entonces aborrecía la historia y además no me la creía, nada de lo que venía en los libros de historia ni en los periódicos me lo creía, la culpa la tenían los que se lo creían, estaba harta de oír la palabra fusilado, la palabra víctima, la palabra tirano, la

> palabra militares, la palabra patria, la palabra historia. (Martín Gaite, *El cuarto* 54)

This childhood abhorrence of history is linked to the conflicts of the war and postwar. At the time, words like "shot to death," "tyrant," "victim," and "soldiers" were everyday descriptors of a dictatorial society and political system grounded in the view that the Nationalists were victims of Republican tyranny. Her hatred of history seems to have drawn C. to a world of illusion: she writes the first half of *El balneario* as a dream. When the man in black criticizes her for breaking this fantastic aspect of her first novel, she realizes that "[p]osiblemente mis trabajos posteriores de investigación histórica los considere una traición todavía más grave a la ambigüedad; yo misma, al emprenderlos, notaba que me estaba desviando, desertaba de los sueños para pactar con la historia, me esforzaba en ordenar las cosas, en entenderlas una por una, por miedo a naufragar" (Martín Gaite, *El cuarto* 55). It is difficult for C. to reconcile her interest in fantasy with her interest in reality, given her early feelings about history. She implies that to write about history one must abandon dreams. Still, it is clear from the way both C. and Martín Gaite resort to historical memory that the author and her protagonists are not interested in fully deserting history in favor of fantasy or dreams. Indeed, in her dream states, C. is able to access personal details locked in her memory that expand historical representation beyond dates and major events.

Her interlocutor's question about whether she finds refuge in literature prompts C. to remember that when she first began to investigate eighteenth-century Spain she "había empezado a refugiar[se] en la historia, en las fechas" (Martín Gaite, *El cuarto* 59). She then pushes even further back in time to imagine the literal refuge she and her family took from bombardments during the Spanish Civil War. In her flashback to the bomb shelters, she remembers highly personal details about the war. Scenes such as a neighbor's father scavenging religious relics from abandoned churches to use as decoration in his apartment, and the family of a neighborhood baker who died when he refused to seek shelter during a shelling would not appear in a traditional historical account of the conflict that omits the testimony of everyday citizens. Martín Gaite moves with fluidity between theorizing about history as a space of refuge to remembering neighborhood bomb shelters and the intensity of the Civil War. This technique makes historical writing accessible and relatable on a personal level for the author and her readership. It opens history up to the experiences of those caught helpless in the background to the conflicts, omitted in a traditional historiograpic text focused on the front lines of the war.

History has its precise points of contact between the personal and the national for C. The man in black's questions about her childhood in Salamanca, where Franco stationed his central barracks, leads C. to recall encountering the dictator's daughter. She narrates locking eyes with "Carmencita" Franco: "'Claro; una vez, me acuerdo, después de no sé qué ceremonia en la catedral… se cruzaron nuestras miradas… se me quedó grabada su imagen para siempre, era más o menos de mi edad, decían que se parecía algo a mí'" (Martín Gaite, *El cuarto* 63). C. identifies with the dictator's daughter as a member of her generation and someone whom she envied above all for her hairstyle, not her politics, since, as C. emphasizes: "'En mi casa, además, no eran franquistas'" (Martín Gaite, *El cuarto* 68). For Martín Gaite, historiography, even within the confines of a fictional narrative, constitutes an intermingling of the personal—C.'s envy of Carmencita's fashionable hairstyle, their physical resemblance—and the political—her encounter with Franco's family differentiated from her family's political leanings.

C.'s thoughts turn to her project of recording postwar courtship customs in the novel's next chapter. This long digression, which takes place entirely in the narrator's mind, eventually becomes cohesive when, through genre fusion, we compare it to how the sentiment is repeated in the published version of *Usos amorosos de la postguerra*. In the novel, C. imagines the project as:

> un poco el mundo de "Entre visillos" pero explorado ahora, con mayor distancia, en plan de ensayo o de memorias, no sé bien, la forma que podría darle es lo que no se me ha ocurrido todavía; lo ordené todo por temas: modistas, peluquerías, canciones, bailes, novelas, costumbres, modismos de lenguaje, bares, cine, en un cuaderno de tapas verdes y azules, fue a raíz de la muerte de Franco. (Martín Gaite, *El cuarto* 73)

C.'s thoughts outline a unique principle that organizes a social history thematically rather than chronologically. C. demonstrates this thematic ordering by thinking about a song from the postwar,

Chapter Three

the trips to the dressmaker in Madrid she made with her family, and the arbitrariness of the rules applied to women by the Sección Femenina that curtailed the liberties they had enjoyed before the Civil War.[15] Martín Gaite repeats this stream-of-consciousness route through different aspects of postwar culture in a more systematic way in *Usos amorosos de la postguerra*, where she divides the text into thematic chapters, but retains the loose overall organization of her research, indebted to the postmodern storytelling quality of *El cuarto de atrás*. The fact that the author self-consciously follows the same organizing principle in both texts promotes their overlap through genre fusion.

C. enters a momentary dreamlike state in which her thoughts magically appear typed on a page in the typewriter, on the same numbered page where these thoughts appear in the novel the reader holds in his hands. Returning to her conversation with the man in black, she mentions the history of Spain and her book on courtship customs, and then reflects that:

> el libro sobre la postguerra tengo que empezarlo en un momento de iluminación como el de ahora, relacionando el paso de la historia con el ritmo de los sueños, es un panorama tan ancho y tan revuelto, como una habitación donde cada cosa está en su sitio precisamente al haberse salido de su sitio, todo parte de mis primeras perplejidades frente al concepto de historia, allí, en el cuarto de atrás… (Martín Gaite, *El cuarto* 104)

Even as C. is thinking about the moment when she should begin her book on postwar courtship customs, she is beginning it. In fact, this thought occurs to her immediately after her fugue state and the fantastic self-producing pages, blending into the rhythm already established of dreams interrupted by memories of cultural history, or vice-versa. This intermingling reflects the unordered process of memory itself, in which the mind groups subjects by their interconnections, not by dates or names as in a traditional historiography, and is interrupted by digressions and out-of-context thoughts. Further, C. relates the novel *El cuarto de atrás*, to the actual back room where she and her sister had their childhood playroom, to the intangible space of unordered memory that retains the personal quality of both the room and the novel. This confluence of seeming opposites melds order with disorder, reality with fantasy, and spaces outside the text with spaces inside the narrative. These overlaps, in turn, capture the project of a social history framed by a subjective memoir that Martín Gaite undertakes in both this novel and her nonfiction study. History, as it has been constructed within the confines of a mythic and "truthful" ideology during the Franco regime, is diametrically opposed to these personal, subjective interventions. Genre fusion, on the other hand, thrives on personal memory and unconstrained genres in the creation of a counter-history.

Moments after these thoughts occur to C., the man in black gives her a pill which is said to delightfully shuffle her memory, which was clearly already disorganized. The man in black calls her "una fugada nata" (Martín Gaite, *El cuarto* 123), meaning that she allows her memory to veer wildly from one topic to another. This heterogeneity is the nature of memory. C. also sees herself as having fled the established order by escaping to a fictional island she invented as a child, avoiding the Social Service, and maintaining leftist ideals under a right-wing regime. Thus this escapist metaphor also applies to Martín Gaite's manner of avoiding the traditional role of historian or novelist in favor of an intermediate position between the two. When C. finally tells the man in black about the book she has been formulating on the cultural history of the postwar, she places it in the context of a "plague" of post-Franco memory texts, admitting that "'[s]e me enfrió, me lo enfriaron las memorias ajenas. Desde la muerte de Franco habrá notado cómo proliferan los libros de memorias, ya es una peste, en el fondo, eso es lo que me ha venido desanimando, pensar que, si a mí me aburren las memorias de los demás, por qué no le van a aburrir a los demás las mías'" (Martín Gaite, *El cuarto* 128). As an alternative to copying the memoir genre that she finds boring and too focused on one individual's memories instead of a collective memory, she tells the man in black that she is "'esperando a ver si se me ocurre una forma divertida de enhebrar los recuerdos'" (Martín Gaite, *El cuarto* 128). This novel is one such way of encapsulating her memories in an engaging and entertaining narrative. *Usos amorosos de la postguerra*, as we will see, is another. When C. considers her promise to Todorov to write a fantastic novel and her promise to herself to record her memories of the postwar, she has an epiphany: she can combine both projects into one.

C. tells the man in black that the inspiration to write a nonfiction book on the postwar occurred to her while watching Franco's

Chapter Three

burial on television, and she realizes that this is a good episode with which to inaugurate the book itself. Her thoughts on the day of the dictator's funeral draw her back to her childhood. She considers how confusing Spanish politics were to her as a child, "'un enredo incomprensible y lejano'" (Martín Gaite, *El cuarto* 130), and remembers the pervasiveness of Franco in postwar culture. The dictator "había conseguido infiltrarse en todas las casas, escuelas, cines y cafés" (Martín Gaite, *El cuarto* 132), invading Spanish culture so thoroughly that he had "'paralizado el tiempo'" (Martín Gaite, *El cuarto* 133). The dictator and his family had even infiltrated C.'s hometown. She contemplates her identification with Carmencita Franco, both of them "'víctimas de las mismas modas y costumbres, [han] leído las mismas revistas y visto el mismo cine'" (Martín Gaite, *El cuarto* 136). Although the events of history—Franco's rise to power and the Nationalist victory in the Spanish Civil War, the passage of censorship laws and strict control of the press, and the sense of political instability as Franco neared death—may be obliquely reflected in the styles, magazines, and movies of the era, these cultural touchstones more aptly reflect personal memories of the time. C. wants to focus on these popular cultural trends as opposed to the specific trail of historical events in her research: "'lo que yo quería rescatar era algo más inaprensible, eran las miguitas, no las piedrecitas blancas'" (Martín Gaite, *El cuarto* 138). The "white stones" are these major notches on a historical timeline, but genre fusion, too, is more interested in the "crumbs" of history: the day-to-day experiences of the past that would never appear in a timeline.

Martín Gaite combines C.'s digressions through memories of her childhood with an on-going conversation with her interlocutor about how best to reflect on her experiences of the postwar. The reader is privy not only to the content of C.'s next book on postwar culture, but to its composition as well: we see the historian at work. On the day of Franco's funeral, C. inaugurates a project of historical recuperation at a moment when Spain has stopped in its tracks to contemplate the end of the political system under which it has languished for forty years. By restarting the historical clock, C. moves forward with her project to examine the past and thus memorialize the end of a ruler who paralyzed time.

When a mysterious woman phones for the man in black and accuses him of being unfaithful, the novel begins to mimic a novela rosa, the pulp love stories tinged with fantasy and mystery popular during the postwar. C. delights in the ambiguity, thinking that:

> lo más excitante son las versiones contradictorias, constituyen la base de la literatura, no somos un solo ser, sino muchos, de la misma manera que tampoco la historia es esa que se escribe poniendo en orden las fechas y se nos presenta como inamovible, cada persona que nos ha visto o hablado alguna vez guarda una pieza del rompecabezas que nunca podremos contemplar entero. (Martín Gaite, *El cuarto* 167)

This argument for the collective nature of history also admits that historians are not the harbingers of truth: if history is a collective tale, no one person will be able to reconstruct the whole story. Still, these "contradictory versions" are what add intrigue to history, along with the techniques that lie beyond an ordered narration and the stagnant presentation of events and dates. The popular, low-brow novela rosa—a genre no intellectual would dare admit to having read and enjoyed—becomes emblematic of a collective telling of history. It is engrossing, exciting both for what it includes and what it omits, and written for a popular audience. *El cuarto de atrás*, too, combines elements of the novela rosa into Martín Gaite's particular blend of fantasy and reality. C.'s thought reveals another moment in which literature and history find common ground, and demonstrates her conscious assessment that this intermingling imbues both genres with interest and excitement.

In the next chapter, C. intercalates the story of her creation of a fantastic island as a childhood refuge. The island mirrors the back room, where she and her sister were able to escape from the adult world. Historical events broke into the narrator/protagonist's fantasies during the postwar, and her privacy was disturbed: the back room was commissioned as a pantry to stave off the family's hunger. The back room also represents C.'s family's leftist leanings, necessarily hidden from the public. C. tells the man in black: "'A un tío mío lo habían fusilado y mi padre ni nos había mandado a colegios de monjas ni quiso tener alojados alemanes en casa, siempre nos estaba advirtiendo que en la calle no habláramos de nada…'" (Martín Gaite, *El cuarto* 193). Indeed, Martín Gaite invented the "isla de Bergai" with a childhood friend, her uncle was shot because he belonged to the Socialist Party, and she and her sister remained in secular schools at a time when most children attended religious schools.[16] These episodes from Martín Gaite's life reveal her desire to speak out after so many years of silence imposed on her by dictatorship social norms. They also underline the author's confidence that her historical narration is no less authentic because it is based on her own experiences; she is the arbiter of historical truth in the novel.

Historical events play a pivotal role in C.'s life, and move her to encounter ways to escape the realities of the postwar, developing a keen sense of imagination. Now, in this transitional moment after Franco's death, C. as an adult can look back and reexamine the interplay between fantasy and history in her life during the postwar and, moreover, speak about it publicly. The man in black tells her that "'lo importante es saber contar la historia de lo que se ha perdido…, así vuelv[e] a vivir'" (Martín Gaite, *El cuarto* 195–96), an insightful description of the immediacy of narrative historiography. At the same time, when C. tells him that she is thinking of naming her historiographical work "Usos amorosos de la postguerra," he dislikes the title, saying that it "'tiene resonancias de sus investigaciones históricas. Con ese título, ya la veo volviéndose a meter en hemerotecas, empañándose en agotar los temas, en dejarlo todo claro'" (Martín Gaite, *El cuarto* 198). The man in black, thinking that this more traditional form of historiography will distract from the narrative and unordered threads C. has been weaving through their conversation, expresses a general criticism of the intermingling of fiction and history: if neither exists in its "pure" form, both are tainted. Instead, he encourages her to grasp her confused state between dreams and reality and "'atrévase a contarla, partiendo justamente de esa sensación. Que no sepa si lo que cuenta lo ha vivido o no, que no lo sepa usted misma. Resultaría una gran novela'" (Martín Gaite, *El cuarto* 197). This criticism, emerging from Martín Gaite's own character, not only forms part of the doubling that takes place in the novel—the author creates her own dissenter, to directly criticize her work—but also shows a self-conscious element in *El cuarto de atrás*. In that Martín Gaite later realizes her historiographic study of postwar culture, and titles it *Usos amorosos de la postguerra española*, it is clear that her inner critic, personified as the man in black, has been considered but ultimately rejected. *Usos amorosos de la postguerra* is not fantasy; it is a form of historiography. But C. has also written the "great novel" the man in black suggests by following a narrative methodology unknowingly patterned after the practice of genre fusion in the novel.

When C. awakens in the final chapter, the man in black has disappeared and been replaced by her daughter. C. wonders if her interlocutor ever existed at all; however, his box of memory pills and the self-multiplying pages forming the novel itself remain. The historical aspects of *El cuarto de atrás*, intermingled with these fantastic details and the dreamlike state of the narrative, lay the groundwork for a fascinating foray into narrative historiography in *Usos amorosos de la postguerra* that picks up where the novel leaves off. It is as though the box of memory pills left at the end of her novel are the crumbs Martín Gaite will follow toward the next phase of her melding of fiction and history. The fantasy that structures *El cuarto de atrás* is translated into personalized storytelling in *Usos amorosos de la postguerra*, both based on Martín Gaite's historical memory and the experiences of her marginalized collective of nonconformist girls. Genre fusion demonstrates how Martín Gaite self-consciously overlaps her two texts to draw attention to their common historical bond: young women coming of age on the margins of Francoist society.

Usos amorosos de la postguerra española: Postwar Society Reinterpreted

The United States and Spain signed their first military base agreement in September, 1953; a month later, Martín Gaite was married. She juxtaposes a concrete historical event with a personal moment in her life—both representing a new union—in the introduction to *Usos amorosos de la postguerra española*. It is a motif she will weave throughout the text, constantly demonstrating the intrinsic connection between history and the people who lived it.

In 1987, when Martín Gaite won the Anagrama Essay Prize for *Usos amorosos de la postguerra*, the author spoke about her return to the theme of courtship customs in postwar Spain: "'Ya toqué el tema en mi novela *El cuarto de atrás*, y creí que con ese libro ya estaba todo contado. Pero el deseo me volvía y me volvía, el deseo de hacer con ello no una novela, sino un estudio sociológico…'" (Montero 34). Martín Gaite's assertion that *El cuarto de atrás* is a novel, whereas *Usos amorosos de la postguerra* is a sociological study, betrays the author's sense of herself as a "mezcla desbarajustada" (*Agua pasada* 365) of historian and novelist. However, this generic division also establishes the fundamental difference between the texts—one is fiction; the other is nonfiction—that the author proceeds to self-consciously and systematically muddle in her writing.

By the time of *Usos amorosos de la postguerra*'s publication, Spain had left the political tumult of the Transition behind, and entered the fully democratic post-Franco era. As C. points out in *El cuarto de atrás*, the literary market was overwhelmed with memoirs, histories, novelized accounts, and fictionalized histories of the postwar period and the dictatorship: Martín Gaite's version could have become one among many. Her particular social and collective approach to history, her unorthodox narrative discourse, and her concentration on a single generation of (mainly female) adolescents, however, has distinguished this work from its contemporaries. And yet, *Usos amorosos de la postguerra* is consistently overshadowed by Martín Gaite's fiction and her nonfiction literary essays in critical studies.[17] *El cuarto de atrás* has prepared the astute reader for what is to come. C., as a foil for the author, addresses her initial dislike of history, her doubts about historiography, her inspirations, and how history has personally affected her. Although she frames these discussions in a fantastic setting, they are representative of a serious and sophisticated approach to historiography. The reader can be assured that Martín Gaite will continue to treat her subject matter in an unapologetically unique style in *Usos amorosos de la postguerra*. Unlike Roig, Martín Gaite does not quote directly from one volume in the other. Rather, applying genre fusion to the two volumes focuses on the thematic overlaps and melding of fantasy and reality common to both.

Martín Gaite stands out from other Spanish authors who blend fiction and history in that she has a PhD in history. At the presentation of her doctoral thesis on the courtship customs of eighteenth-century Spain, she announced:

> todo el material, tanto el tomado de historias particulares como de ficción, lo he seleccionado y ordenado—aunque quizá sería mejor decir desordenado—con arreglo a criterios y preferencias de tipo claramente literario; pero es que eso yo no lo puedo remediar. Cada uno tiene su forma de contar las cosas. (Martín Gaite, *Agua pasada* 366)

Martín Gaite organizes her material according to her own inner narrative cohesion (one might imagine her committee giving her some leeway with her methodology, as an already famous novelist). Despite being the only formally trained historian among the other authors in this study, Martín Gaite feels no obligation to adhere to the traditional manners of ordering historiography chronologically.

By inspecting *El cuarto de atrás* and *Usos amorosos de la postguerra* through the lens of genre fusion, one is able to discern their similar literary approach to what is effectively the same historical material, differentiated by the primary source quotations and footnotes the author has added to her nonfiction text. While Martín Gaite labels *Usos amorosos de la postguerra* a "sociological study," history is an essential factor in her analysis of the postwar era. Although concerned with social and collective movements, the author also examines archives of newspapers, magazines, and political propaganda, contextualizing her study of mass culture in the historical circumstances of the era. The recesses of the author's own memory also become an archive in the work, as is clear when Martín Gaite encourages someone else to continue the investigation of courtship customs in later decades, someone who has "la paciencia de reunir los materiales de archivo y de memoria suficientes para contárnosla bien" (*Usos amorosos de la postguerra* 218). *Usos amorosos de la postguerra* is a socio-historiographic study; a unique moniker for the author's individualistic interpretation of historiography.

The opening paragraph of *Usos amorosos de la postguerra* illustrates how Martín Gaite envisions the project as a response to a typical work of historiography:

> Siempre que el hombre ha dirigido su interés hacia cualquier época del pasado y ha tratado de orientarse en ella, como quien se abre camino a tientas por una habitación oscura, se ha sentido un tanto insatisfecho en su curiosidad con los datos que le proporcionan las reseñas de batallas, contiendas religiosas, gestiones diplomáticas, motines, precios del trigo o cambios de dinastía, por muy convincente y bien ordenada que se le ofrezca la crónica de estos acontecimientos fluctuantes. Y se ha preguntado en algún momento: "Pero bueno, esa gente que iba a la guerra, que se aglomeraba en las iglesias y en las manifestaciones, ¿cómo era en realidad?, ¿cómo se relacionaba

> y se vestía, qué echaba de menos, con arreglo a qué cánones se amaba? Y sobre todo, ¿cuáles eran las normas que presidían su educación?" (11)

Martín Gaite does not intend to write a conclusive history of postwar Spain, a methodical survey of political conflicts, dynasties, and economic turmoil. Her goal is to answer her own questions of history. While never doubting the importance of the chronicle style of historiography, she notes the omission of more personal and cultural data showing what Spaniards experienced on a day-to-day basis during these major historical moments. Above all, she identifies a need to look into education, which can be interpreted as both familial upbringing and institutional learning: both influential arenas in the lives of adolescent Spaniards over which the Franco dictatorship exerted a heavy-handed control. The fluidity with which Martín Gaite describes her investigative practice and its application in the fields of fiction and historiography only emphasizes the fact that the basic material for both works remains the same: the cultural and social norms for adolescent girls during the postwar. In that she utilizes the same archival research, it is the tone of the narrative, how she orders her thoughts and impressions, and the ultimate decision of whether to wrap the material in a fantastic tale or build it into a historical framework that determines the genre of her published work. In *El cuarto de atrás* and *Usos amorosos de la postguerra*, the material itself—historical in nature—remains unchanged.

Martín Gaite's archival investigations of postwar courtship customs grew out of an interest in "la relación que tiene la historia con las historias" (Martín Gaite, *Usos amorosos de la postguerra* 11), that is, how the price of wheat relates to what girls wore to parties. But the author admits that at the outset of her investigations, the archival material she researched "[le] tentaba más como divagación literaria que como investigación histórica" (*Usos amorosos de la postguerra* 12). This pull toward a more novelistic realization of her historical inquiry affects how she comes to view the material before her, paying more attention to the tone that she wants to strike in her novel than "el análisis y la ordenación de los textos que iba encontrando" (*Usos amorosos de la postguerra* 12). Only later does she come to realize that her shelved project to write a social history, debated in the pages of *El cuarto de atrás*, still held an appeal for her, and she returns to her role as a historian. As Martín Gaite

Carmen Martín Gaite

undertakes this historical investigation, however, her narrative sensibilities as a novelist continue to provide inspiration.

She limits her study to a period of approximately fifteen years during the 1940s and 1950s, when she was an adolescent in Spain. Still reeling from the bombs of the Civil War, the country was saturated with:

> [l]a propaganda oficial, encargada de hacer acatar las normas de conducta que al Gobierno y a la Iglesia le parecían convenientes para sacar adelante aquel período de convalecencia, [que] insistía en los peligros de entregarse a cualquier exceso o derroche. Y desde los púlpitos, la prensa, la radio y las aulas de la Sección Femenina se predicaba la moderación. (Martín Gaite, *Usos amorosos de la postguerra* 12–13)

The text's central motif of moderation and self-control—presented to the Spanish public as norms of "'restricción' y 'racionamiento'" (*Usos amorosos de la postguerra* 13)—stand in stark contrast to Martín Gaite's unrestricted freedom decades later to recount the actual state of unease, contradiction, and fantasy of the era. Above all, the period is marked by one rule: "Prohibido mirar hacia atrás" (Martín Gaite, *Usos amorosos de la postguerra* 13). If, looking back, the primary activity of historiography and historical research, was prohibited, clearly any sort of far-reaching historical project was severely constricted during the dictatorship years. Even the statements that Martín Gaite makes in the introduction to *Usos amorosos de la postguerra*, plainly detailing Francoist restrictions, would have been censored under the dictatorship. The author carefully manipulates the propaganda of the Franco era, juxtaposing it with both a cultural acquiescence and quiet resistance to those Francoist norms in order to uncover its effect on members of her generation and their courtship customs, resulting in a sociohistoriographic study that is anything but reserved.

Usos amorosos de la postguerra is divided into nine chapters,[18] each focused on a different aspect of postwar culture and society alluded to in the popular aphorism, lyric, or quotation from a book or magazine that constitutes the title of each chapter. The chapters are loosely divided thematically, as the protagonist/narrator in *El cuarto de atrás* had considered doing. Within each chapter, the subject matter veers around a central theme, at times in a stream-of-consciousness fashion, from Martín Gaite's personal experiences, to archival material, to the historical background of the era. The author's inclusion of song lyrics, advertising jingles, snippets of short stories from magazines, advice columns, jokes, and idioms, among other relics of popular culture, are all carefully footnoted and constitute a concrete documentation of the era. Popular culture during the early years of the dictatorship, as Helen Graham has noted, "was perceived as useful to the regime because... it was seen as pacificatory, offering malnourished and unhappy Spaniards a form of—ostensibly depoliticized—'escapist' entertainment" (Graham and Labanyi 238). Martín Gaite reveals the subversive reactions marginalized teenage girls had to such escapist mass culture. She demonstrates how these seemingly "depoliticized" cultural products could, in fact, lead to a counter-discourse against hegemonic Francoist mythology.

Although these cultural manifestations historically contextualize her narration, Martín Gaite also includes discussions about the fictional spaces of the era, like the novela rosa, "dangerous" literature, and the feminine ideal, which represent equally important fantasies of the postwar. The sheer quantity of information in *Usos amorosos de la postguerra* is a staggering testament to the long hours Martín Gaite spent pouring through materials in Spanish archives. Three overriding subjects demonstrate Martín Gaite's unique approach to historiography in the text: the revision of Francoist historiography through a counter-discourse; the author's personal connection to the era and its cultural touchstones; and the opposition between reality and fantasy (and thus history and fiction) prevalent during the postwar. In that these were elements fundamental to *El cuarto de atrás* as well, they form the essential bonds that create genre fusion between Martín Gaite's two texts.

* * *

Postwar Spain, explains Martín Gaite, was embodied by Franco: "La verdadera España la representaba él. Más todavía: era él mismo" (*Usos amorosos de la postguerra* 19). The dictator exerted a monolithic power over the country, leading to an equally monolithic control over the history of postwar Spain. Martín Gaite's aim is to show the side of Spain that was out of reach of Franco, calling on communal, generational stories to provide a counter-discourse to the dictatorship's strictly unified, official history. Delving into the unspoken territory of male/female relationships and cultural influences on girls, she uncovers a rebellious undercurrent below the surface comportment of the obedient, conservative, postwar Spaniard. The author achieves some of her counter-discourse with humor. In explaining that Spaniards were expected to uphold a façade of "alegría tensa, sublime y como atormentada," she responds: "Con música de himno quedaba bonito, pero ¿quién podía identificarse con aquello a la hora de la merienda?" (Martín Gaite, *Usos amorosos de la postguerra* 24). This is a comical way of pointing out the inadequacies of the Franco ideal when applied to actual people. Adolescent hungers and feelings, according to Francoist doctrine, were irrelevant. If, perchance, this false and tormented happiness did not adequately express one's sense of self, boys and girls had different ways to respond. Although antithetical to the institute of chaste dating and long-term engagement (*noviazgo*), it was an unspoken norm that boys would not arrive at marriage as virgins and thus would take the proactive measure of visiting prostitutes. The authorities may have outwardly denounced this kind of immoral behavior, but it was tacitly accepted. Moreover, although it would be socially unacceptable to marry a lower-class girl, a sexual encounter with one was a different story: indeed, it was implicitly acceptable for a boy to sleep with a girl below his social and economic standing.

Middle-class girls who found themselves outside the mold of the sublimely happy youth, on the other hand, were branded *chicas raras* ("strange girls"), instead of the spoiled, vapid, rich *niñas topolinos* ("platform-shoe girls") who focused all their energies on clothes and boyfriends. Although it was presumed that a *chica rara* was unable to find a husband, often it was an active choice on the young woman's part to remain single, an affront to the teachings of the Sección Femenina. The *chica rara* looked instead to the female model of the Second Republic, when women could be independent and educated. These self-sufficient women were a disgrace and an embarrassment to Franco-era society. Cultural norms during the regime imposed a strict division between the feminine ideal of the Sección Femenina and the anti-Franco femininity promoted by the Republic, thus superimposing a gendered political interpretation on differing modes of female comportment during the postwar.

This binary between the Falange as good and the Republic as bad was applied to the divisions between model Spanish woman in postwar society. The smiling woman was "fuerte y animosa" and

Chapter Three

"'airoso,' con claras connotaciones triunfalistas" (Martín Gaite, *Usos amorosos de la postguerra* 40–41), whereas the glum, rejected, single Spanish woman reflected "[l]o contrario [que] era darse por vencido, 'quedar desairado,' en mal lugar" (41) or was "la chica 'que iba para soltera'" (42). Language marks a social division more commonly associated with the winners and losers of the Spanish Civil War. Martín Gaite makes this political/cultural association apparent when she writes: "Dentro de esta retórica del éxito y el fracaso, la solterona que no había puesto nada de su parte para dejar de serlo era considerada con el mismo desdén farisaico que el gobierno aplicaba a los vencidos" (*Usos amorosos de la postguerra* 42). The only exception to the rule that good, patriotic Spanish women must find husbands is the young woman who chooses to remain true to a boyfriend or husband who has died in the war. These women were "heroína[s]" and "novias eternas" (Martín Gaite, *Usos amorosos de la postguerra* 43–44).

A young woman in postwar Spain was expected to take great pride in her hair and clothes; only the *chica rara* would consider leaving the house in a state of disarray. This kind of carelessness, within the paradigm of Francoist society, could only lead to a total breakdown of the political regime: "La alerta contra la anarquía, que vertebró toda la política interior y exterior en los años de consolidación del franquismo, tuvo su correlato más fiel en el ámbito de lo doméstico" (Martín Gaite, *Usos amorosos de la postguerra* 118). If the *chica rara* refused to take the same kind of care in her appearance as "normal" girls did, she also might refuse to follow the extensive social norms as to meeting, courting, and marrying a boy. This would ostensibly pave the way for the destruction of Franco's carefully established political and cultural objectives. Although Martín Gaite defends the *chica rara*'s decision to isolate herself with "una razón tan noble como la de su afición a los libros" (*Usos amorosos de la postguerra* 182), reading was, in practice, not a good enough reason for a girl to exclude herself from the social standards of the time. In fact, as it smacked of the Republican ideals of femininity, it was essentially an affront to the state. The author's counter-discourse is evident in her revelation that these girls did, indeed, exist. Martín Gaite even goes so far as to divulge that the courtship model the *chica rara* abhorred was fundamentally flawed. The interminable *noviazgos* that ended either in marriage or a breakup were a time of repressed sexuality. The couple arrived at the wedding "[t]otalmente a ciegas" (Martín Gaite, *Usos amorosos de la postguerra* 208), and this lack of information forced the couple to lose respect and sincerity for one another. Martín Gaite interprets this absence of sexual information as a failure of early postwar society that has continued to have a lasting effect in the male-female relationships of modern day Spain.

Although Martín Gaite eventually married and became a mother, it is clear that she identifies with the against-the-grain attitude of the *chica rara*, disassociated from Franco's ideal Spanish behavior but nonetheless a rampant figure in postwar society. She expresses her attraction to the Republican feminine ideal, idolizing the independent, studious, artistic, short-haired women of the Republic whom she "veneraba en secreto. Fueron las heroínas míticas de mi primera infancia" (Martín Gaite, *Usos amorosos de la postguerra* 49). Martín Gaite's use of the word "mythical" draws the distinction between the fantastic ideal of the Spanish female during the Republic and the venerated female ideal of the postwar. The *ama de casa* focused on her husband and family, and did not try to seek some other kind of validation outside the home. Martín Gaite offers another alternative to the official record by revealing her own secret idealization of the type of woman who would become a "bad" model for Spaniards during the postwar.

With a basic knowledge of her autobiography, the identification between Martín Gaite and her adolescent subjects in *Usos amorosos de la postguerra* is apparent, just as it was between C. and the author in *El cuarto de atrás*. However, the author is equally cagey in both texts about these direct connections. While she rarely narrates with a first person singular "I" in *Usos amorosos de la postguerra*, there are moments when her use of the first person collective "we" draws attention to her personal feelings about the subject matter. Confronted with the tempered behavior of an ideal postwar "Spanishness," she writes that: "Los niños de la postguerra, que lo que queríamos era ir al cine o que nos compraran una bicicleta, estábamos hartos de la vida sacrificada, vigilante y viril…" (Martín Gaite, *Usos amorosos de la postguerra* 23). Skirting societal norms, some of these children attended secular schools and avoided their Social Service requirements, just as Martín Gaite did. She only alludes to her personal connection to this group of nonconformists by writing about those that "no quería—y éramos muchas—cumplir aquellos seis meses a destajo, en plan de sufrido

Chapter Three

recluta, y prefería darle largas al asunto" (Martín Gaite, *Usos amorosos de la postguerra* 64). Martín Gaite's subtle pertinence to her focus group communicates her authority to write an accurate historical representation of this era and its contradictions.

These rebellious girls had to face their national requirement upon their return, sometimes with an additional term of service, in which case "el remedio venía a ser peor que la enfermedad, y no acababa una de quitarse de encima aquella pesadilla de las genuflexiones gimnásticas, la tarta de manzana y los bodoques e iniciales bordados en el embozo de la sabanita infantil" (Martín Gaite, *Usos amorosos de la postguerra* 64). Martín Gaite's connection to the text reveals itself not only because she, too, traveled out of the country to avoid her Social Service, but also in her transparent cynicism toward the entire Francoist system. The level of detail she assigns to this description allows the reader to understand more thoroughly the experiences of a typical postwar girl, down to the sheets she had to embroider, in a way that the majority of traditional historiographic texts would, or could, not provide. However, the fact that this text follows the conventions of an objective historiography by avoiding, for the most part, subjective valuations, may be what prevents Martín Gaite from stating the obvious. The author was a "strange girl" who admired the long-vanquished Republican feminine ideal over the state-sanctioned Falangist paragon and struggled with the regime's societal norms as antithetical to her interests. Martín Gaite may have become one of Spain's most admired authors, but she lived an inner life on the margins of postwar society.

The Franco regime's outwardly fantastic conception that life had returned to normal after the war was mitigated by the reality that a murmur of uneasiness could be heard below the voices of enforced triumphalism. For Martín Gaite, this opposition is encapsulated in the dialectic between fantasy and reality for adolescent girls. They are denied basic information about class struggles, sexuality, or the war because it is considered dangerous, but their submersion into the fantastic world of novelas rosas and advice columns is seen as harmless. In one advice column Martín Gaite quotes, the columnist tells the letterwriter that he or she needs to accept the realities of the world: "'No seré yo quien te coloque las gafas del desencanto y la desilusión, pero sí me gustaría graduarte la vista para que puedas apreciar todo en sus verdaderas proporciones'" (Martín Gaite, *Usos amorosos de la postguerra* 160). However, this same columnist effectively dons rose-colored glasses when she concludes her advice by stating that: "'El mundo es maravilloso y todo aquello en que palpita la vida debe despertar en nosotros un eco de entusiasmo'" (Martín Gaite, *Usos amorosos de la postguerra* 160). Martín Gaite's tone in narrating Spanish dictatorship-era courtship customs mirrors the confusing blend of reality and fantasy that saturated the postwar. Martín Gaite includes herself as one of these postwar girls, saying that "[l]as jovencitas vivíamos de ilusiones" (*Usos amorosos de la postguerra* 159). These are the kinds of illusions that fantasy produces more readily than reality. As much as adolescent girls struggled to see the world and society around them as it really was, they were constantly encouraged to live in an alternate, fantastic reality.

One of the ways this fantasy took hold was through various stages in the courtship process. The fleeting moments when a young woman felt in control of her relationship are as illusory as dreams. Some girls would write to soldiers wounded in Spain's military support of Hitler's invasion of Russia, the División Azul, imagining that their epistolary relationship would blossom into a full-fledged romance. The reality was that, for the former Nationalist soldiers who returned from Russia, a "normal" postwar romance was often inconceivable. Establishing a relationship with "un soldado del que podían acabar enamorándose sin haberlo visto nunca" (Martín Gaite, *Usos amorosos de la postguerra* 153) was a difficult proposition, especially since many soldiers, if they returned at all, came back sick, traumatized, or impotent.

Once established in an informal relationship, the only time a girl gained control was at the moment of a formal *noviazgo*, when she could opt to declare her love or not. Martín Gaite explains that "solamente durante ese plazo intermedio entre el sueño y la realidad se sentían dueñas de su destino, libres de elegir o dejar de hacerlo, protagonistas" (*Usos amorosos de la postguerra* 198). The author's terminology here is revealing: the moment between dating and engagement is a space between dream and reality, and she asserts that this is a rare time of liberty for a young woman. Further, by calling the girls "protagonists," Martín Gaite highlights the contradiction between a taste of free will and the pure fiction of the rest of their lives, when Franco's social norms controlled these young women's trajectories.

Chapter Three

The wedding dress constituted another sign of the liminal space between reality and fantasy during the postwar. In a tightly controlled environment dominated by caution and restraint, the ostentatious display of the wedding dress was a singular moment when women could enter into fantasy. Martín Gaite says that the veil, the illusion tulle, "marcaba la frontera solemne entre el ensayo y el estreno, entre la ficción y la realidad" (*Usos amorosos de la postguerra* 124). The dictator's own daughter, however, had to be a symbol for a controlled, sacrificing Spanish society. Carmen Franco's example was simplicity in her dress and comportment, to wit, her wedding is a simple affair: "'El almuerzo, señorial y sin alarde. Franco come siempre el pan de ración que comen los españoles'" (Martín Gaite, *Usos amorosos de la postguerra* 126). In 1950, the regime promoted the all-pervasive notion that all Spaniards—and even Franco himself—were sacrificing for the good of the populace. Middle-class Spanish women took the opportunity of their weddings to allow themselves a consumer-culture fantasy for one fleeting moment. In general, however, Martín Gaite sees a woman's choice of clothes as symptomatic of her relationship to her husband: modest, conventional, and submissive. After enjoying dreamlike moments during the courtship and wedding, the young wife is quickly awakened to the realities of marriage and, by extension, of the postwar. The toggling between dream states and reality in *Usos amorosos de la postguerra* matches C.'s fugues in *El cuarto de atrás*. Both reflect the disordered and fantastic role of memory in creating a history fleshed out with the illusions and aspirations of everyday Spaniards.

Many of the romantic dreams of postwar girls were fueled by fiction and, in particular, by the melodramatic romance of the novela rosa. But other forms of fiction, including high works of Spanish literature, were also considered dangerous. These books fed false hopes or, alternately, laid bare issues of poverty and class struggle in Spain from which girls should be shielded. There was a general mistrust of literature, and young women were in risky territory if they lived "alimentándose de novelas" (Martín Gaite, *Usos amorosos de la postguerra* 147). Girls devoured these novels and formed the basis of their ideas about relationships and adulthood with them as guides. While it is clear that the novelas rosas drew young readers away from the realities around them, they were relatively harmless: "la novela rosa siguió considerándose durante mucho tiempo como un mal menor, comparada con otros modelos mucho más peligrosos de la literatura" (Martín Gaite, *Usos amorosos de la postguerra* 157). Leopoldo Alas's classic nineteenth-century Spanish novel *La Regenta*, on the other hand, became a work not to be trusted. One source deemed the book to be an "*admirable novela, pero no apta para señoritas*" (Martín Gaite, *Usos amorosos de la postguerra* 149; emphasis in the original). In *La Regenta*, the protagonist consumes novels and their romantic ideals, thus demonstrating the dangers of popular fiction: she becomes involved in Don Juan-esque affairs, but is left unaware of the underlying aggression of her suitors, and exchanges her sexual honor for a romantic fantasy. Although the novel's ironic central thesis proving that the *chica rara* will inevitably be misguided by literature seemed to uphold Francoist norms, its concurrent demonstration of the sexual pleasure that accompanied this literary fantasy was too scandalous for proper young ladies.

Martín Gaite's focus on the novela rosa in *Usos amorosos de la postguerra* underlines the connections between fantasy and reality for young girls by combining these dualities in her narration. In one passage, the author flows from an imaginary scene of a girl dreaming of her adolescent infatuation at the window one night to a scene in a novela rosa:

> ¿Estaría pensando en ella aquel muchacho a quien aureolaba en sus insomnios? ¿Hablando de ella con alguien? ... Pero la incógnita estremecedora era la de adivinar cómo se comportaría a partir de las diez de la noche. ... Le diría, por ejemplo, "Te rapto para mí," como Felipe Arcea a Sol Alcántara en la novela *Vestida de tul*, literalmente devorada por las jovencitas de postguerra. (Martín Gaite, *Usos amorosos de la postguerra* 141)

The author, moving from an imagined scenario to a direct quotation from a novela rosa to a re-evaluation of the powerful influence this text had on young girls in the social context of the postwar, quickly transitions from a space of fiction to a space of history. Martín Gaite places these romantic, fantastic scenes into context. She explains the traditional coming-out party for girls, and that young women were not given the key to their houses because they were commonly prohibited from going out without a family chaperone after the evening meal at 10 p.m. This blend of the concrete, social norms of the era with common fantasies of young women filtered through the fiction of the period demonstrates Martín Gaite's adept manner of blending genres around a constant historiographic foundation. The author's firsthand knowledge of these customs only gives her socio-historiographic evaluation of this period more depth and authority.

In the Provisional Epilogue, Martín Gaite returns to the same moment with which she inaugurated the text. From 1952 to 1953, Spain signed a military accord with the United States, rationing was terminated, and the regime founded Televisión Española. In the book's introduction, Martín Gaite juxtaposes this moment with her own wedding; here she centers on a more concrete historical context. She uses the epilogue to introduce some of the transformations brought about during the 1950s, reflected in changing attitudes toward sex, poverty, and the Church. These shifts were echoed in the literature of Martín Gaite's own Generación de medio siglo, by authors such as Miguel Delibes, who began to write about previously untouchable issues. Martín Gaite quotes one young author who demands a movement away from all-encompassing myth as the basis of Spanish society, seeing the representation of truth as the "'verdadera revolución'" (*Usos amorosos de la postguerra* 216). Although this call to the arms of veracity was written in 1955, *Usos amorosos de la postguerra* responds, thirty years later, by combating dominant Francoist historiography with a more personal and accurate examination of postwar society, and incorporating into its narrative style some of the same fantasy/reality oppositions at work during the regime.

* * *

In *El cuarto de atrás* and *Usos amorosos de la postguerra española* fantasy constantly collides with history. Martín Gaite has defined the fantastic as a "brecha en la costumbre, como algo que nos sorprende y rompe nuestros esquemas habituales de credibilidad y aceptación, un descubrimiento, a veces banal y fortuito, pero que provoca—y eso es lo importante—un nuevo punto de vista" (*Agua pasada* 158). By this definition, the fantastic can be something as surprising as a self-producing novel, whose pages magically appear at a typewriter, or something that breaks away from our conceptions of normal, such as the notion that postwar girls who weren't overly interested in marriage and liked to read books were not as strange or uncommon as they seemed. History is not far removed from these dual applications of the fantastic. In *El cuarto de atrás*, Martín Gaite's personal experience of history weaves its way into a fantastic tale. In *Usos amorosos de la postguerra*, fantasy is a constant not only as an escape from the realities of real life for postwar girls, but also in Franco's refusal to acknowledge that postwar Spain was not the united, morally upstanding, egalitarian society he insisted it was. In this way, Martín Gaite's definition of the fantastic reaches into the preconceived notions of Franco's historiographers. Her new historical outlook, based on the perspectives of adolescent girls and her own memory, breaks the postwar mold of historical examination by valuing subjectivity. Francoist mechanisms of social control such as the Sección Femenina assumed that popular culture could be harnessed for the state but was unimportant in the annals of history. Martín Gaite's study proves this assumption wrong. Yet despite its subjectivity, *Usos amorosos de la postguerra* is neither fantasy nor fiction. It is a socio-historiography of an often-ignored population during an influential period in twentieth-century Spain. Its accuracy lies in the firsthand experiences of its author, as judged by the reader.

The application of genre fusion to *Usos amorosos de la postguerra* and *El cuarto de atrás* converges around the persona of Carmen Martín Gaite. The author's life story is filtered through her memory and demonstrates her life-long interest in unique methods of historical representation. While the author establishes a chronology and nods toward the conventions of a traditional historiographic study, a genre fusion reading shows that her ultimate goal is to concentrate on the untold stories of history and break the silences imposed by Francoist dogma. For Martín Gaite, elements of a postwar adolescence such as fashion, pulp fiction, teen magazines, slang, and first dates constitute the history of Spain in the same way traditional details of history do. In fact, the economic state of Spain after the Civil War, postwar political propaganda, the resurgence of tourism in the 1950s, Franco's death, and the politics of Spain in the dictator's wake are all reflected to one degree or another in Spain's popular culture over the years. Martín Gaite delves into the character and dysfunction of a collective marginalized by prevailing social norms through this examination of the material culture and customs of an era. Genre fusion exposes how she assembles a personal and collective memory and establishes a new historiographic approach that stands in contrast to the dominant paradigm of Francoist historiography. While it must be stressed that the absolute difference between *El cuarto de atrás* and *Usos amorosos de la postguerra española* is that the former is a novel and the latter is a work of historiography, read in congruence via genre fusion, these two texts relay an identical and rarely seen history. In a new period of Spanish historical discourse, genre fusion's unconventional approach to history is not only entirely valid, but fills a gaping void.

Chapter Four

Carlos Blanco Aguinaga
The Spanish Other in Mexico

> *Y lo que contemos, por insignificante*
> *que parezca ser, estará inscrito*
> *inevitablemente en la Historia.*
> Carlos Blanco Aguinaga
> *Por el mundo*

Theorizing Exile Identity: Fluid Borders and Genres

The *Sinaia*, sailing from Sète, France to Veracruz, Mexico in the summer of 1939, published its own newspaper, the *Diario de la primera expedición de republicanos españoles a México*. The May 30, 1939 edition included a summary of Professor Modesto Bargallo's recently held mid-sea conference on Mexico's geography: "Estados Unidos, al Norte; al Este, el Golfo de México; al Sur, la América Central y al Oeste, el Pácifico" (Ruiz Funes and Tuñón 73–74). This was necessary information for the refugees aboard, seeing as how many had almost no conception of their destination. "'No tenía ni la menor idea de lo que era México. Con decirle a usted que yo aún creía que Texas era de México. No tenía ni la menor idea'" (Ruiz Funes and Tuñón 75), one passenger recalls. Many would unwittingly spend the rest of their lives there. Although Mexico's geography would remain unchanged, the exiles would arrive and start their displaced lives in a country unique to each.

As the Nationalist victory in the Spanish Civil War became imminent, scores of left-leaning Spaniards began the arduous process of crossing borders, boarding ships like the *Sinaia*, and repatriating themselves in countries abroad. These exiles brought their children, some old enough to understand the motivation behind their family's departure, others too young to comprehend much beyond the name of their country of origin. These second-generation exiles were Spanish by birth, but their life experiences connected them to their adoptive country. Many eventually became naturalized citizens. First-generation exiles identified themselves as Spanish. Third-generation exiles, the grandchildren of the initial wave of adult exiles, were, arguably, not exiles, having been born in their parents' adopted country. This is, however, a contentious point: which generation is no longer considered an exile generation? Individuals who uprooted themselves from Spain after the Civil War as adults were prompted in part by political motivations. Their children, however, may have maintained only peripheral notions of the politics of exile, leaving Spain primarily of their parents' accord. Does the demarcation of exile lie along strict boundaries of country of birth, or along a scale of political consciousness? On a spectrum of intentionality, children can be located at the "collateral exile" pole, participating in an involuntarily movement across borders but completely unaware of its implications; at a "politically conscious exile" pole, aware of the political implications of exile and also voluntarily participating in the diaspora; and in every intermediate category in between.

Thus, these second-generation exiles inhabit a middle ground of exile, consistently eluding a strict national definition. For them, even the term *exile* is problematic. Eduardo Mateo Gambarte has postulated that second-generation exiles who arrived in Mexico were neither Spanish nor Mexican, and that perhaps the only solution to this dialectic is for the exiles to form "una nueva nacionalidad: la de exiliado" ("La segunda generación" 175). Second-generation Spanish exile Carlos Blanco Aguinaga and his peers remained, in relation to Mexicans and Spaniards, "en medio, ni aquí ni allá, ni del todo con ustedes, ni del todo con los míos" ("Aquí y allá" 323).

The exile writing born of the diaspora after the Spanish Civil War has been the topic of considerable critical study, generally focused on those who crossed from Spain to the Americas as adults. Writers such as Max Aub, Ramón J. Sender, María Zambrano, and María Teresa León, among many others, have garnered more attention from scholars than Blanco Aguinaga, a virtually unknown member of the second generation of Spanish exiles who has quietly made a name for himself in the field of literary scholarship. What, then, can isolating the case of this particular exile reveal about the exile experience? Although scholars have studied the first generation of exile writers, second-generation exiles have been left virtually unexamined even at the most basic level of self-identification.[1] Blanco Aguinaga has distinguished himself from his peers by approaching the question of the Spanish diaspora to Mexico from two angles: he theorizes about exile in general while applying these theories to himself and members of the second generation in his fiction and his historiography.

Blanco Aguinaga has uncovered the effects of a diluted national identity on a generation marginalized by virtue of their distance not only from Spain, but also from the attentions of scholars. Much like Montserrat Roig, Carmen Martín Gaite, and Javier Marías, Blanco Aguinaga is self-consciously the subject of his overlapping works. His historiography and fiction reexamine a period in Spanish history that was wholly excluded from history books on the Iberian Peninsula during the Franco dictatorship. Recognizing the inherent contradictions and fissures in a seemingly straightforward trajectory, Blanco Aguinaga questions his own understanding of his exile experience, moving beyond its contours to its innermost depths. As he outlines his early years in an autobiography, he is cognizant that these details spring from his memory. He interrogates the mind's ability to remember the past voluntarily and accurately:

> ¿Dónde está la realidad de lo que uno cree recordar y dónde empiezan los inventos, las falsificaciones inevitables de la memoria, que olvida y se confunde? A más de que a veces uno prefiere callar ciertas cosas. Por supuesto que los hechos centrales de esta historia están claros: una primera infancia bien arropada...; una violenta y larga guerra civil... que acabaríamos perdiendo; un primer exilio difícil y doloroso...; y, luego, un segundo exilio a un país remoto y sorprendente. Eso es así, pero ¿y los detalles? (Blanco Aguinaga, *Por el mundo* 107)

Blanco Aguinaga supplies these details throughout his writing on exile, regardless of genre, returning again and again to his own experiences. Although he recognizes the inherent fallacies of memory, he puts its reliability and the issue of voluntary amnesia to one side in the interest of telling his, and his generation's, untold story.

For Blanco Aguinaga's family and a host of other left-leaning Spaniards, Mexico promised political sympathy and linguistic proximity: a temporary home away from home. After all, the

Chapter Four

political base of the Spanish Republic had fled to Mexico alongside its constituents. For children born in Spain and raised in Mexico, however, these connections were immaterial and did not erase the confusion of maintaining two cultural identities. As years passed with no sign of a return voyage, a once-temporary exile grew permanent. The second-generation exiles' struggle with their peculiar status as both—or neither—Spaniards and Mexicans intensified. This theme of identity crisis, rising from Blanco Aguinaga's life story, is alive in the pages of his essays and fiction, both imbued with testimonial nuance. In his essays on exile, Blanco Aguinaga looks toward Javier de Lucas's discussion of the rights of asylum, isolating "la imposición de la renuncia a la propia identidad, porque se impone la renuncia a la memoria, el olvido como condición de la salida de la transitoriedad" (de Lucas 53) as key losses for the political exiles of 1939 Spain. These exiles struggle against forgetting in order to maintain a sense of their own identity as they simultaneously attempt to integrate themselves into their adopted society. Blanco Aguinaga's work provides a response to de Lucas's assertion, illustrating one exile's reaction to his displacement. Motivated by an unflagging pressure to remember, Blanco Aguinaga embraces the identity crisis common to every exile as a necessary catalyst for his writing and a clear theme in his texts.

It is precisely this reliance on autobiography that the scholar Michael Ugarte identifies as a driving force behind all exile writing. In *Shifting Ground: Spanish Civil War Exile Literature*, Ugarte observes that the boundaries between personal and collective history and fiction are often blurred. "Exile," as Ugarte reminds the reader, denotes not only a person but also a movement of people. The twofold nature of the term signifies the twice-marginalized experience of exile: once via the geographical removal from the homeland; once via the individual's supposedly temporary and segregated presence in the adopted country. Ugarte asserts that "the intensely personal and specific experience of exile is paradoxically a marker of its universality" (19), also characterized by common themes and patterns that manifest themselves in literature, such as tensions with politics and history. While authors interpret their individual exile experiences in unique manners, "exile," as it refers to a politically coerced displacement from the homeland, is a universal concept.

As narrative vehicles, personal testimony and autobiography lend structure to the recorded exile experience. "[A]n ordered construction with a beginning, middle, and end, even if those parts or substructures are not placed in chronological order" (21) is a universal trait of exile writing, according to Ugarte. In the imposition of a fictionlike structure on an actual life story, "[t]he uneasy relationship between language and real life brought to bear by autobiography is also present in the replication of exilic experience with a testimony of that experience" (Ugarte 21). Thus, the same elements inherent in nonfiction life writing—testimony, autobiography, and memory—are central to a fictional approximation of exile, subject to the same tensions and threats of oblivion. The displacement and textual representation of that experience create a number of unresolved conflicts for the author and the text encapsulated in the dualities of the present and the past, the here and the there, the real and the imagined. For the exile, there is a constant conceptual struggle between the return to the homeland versus the permanence in the adopted country, the official history versus the exile's particular life experiences, the former self versus the new self, and memory versus reality. These conflicts form the basis for the exile's individual identity crisis, apparent in Blanco Aguinaga's writing, while also signaling the universal trends present in all exile writing.

Unlike scholars who have theorized Spanish exile writing with a focus either on fictional texts or on forms of historiography, Ugarte makes a case for the interconnectedness between these two genres.[2] Indeed, for the author, it is impossible to divide exile writing into the discrete categories of fiction and historiography. Ugarte argues that fiction informs to a great degree the Spanish exiles' attempts to testify about their life experiences:

> Many exile writers are faced with the dilemma of re-creating their own exile both as a response to their banishment and as a work of fiction. The initial break from the land gives rise to a need to recover a lost identity and thus re-create the former self in a frustrated struggle against oblivion. Their texts must, therefore, remain in the middle ground between real events and created ones without ever losing sight of either. (108)

When we read "real events" as represented by historiography and "created ones" as represented by fiction, it is clear that Ugarte's "middle ground" is the area genre fusion theorizes. Ugarte makes the pointed observation that critics of Spanish literature are reluctant to study realism in fiction, and show a "distaste for the consideration of historical, political, or social concerns in literature" (110). Hayden White's comment that "[t]his affiliation of narrative historiography with literature and myth should provide no reason for embarrassment... because the systems of meaning production shared by all three are distillates of the historical experience of a people, a group, a culture" (*Content* 44–45), answers this critical reluctance by pointing out a common historical point of departure in the text, an entry point central to exile writing. These historical, political, and social concerns converge in the essays and novels of Blanco Aguinaga. Exemplifying Ugarte's model of the conflicted exile writer, Blanco Aguinaga blends fiction and history when he represents his and his generation's displacement. He quiets the distaste and "embarrassment" left by an unwillingness to delve into the two genres in conjunction.

Although Blanco Aguinaga composes fiction in a novelistic or short story form and social/historical criticism in an essayistic form, his genres are not so well defined. Both converge around autobiography and history. He drafts an autobiographical first person as part of the narrative of his essays, while his short stories trace the author's life story within an accurate historical framework. Ugarte recognizes this as a pattern in exile writing: "The autobiographical I serves as the center of a story which orders and structures the real experience; it turns the real story into a fiction, even if there has been no conscious attempt to do so" (21). According to Ugarte, this personal and historical intermingling is a model "not only for the ways in which poetic devices and concepts intrude into the recording of history in general, but for the overlapping literary and historical structures common to exile texts" (57), highlighting the possibility that genre fusion can be applied to exile writing.

This tendency toward genre fusion also results in the encroaching "I" or "we" in the exiles' supposedly intellectually abstract study, demonstrating "how a scholarly essay on exile may become contaminated with literary devices when the writer is an embodiment of the consequences" (Ugarte 62). Ugarte's use of the word "contaminated" suggests that a personal perspective spoils an otherwise intellectually rigorous essay, and that a text cannot be completely objective and personally revealing at the same time. Yet this opposition is the consequence of exile itself: it is the result of the determining political, historical, and social factors of exile mitigated by the personal experience of the exile. Blanco Aguinaga's body of work blends the personal and the communal experience of exile. It provides a nuanced approach to exile as an experience as well as to exile as a human subject.[3] These combinations reveal, in turn, the dichotomy between historiography as the representation of past events and historical fiction as the representation of the human experience of these events. As Paul Ricoeur has observed, this differential demands that "[e]ither one counts the cadavers or one tells the story of the victims" (*Time and Narrative* 3: 188), either chronicling history or engaging in storytelling. However, when Blanco Aguinaga invites both the cadavers and the victims into one unified text, fictional or nonfictional, he functionally demonstrates that historiography and fiction are not mutually exclusive narrative modes. Their combination brings both cadavers and victims back to life.

As a literary scholar, Blanco Aguinaga consistently argues that the key to understanding certain prose and poetry is historical and social context. His treatments of the relationship between history and fiction span genres and continents. He has written about the political state and social reality of Mexico as it appears in Juan Rulfo's *El llano en llamas*, historicity in three of Benito Pérez Galdos's novels, the social and literary influences of Miguel de Unamuno's Generation of '98, and the determining forces Transition-era politics have had on modern Spanish narrative, among other topics.[4] The author's three-volume series on the social history of peninsular Spanish literature extends Blanco Aguinaga's preoccupations into the interactions between literature and society. Both of these key concerns—the historical and the social—also form the cornerstone of Blanco Aguinaga's writing on exile: a movement married to the historical circumstances that created it and the social implications that sustain it.

The author turns to the topic of exile in a series of essays he has edited and re-edited over the last two decades.[5] While each iteration of Blanco Aguinaga's exile essay serves a distinct purpose, all immerse the author in the particular circumstances of those Spaniards who left Spain for Mexico in 1939. This diaspora is a situation the author has called extraordinary within the universal

Chapter Four

history of exile. As one among thousands on ships making the passage across the Atlantic that year, Blanco Aguinaga imbues his essays with the experiences that make him a living example of exile, yet never strays from an objective and historically minded outlook on the subject. The author's individual perspective of exile has spawned a theoretical approach that permeates his texts, forming what he has labeled an "'universo de discurso'" (Blanco Aguinaga, *De mitólogos y novelistas* 4) in other authors. This "discursive universe" influences and is influenced by the varied elements in its surrounding atmosphere, melding fiction and history to form a rounded and personal assessment of exile that lends itself to an examination through genre fusion.

* * *

Blanco Aguinaga was born in 1926 in Irún, a town that touches the border with France in the northernmost reaches of the Spanish side of the Basque Country.[6] His first exile began not far from home. As the Nationalist General Emilio Mola and his forces fought Republican troops for control of Irún, Blanco Aguinaga crossed the international bridge into Hendaye, France with his mother and sister in September 1936. For three years, Blanco Aguinaga's father worked as a consulate representing the northern regions of the Spanish Republic from Hendaye. The family shared a large house with other Spanish exiles, and the children integrated into French schools. In 1939, with the fall of Madrid to the Nationalists imminent and the acute sense that France would not hold out from a Nazi invasion much longer, the family made its second exile voyage to Mexico. Unlike the short walk across the international bridge from Spain to France, this exile involved a three-week passage on the ship *Orinoco*. Blanco Aguinaga, his mother, and his sister joined their father in Veracruz, Mexico on August 21, 1939.[7]

The family integrated into Mexican life as best they could, though uncomfortably. The understanding was that they were only passing through the country: "A fin de cuentas, ¿qué más daba, por un tiempo? ¿No era verdad que estábamos en México de paso?" (Blanco Aguinaga, *Por el mundo* 136–37). This was a belief that, as World War II failed to remove Franco from power and the United States signed a series of military accords with Spain, became less and less convincing. With the support of the Servicio de Evacuación de Refugiados Españoles (SERE) and the Junta de Apoyo a los Republicanos Españoles (JARE), organizations aiding recent Spanish refugees in Mexico, Blanco Aguinaga attended schools operated by the Republic in Mexico. There, he was immersed back in Spanish culture, surrounded by other second-generation exiles and taught by exiled instructors from Spain.[8] He remained in Mexico City until he was 16, when he moved to the United States to continue his studies. His education in the US led him back to the Spanish literary canon and writers such as Unamuno and Antonio Machado, whom his contemporaries in Spain would not have been permitted to study in Franco-controlled schools. This exposure inspired Blanco Aguinaga to embark on a life-long career as a literary scholar. Upon returning to Mexico after graduating, he collaborated with other exiled Spaniards of his generation on the Mexican literary magazine *Presencia* and completed his post-graduate studies. University faculty positions led him back across borders to Spain and the United States, and eventually to the University of California, San Diego, where he was Professor Emeritus of Spanish Literature until his death in 2013.[9]

Blanco Aguinaga's tidal movements mirror his progression through various literary pursuits, both critical and creative, over the course of his career. He maintained ties to the traditional literary studies of Spain through his early academic publications on Unamuno and the Golden Age writers Francisco Quevedo and Miguel de Cervantes. But he soon branched out into the world of contemporary exile literature and literary history, among many other topics, in his extensive studies and critical editions of the exile poetry of Emilio Prados, as well as his definitive work on the social history of modern Spanish literature.[10] It was not until the late-1980s that Blanco Aguinaga began publishing works of fiction, although even in his short stories and novels, he has maintained the connection between his literary knowledge and his self-reflective embodiment of an exile writer. In contrast to his prolific production of literary criticism, however, Blanco Aguinaga's own body of fiction has scarcely been studied.[11]

Moving in and out of history, back and forth from exile to permanence, Blanco Aguinaga's five fictional tomes tend toward fragmented, nonlinear approximations of history and exile. Unlike his novels, the short stories collected in *Carretera de Cuernavaca*, each narrative independent of the one before and after it, nonetheless arrive at the most linear narrative exploration of exile in his body of fiction.[12] The stories in *Carretera de Cuernavaca* are clearly an outcropping of Blanco Aguinaga's meditation on the collective Spanish exile to Mexico. The author's presence in the text is subtle, yet unmistakable. He maintains an involvement with his characters through shared experiences and a common and relentless questioning of the exile experience. Certainly many readers will be unfamiliar with the specifics of Blanco Aguinaga's life, digesting the stories unaware of the author's implied interpretation, but this reading does little to diminish the author's foray into the inner recesses of exile. However, by applying postcolonial theoretical models, historiographic information, and testimonial accounts from Blanco Aguinaga's essays to his short stories, or by reading his essays with an awareness of the personal and narrative approach to history in his short stories, one arrives at an enriched reading of both texts. Blanco Aguinaga develops his fiction and historiography in tandem—literally, as *Carretera de Cuernavaca* and the first of his exile essays are published the same year—with an underlying stake in history and subjectivity, depending heavily on the narrative technique of testimony.[13] Studying the results of this overlapping through a lens of genre fusion shows interdependent genres that continually strive to represent the immensely personal consequences of a life lived in exile. Read together, Blanco Aguinaga's essays and stories explore the inner life and historical context of the marginalized second-generation Spanish exile. Genre fusion allows the full story of this generation's exile experience to emerge.

Total mexicanización or refugiados españoles?

Although traditionally categorized as nonfiction, the essay can include a variety of other literary genres: from autobiography, to historiography, to sociology, to criticism. The modern essay is a blank slate, ready for intertextual and interdisciplinary meditations on a theme. Graham Good has called the form "a kind of hybrid of art and science, an aesthetic treatment of material that could otherwise be studied scientifically or systematically" but that, in the essay, "happily coexist" (14–15). An essayistic examination of the post–Spanish Civil War diaspora, for example, could study the population movement and reestablishment from a strictly historiographic vantage point, providing data on individual exiles and statistics on their collective trends. Or, it could comprise a memoir of one exile's personal experiences and reactions to his or her displacement. Blanco Aguinaga selects the essay form in order to blend these two approaches. His nonfiction treatment of exile epitomizes this hybrid of art and science, or, in this case, of personal narrative, literary analysis, and historiography. Following Roig's testimonial historiography and Martín Gaite's socio-historiographic study, Blanco Aguinaga's personal-historical essays are yet another mode of narrative historiography that captures the lived experience of history.

Blanco Aguinaga's numerous essays examining exile are concerned with the plight of the Spaniards who emigrated to the Americas after the Spanish Civil War. The author touches on the visible scars of displacement apparent in the literary compositions of first-generation exile writers such as Aub and Luís Cernuda in a number of essays.[14] However, in "Otros tiempos, otros espacios en la narrativa española del exilio en América" (1990) and "Sobre el exilio español en México" (2001), Blanco Aguinaga turns his attention toward himself and his generation, proposing that those who left Spain for Mexico as children in 1939 experienced a wholly unique form of exile. Although distinct texts published a decade apart, these two essays have closely matched content. Early on in both works, Blanco Aguinaga cites Prados, a first-generation Spanish exile and Generation of '27 poet. Blanco Aguinaga considers the second stanza of Prados's poem "Canción," published in the 1946 collection *Jardín cerrado*, a literary counterpart to his essay:

> Tengo mi cuerpo tan lleno
> de lo que falta a mi vida,
> que hasta la muerte, vencida,
> busca por él su consuelo.
>
> (Prados, *Jardín cerrado* 83;
> Blanco Aguinaga, "Sobre el exilio" 15;
> Blanco Aguinaga, "Otros tiempos" 249–50)

Loss and absence become defining characteristics of those who have been forced to leave their homelands. But for Blanco Aguinaga, these verses present the exile with a challenge to keep living, to continue a life in Mexico that affirms the possibility of a return to Spain despite the fact that "el comportamiento franquista declaraba a las claras que habíamos sido vencidos y desterrados para siempre" ("Otros tiempos" 250). For exiles such as Prados and Blanco Aguinaga, this struggle between return and permanence becomes a struggle between life and death.

The prominent inclusion of Prados's verses also highlights the hybrid nature of Blanco Aguinaga's essay form, as he weaves elements common in poetry and prose into an ostensibly nonfiction text. Citations of verses, personal anecdotes, and the memories of the exiles' collective frustrations and aspirations reflect similar moments in the author's fiction. Blanco Aguinaga's essays are narrative works of historiography infused with memoir, testimony, objective data, and historical background that reflect the individual and collective limbo of exile. The author and his essays reside in a middle territory between Mexican and Spanish politics and culture, between first and third generations, between history and fiction, and between exile and return, all of which contributes to an identity crisis both personal and generational.

Blanco Aguinaga distinguishes "Otros tiempos" by looking at exile through the lens of its constituent literature. These literary works often blend historical fact with personal experience through a first-person narrative voice, as demonstrated by Prados's poetic declaration. They are also attentive to language, one of Blanco Aguinaga's primary preoccupations. The ways exiles refer to themselves and the labels others bestow on them is, for the author, a fluid measure of identity. Blanco Aguinaga's use of the first-person *nosotros* in his recollections of this volatile terminology demonstrates that these labels also constitute one of the many roots of his own ever-changing identity: "Porque nosotros nos considerábamos *refugiados*. De refugiados nos trataban también nuestros países de asilo y las organizaciones internacionales que intentaban ayudarnos. Y, en cuanto *refugiados*, esperábamos un día dejar México" ("Otros tiempos" 250; emphasis in the original). The exiles consider themselves refugees when they are confident of their imminent return to Spain: both a cause and an effect of being treated as temporary guests by their Mexican hosts.

However, as they begin to doubt their temporary refugee status, after more than a decade in Mexico, the terminology used to describe the Spanish exiles shifts: "[Y]a casi ni los americanos de siempre nos llamaban *refugiados*. Creo que es por entonces cuando empiezan a circular ya muy abiertamente los términos *destierro* y *desterrado(s)*, términos que apuntan a la posibilidad de que nuestros *refugios* podrían ser permanentes" (Blanco Aguinaga, "Otros tiempos" 250; emphasis in the original). Blanco Aguinaga notes that a "refugee" by definition cannot be a permanent resident. Yet as the second generation of Spaniards grew up in exile, Mexico began to mutate into a less temporary refuge in their minds. As the first generation settled into jobs and situated their uprooted families, and a third generation was born in Mexico, the second generation continued to inhabit an uneasy middle ground represented by yet another term that left both their permanence and temporality undiagnosed. The exiles became "*trasterrado(s)*: al parecer no éramos ya, sencillamente, sino los que habíamos pasado de una tierra a otra, en la cual íbamos haciendo nuestras vidas" (Blanco Aguinaga, "Otros tiempos" 251; emphasis in the original). "Trasterrado" indicates a benign transition from one country to another.[15] This nomenclature crops up at every juncture in the essay. By extension, it is ever-present in the lives of the exiles as reminders of their changing interpretation of their own exile status in Mexico and of their relation to the native people in their adopted country. The exiles are never simply *exiliados* or *exilados* in Blanco Aguinaga's essay. Their alternate signifiers contain more complex layers of temporality, permanence, sense of voluntary or forced movement, and level of integration into their adopted society.[16]

For Blanco Aguinaga, state- and self-imposed restrictions on the exiles' participation in Mexican life mean that the most effective vehicle to tease out "los tranquilizadores significados posibles del término *trasterrado(s)*" ("Otros tiempos" 251; emphasis in the original) and thus to gain a greater understanding of the exile's inner acclimatization, is through literature. Literature has the ability to represent what the ample documentation of the diaspora after the Spanish Civil War cannot. Blanco Aguinaga asserts that facts and data about exile "no dan cuenta de las ambigüedades y contradicciones, de las procesiones y fantasmas que seguían (y siguen) yendo por dentro, en el interior de la vida de los exilados" ("Otros tiempos" 251). As such, a more profound examination of the exile experience, beyond that which a traditional historiographic chronicle offers, is necessary to comprehend fully the unique experience of this particular generation of exiles.

Blanco Aguinaga writes that in literature one finds evidence of the exile's inner torment and doubt; of the "incurable herida que marcó aquel exilio tan largo que resultó ser permanente" ("Otros tiempos" 251). Poetry and narrative by such writers as Prados, Aub, and Francisco Ayala manifest the void that remains hidden in the lives of exiles who are outwardly adapting to their adopted country. In Mexico these and many other exiled authors continue a long literary tradition, complete with a litany of problems particular to exile writers. One of the fundamental disadvantages of exile writing, according to Blanco Aguinaga, is its lack of acceptance in the literary milieu of the adopted country. For the most part, the literature of Spanish exiles in Mexico was collected neither in Mexican nor Spanish anthologies. Instead, it was published almost exclusively by the exiles' own publishing houses.[17]

The critical reception of exile literature is a concrete representation of the identity crisis suffered by Spaniards in Mexico. Overlooked by country-specific literary scholars, both author and text languish in a cross-national limbo. Spanish exile writers in the Americas were isolated from the literature of Spain and their adopted countries. They were exiled from literature, not connected to any literary body or nationality. In response, these writers adopt a blended literature that draws from both Spain and the Americas, but belongs to neither. Blanco Aguinaga's descriptions of the responses of exiled Spanish novelists reflect the world the author created in his fiction in order to adapt to his exile status. He writes that "la narrativa española del exilio del 39 se ocupa principalmente del mundo que los narradores han dejado atrás" but, unlike the tradition of exile writing established by their literary predecessors, "ofrece también una notable voluntad de narrar sobre aspectos de la vida de los países de asilo" (Blanco Aguinaga, "Otros tiempos" 254). By incorporating the adopted nation into their publications, Blanco Aguinaga asserts, Spanish exile writers in Mexico differentiated themselves from other canonical exile writers. Thomas Mann, James Joyce, and Unamuno suffered much shorter periods of displacement, focused their attention primarily on their country of birth, and were able to integrate into the national body of literature of their homelands. As we will see, Spanish exile writers who wrote about the Americas were disparaged for tackling a topic with which critics presumed they were not familiar.

Blanco Aguinaga posits that the Spanish authors in Mexico combined national interests for a number of reasons: "porque era más que dudoso que fuésemos a volver a España" ("Otros tiempos"

254), because they were exiled to countries where they spoke the same language and had similar cultural backgrounds, and because they experienced "grandes transformaciones sociales que no podían menos que importar a las gentes de un exilio que, en principio, se presentaba ante el mundo como de izquierdas" ("Otros tiempos" 255). This confluence of factors makes itself plain in *Carretera de Cuernavaca*, a collection of narratives beginning in Civil War–era Spain and moving to Mexico during the latter half of the twentieth century. This temporal and spatial movement mirrors the exile's shift in focus as he realizes his "temporary" exile has encompassed a lifetime. The exile's progressive awareness of his new reality occupies Blanco Aguinaga in this series of stories.

As Spanish exiles developed a deeper connection to their adopted country in their writing, their personal and professional distance from Spain grew:

> [M]ientras aquellos narradores producían desconectados de los lectores españoles (desconexión impuesta por la censura y por los intereses propios de quienes iban haciendo su vida en España), la narrativa española, según sabemos, iba haciendo su propia historia interna sin contacto real alguno con lo que producían [los escritores exilados] en América. (Blanco Aguinaga, "Otros tiempos" 256–57)

Barred from both Spain's and Latin America's literary canons, and consequently at a loss as to their own national authorial identity, these exile writers created their own canon, their own blended nationality, and their own unique path through exile. Blanco Aguinaga writes that "las obras literarias no son personas" ("Otros tiempos" 257). However, second-generation Spanish exiles occupied the same undefined territory between two countries as the books and poetry they wrote that never fully entered into any national canon.

This exclusionary tendency, along with the title of "Otros tiempos, otros espacios," hinges on the notion of "otherness." In *Orientalism*, Edward Said theorizes the postcolonial "other" in terms of the culturally constructed distinction between the hegemonic Occident and the exotic Orient. In the case of the Spanish exiles, however, this dichotomy is turned on its head. The Spaniards, once the colonizers, are the subjugated other, while the Mexicans are the dominant culture. Homi Bhabha looks at the conflict inherent in "otherness" as stemming from the definition of the other as "at once an object of desire and derision, an articulation of difference contained within the fantasy of origin and identity" (96). The Spanish exiles are, as Blanco Aguinaga enumerates, at once desired for their unique status and derided for their difference. Moreover, they and their hosts are stymied when faced with defining their "fantastic" origins, as their fluid terminology demonstrates, adding to the identity consternation the Spanish exiles face. Bhabha writes that "the recognition and disavowal of 'difference' is always disturbed by the question of its re-presentation or construction" (116). This fragmented representation of difference becomes apparent in the prejudices experienced by the Spanish exiles and their own mutable self-identification. Blanco Aguinaga has argued that Spanish otherness was more evident in practical rather than theoretical terms. In his autobiography, he explains how his concept of the other was molded as a child during his first exile in Hendaye, France: "Para saber por qué, para entender qué era lo que nos estaba ocurriendo—por fuera y en el interior más privado—no nos hicieron falta teorías sobre 'el otro' o 'la otredad': lo otro era aquella Hendaya, antes neutra de significado, para la cual la otredad (indeseable, además) éramos nosotros" (*Por el mundo* 60–61). Nevertheless, it remains clear that the Spanish exiles' movements across borders and their "undesirability" relates them to definitions of the other provided by postcolonial theory. Even as they yearn to belong to a group, a nationality, or a country, they face cultural constructions of difference as exiles.

Blanco Aguinaga pushes back against these traditional notions of the other: "en el mundo en que vivimos, result[a] intolerable que todo lo que es y/o aparece como *otro* tenga que seguir existiendo en las afueras de lo hegemónico" ("Otros tiempos" 256; emphasis in the original). It is precisely this marginalization on the "outskirts of the hegemonic" that the author combats by writing about the Spanish exile community in Mexico. Blanco Aguinaga acknowledges the otherness of the exiles, which only makes him more determined to legitimize their struggle by telling their—and his—story. He also disputes the idea that the other has no grasp of the dominant culture. Exile writers like Sender and Ayala have focused on issues pertaining to the Americas in some of their works. But Latin American critics "se desentiende[n] de la existencia" (Blanco Aguinaga, "Otros tiempos" 255) of these texts, because the topic is supposedly outside the author's range of knowledge. Yet Blanco Aguinaga argues in "Otros tiempos" and demonstrates in his fiction that narrative is able to represent "no sólo las ambigüedades y contradicciones del interior de una 'tribu', sino las ambigüedades y contradicciones que surgen inevitablemente en las relaciones de esa 'tribu' con otras" ("Otros tiempos" 256). Just as he bridges the gap between genres in this essay and in his short stories, Blanco Aguinaga sees a point in the future when the exile writing of 1939 will be understood as a hybrid Spanish-Mexican discourse. "[P]ara que eso ocurra, tendremos que inventarnos otra manera de entender y de historiar no sólo el exilio español sino, claro está, la Guerra Civil misma" ("Otros tiempos" 257), a revisionist task that Blanco Aguinaga has begun in his texts.

* * *

As the otherness discussed in "Otros tiempos" explodes into a full-blown identity crisis, Blanco Aguinaga further elaborates on the personal and collective experience of exile in "Sobre el exilio español en México." Although the two essays share points of convergence, "Sobre el exilio" is more personal than "Otros tiempos." It relies on Blanco Aguinaga's memories of his childhood and his research on 1940s and 1950s Mexico in order to reconstruct the exile experience. As a member of the second generation, "los niños que llegamos a México en 1939 o 1940" ("Sobre el exilio" 23), Blanco Aguinaga often writes in the first-person collective voice. He delves into the peculiar status of a group that at once looked back to Spain and forward to Mexico. Blanco Aguinaga's personal account of these years in exile is based on the caprices of his own memory, as he admits: "No sé si la memoria me engaña excesivamente, pero recuerdo..." (Blanco Aguinaga, "Sobre el exilio" 27). Memory is again the backbone of a narrative where the author seeks to explore a collective history that lies outside the boundaries of a traditional historiography.

In the opening paragraph Blanco Aguinaga demonstrates the conflicted personal connection he maintains with a topic that also interests him on a more scholarly level:

> El asunto que hoy nos ocupa me produce siempre sentimientos encontrados. Tengo claro, por una parte, que es una cuestión que, en general, no interesa mayormente en este país, y mucho

> menos a la gente joven. Sesenta años de distancia histórica son muchos años, sobre todo en un siglo tan lleno de hechos que, además, si antes eran para nosotros principalmente hechos *occidentales*, ahora son mundiales. Cierto que los exilios y las emigraciones siempre fueron hechos *mundiales*, pero vivíamos como si no lo supiéramos. Ahora, en cambio, ¿qué lugar de importancia puede ocupar en la historia mundial un exilio como el español de 1939 comparado con las enormes emigraciones en medio de las que vivimos y de las que tenemos conciencia? ("Sobre el exilio" 13; emphasis in the original)

Blanco Aguinaga imagines the younger generation in Spain will have little interest in an exile so distinct from "modern" diasporas. But the universal exile experience, here and in his previous essay, is made unapologetically personal. Blanco Aguinaga is the protagonist in his account of exile. He may express conflicting emotions when revisiting the topic, just as he has conflicting emotions about his own exile, but his experiences serve as a case study. He demonstrates not only his theoretical reading of exile but also the relevance of the Spanish migration of 1939 in a global discussion of exile. This passage also introduces the liberties Blanco Aguinaga will take with the adaptable essay form. His personal experiences of exile establish an underlying narrative thread while his scholarly approach to the topic constitutes a more historiographic approach. In essence, the author creates an amalgamation of historiography and autobiography through a narrative that seamlessly flows from chronicle of events to personal anecdote. It is this intermingling of form that creates a narrative historiography.

    Blanco Aguinaga examines key moments in the exiles' passage from Spain and first years in Mexico with quantifiable data. Analyzing first-person accounts and data of passengers on the *Sinaia*, the first of the many ships bound for Mexico, the author identifies the average age of the adults as 34 (Blanco Aguinaga, "Sobre el exilio" 20). His statistical breakdown of the profession of the passengers shows the Mexican government's preference for an influx of intellectuals and professionals: "Si vemos, por ejemplo, la lista de pasajeros del *Sinaia*, encontramos un 34,8% de obreros, un 26,8% de 'profesionistas,' 18,9% de 'agricultores,' 13,5% de empleados, y un 5,2% de maestros" (Blanco Aguinaga, "Sobre el exilio" 20; emphasis in the original). These figures highlight the historical precision of Blanco Aguinaga's essay. The author's firsthand experience as an exile coupled with his attention to detail lends his essay an authority that communicates historical accuracy to the reader.

Given the Mexican government's leftist political tendencies, the country's economic opportunities, and its distance from the brewing second World War, these well-trained and educated Spaniards enjoyed what Blanco Aguinaga calls "nuestro privilegiado exilio" ("Sobre el exilio" 27). The displaced Spanish Republican party had exiled to Mexico with many of its constituents and formed a close relationship with Mexico's government under the leadership of Lázaro Cárdenas. Along with the Spanish refugee aid agencies, the Mexican government helped the Republic establish medical practices, factories, and schools, all designed to serve the exile population. Yet despite this privileged treatment, "todo aquello tenía ciertas limitaciones" ("Sobre el exilio" 25), explains Blanco Aguinaga. Indeed, there were two barriers to the exiled Spaniards' complete integration into Mexican life that had wide-ranging implications for the second and third generations. First, Spaniards, whether or not they were naturalized Mexican citizens, were barred from participating in Mexican politics, a rule written into the Mexican Constitution. Second, although the Mexican government welcomed the exiles with open arms, the country's population was not as eager for their arrival. Blanco Aguinaga relates that many of Mexico's population was more religious and conservative than its government, and this produced a "profundo sentir *antigachupín* del pueblo mexicano" ("Sobre el exilio" 26; emphasis in the original). These Mexican-Spanish relations are the undercurrents of the historical record of the Spanish exile.

For the second-generation exiles in Blanco Aguinaga's studies, nationality is key to the determination of a unique personal identity. This identity is threatened when the exile's nationality revolves around his affiliation first to his birth country, Spain, about which he may only have the vaguest of personal memories, and second to his adopted country, Mexico, where the exile has lived his formative years, yet from which he may continue to feel culturally and socially alienated. The exile's or his parents' banishment from their native Spain and their inability to participate in the Mexican political system only complicates matters of nationality. This second generation, having grown to maturity in exile, maintains a deeper emotional connection to Mexico than their parents and a stronger stake in the country's politics. However, the Spanish

Chapter Four

Republic's new infrastructure, built on the fundamental separation of Spaniards from Mexicans, is a formal determinant of national identity that is not obvious to the young exile. What is obvious to Blanco Aguinaga as a child is the treatment he and his exiled peers receive from a Mexican population wary of their presence: "el mexicano medio no [veía] a los refugiados con buenos ojos y que hasta los niños [teníamos] la impresión de que se nos toleraba por imposición de un gobierno y de unos intelectuales progresistas, con los cuales gran parte del pueblo no compartía muchas cosas" ("Sobre el exilio" 26). First physically marginalized from Spain, the second-generation exiles continue to reside on the margins of society in Mexico. Under these conditions, a determination of their own nationality is doubly complicated.

As in the previous essay, the ever-shifting terminology Mexicans use to refer to the exiles reveals the personal and social identity crises that molded the second-generation exiles' self-impression. Blanco Aguinaga illustrates this linguistic conflict by drawing on the microcosm of a soccer match between Mexicans and Spanish exiles:

> [E]n los partidos de fútbol que jugábamos por todos los campos del Distrito Federal, en cuanto había una jugada dudosa o disputada se nos insultab[an] [los niños mexicanos] llamándonos *gachupines*, lo que llevaba a no pocas peleas porque nosotros teníamos muy claro que no éramos gachupines sino *refugiados*, a lo que, cuando lo decíamos buscando guerra, se nos replicab[an] que no éramos sino unos *pinches, refugíberos* o *refugachos*. ("Sobre el exilio" 26; emphasis in the original)

Blanco Aguinaga explains elsewhere that this *gachupín* label is evidence of the residual resentment toward Spain's colonial oppression and exploitation of the Mexican population ("La cuestión de la vuelta" 440). The second-generation exiles were not only struggling to assert their own identities in the face of a complicated sense of nationality, they were also attempting to defend themselves. Mexican children were, meanwhile, just as confused about the identities of their newly arrived counterparts and, moreover, on the defensive due to this Spanish invasion. In movie theaters, the young Mexicans would applaud the image of Francisco Franco on the screen, "cosa que, claro está, también nos enfurecía y nos llevaba a no pocas broncas" (Blanco Aguinaga, "Sobre el exilio"

26). These Mexican children may not have fully comprehended the implications of applauding the man who had driven the Spanish exiles from their homes. Nevertheless, these scenes illustrate the political dimensions of the struggle between the other and the dominant culture.

These playground conflicts were undoubtedly exacerbated by the privilege Spanish children enjoyed in attending private schools composed exclusively of Spanish students and teachers. When it became clear that the exiles' return to Spain was no longer imminent, the Spaniards were no longer refugees. Rather, they were "destierro y desterrado(s)… trastierro y trasterrado(s)" (Blanco Aguinaga, "Sobre el exilio" 28). These fluid labels are fundamental markers of identity in Blanco Aguinaga's writing on exile, as will be apparent in *Carretera de Cuernavaca* as well. The language is a manifestation of the unstable relationship of the exiles to their native Spain: were they banished or did they leave voluntarily? Despite a modicum of integration into Mexican life and society, Blanco Aguinaga asserts that the Spanish exiles and their children never reached a "total mexicanización" ("Sobre el exilio" 27), or immersion in Mexican culture and society. For the second generation, this "manera de estar y no estar… en México" (Blanco Aguinaga, "Sobre el exilio" 33), coupled with a constantly changing dynamic with Spain fed an on-going identity crisis, founded on a continued uneasiness toward complete integration and acceptance on the part of both nationalities.

Second-generation exiles had little control over their movements: the first-generation exiles made the decision to leave Spain, bringing their children with them. In "Otros tiempos" Blanco Aguinaga focuses primarily on the first generation when he describes the difficulty Spanish writers encountered in participating in the Mexican literary community as allegorical to the Spanish exile's identity crisis when caught between two nationalities. In "Sobre el exilio," however, this identity crisis is more personal for the author: "¿Existe alguna manera más real, más material de pertenecer al país en el cual uno radica que por el trabajo y la descendencia con que uno contribuye a la vida de ese país?" (29). What else can the exile do to gain acceptance but work and contribute his own offspring to his adopted nation? This is what Blanco Aguinaga and his contemporaries have done, and he is just as conflicted about his identity as his exiled peers. Perhaps more so, given his second exile to the United States in the 1960s. Mari Paz Balibrea has for this reason called Blanco Aguinaga a thrice-marginalized exile writer: "al marchar a instalarse en los EEUU durante más de 30 años, ha perdido, aunque no totalmente, ese reconocimiento [como escritor] en México" (13).

One of the seminal moments repeated verbatim in both of Blanco Aguinaga's essays is when "el *refugio* se [convirtió] en *morada*: tirar las viejas maletas; comprar muebles algo mejores; empezar a pagar a los médicos que tantas veces nos habían atendido gratis; pensar en casarse, o en tener hijos y nietos" ("Sobre el exilio" 28; emphasis in the original). This is the moment when the Spanish exiles realize they are not returning to Spain. Based on Blanco Aguinaga's description, it is a crossroads that results in the resumption of everyday life, put on hold when the exiles fled their homeland. Yet evident in both of these essays is that despite their outward assimilation, the exiles' self-doubt is not magically cured:

> La verdad es que los datos de esa amplísima y profunda participación del exilio del 39 en la vida mexicana, participación hace ya tiempo documentada y reconocida por todos, siendo, como son, el rastro visible de lo vivido hacia fuera, no dan cuenta de las ambigüedades y contradicciones, de las procesiones y fantasmas que seguían (y, hasta cierto punto, siguen) yendo por dentro, en el interior de la vida del exilio e, incluso todavía, en la de algunos de sus descendientes. (Blanco Aguinaga, "Sobre el exilio" 30)

The difference between this passage and the nearly identical passage from "Otros tiempos" cited previously is that here Blanco Aguinaga explicitly emphasizes the identity crisis in the lives of first-, second-, and even third-generation exiles as especially profound and longevous. And, although others may have skimmed over the complications that arose even from a "privileged" displacement, Blanco Aguinaga confronts the invisible "ambiguities and contradictions" that only exist in the inner recesses of his generation's psyche in these essays. The author amends the official historical record of the 1939 Spanish exile with the intimate struggles only the exiles themselves can recount.

Taken as a whole, "Otros tiempos" and "Sobre el exilio" hinge on the question of identity for Spanish exiles in Mexico. They focus on the unique position of second-generation exiles, who sought a more stable identity through naming, literary acceptance, poetic and narrative representation, and national allegiance, according to Blanco Aguinaga. These are the thematic threads that run through *Carretera de Cuernavaca*, positioning Blanco Aguinaga's nonfiction theories of exile identity crisis as a corollary to his fictional rendering of a life lived in exile. The author's personal experiences assert themselves in his nonfiction essays as they do in his fiction, where he channels his own trajectory through his characters. Additionally, just as personal and subjective anecdotes, subject to the whims of memory, shape his historiographic essays, historiography will guide his fictional text. The application of genre fusion on these overlapped texts illuminates the outward treatment and innermost anxieties of the Spanish exiles. Through Blanco Aguinaga's nonfiction essays and his fictional narratives, genre fusion tells a story of the author's and his generation's marginalization that provides a more exhaustive representation of Spain's collective memory.

Carretera de Cuernavaca: A Generation Adrift

In a series of thematically interconnected narratives, *Carretera de Cuernavaca* follows second-generation exiles as they are uprooted from Spain and transplanted to Mexico after the Spanish Civil War. The stories linger on the difficulties exiles encounter in assimilating to the Mexican cultural landscape during adolescence and young adulthood, and delve into nagging doubts about identity well into an exile's prime. In a variety of narrative voices, most often the first-person *yo* or the second-person *tú* or *vosotros*, the stories in *Carretera de Cuernavaca* envelop the reader in the unique perspective of a second-generation Spanish exile. They approach the exile experience from mundane situations contextualized in history, arriving at transformative moments and observations about displacement and assimilation.

Although independent narratives, the three sections of stories in *Carretera de Cuernavaca* are a complementary series. In "Aquella casa," the Spanish children living in a giant house just over the border in France are to be reunited with their father in America. They must leave their grandfather behind, watching as he carries his suitcase back over the bridge to a now indelibly changed Spain. In another story, young Antonio finally sees his new surroundings as more than just a distant and foreign land when he meets an older Mexican neighbor. She seduces him, becoming his "new world Aphrodite." In the title story, a group of expatriate adult friends sort out their prolonged exile over dinner parties, poetry, and tumultuous relationships among each other. They want to differentiate their situation from that of the previous generation and "aclarar el problema del exilio, del suyo, no del de sus mayores, que ese es un problema elemental" (Blanco Aguinaga, *Carretera* 160). The stories in *Carretera de Cuernavaca* represent a cross-section of the second-generation exile experience, touching on children's thoughts of war, difficulties in determining nationality, representations of exile in literature, and the trustworthiness and fragmentary nature of memory. These narratives also obliquely tell Blanco Aguinaga's own story without falling into memoir. As a result, *Carretera de Cuernavaca* is an example of the exile literature about which Blanco Aguinaga theorizes in his essays. By filling in the gaps left by historical information, the book shares a communal experience, training a spotlight on the personal stories that constitute the exile's history.

The opening story, "El armario," establishes a mythical backdrop to a child's imaginings of war. A young Basque boy is mesmerized by the town carpenter, Etxepare, as he builds an armoire for the boy's parents. The carpenter measures without a ruler, and the piece is said to last "mucho más que una vida" (Blanco Aguinaga, *Carretera* 12). The boy watches Etxepare build the armoire day after day, until one night "a lo lejos se oían bombas y mucho ruido de gente corriendo por la calle" (Blanco Aguinaga, *Carretera* 15)—the war arrives—and the boy hides in the armoire. There is a "largo silencio" (Blanco Aguinaga, *Carretera* 15) as years pass, and the boy emerges as though from a dream into a field of flowers and tombs. His explanation for the years spent in the armoire recognizes Etxepare's magic: "Y ahora ya sabes que es verdad; que si mides bien, cualquier cosa que hagas puede durar más que una vida" (Blanco Aguinaga, *Carretera* 16).

As the only tale in *Carretera de Cuernavaca* to contain fantastic elements, "El armario" establishes a metaphor for exile. The mythical Etxepare understands not only abstract measurements of time and space, but also that something as sturdy as the armoire could last a lifetime, like exile itself. The Basque carpenter is the only one who accurately predicts the future. Most exiles assumed they would return to Spain in their lifetime, if not within a few years, as Blanco Aguinaga emphasizes in his essays. However, even "measuring well" cannot quantify the unknown factors and duration of exile. The boy's view of the war as a long silence is analogous to the exiles' removal from Spain. For some, like Blanco Aguinaga, this exile has lasted a lifetime; for others, it has left them silent, without a voice in any national discourse. The mythical qualities of "El armario" set it apart from the real war and displacement experienced by the author and his contemporaries. Still, as the Spanish exile stretches across generations, it is clear that it is a phenomenon that has lasted "mucho más que una vida." "El armario" establishes a magical tone absent later in the collection, as the remainder of the stories shift to a starkly realistic worldview. However, Blanco Aguinaga's exile lies just below the surface of the narrative, a life story the author mines for inspiration and background throughout *Carretera de Cuernavaca*.

"El hermano mayor" appears just after these mythical beginnings and sets the collection's tone by referencing historical details while still maintaining a child's perspective of war. The big brother in question is Pedro, who lives in a Basque village. The young narrator idolizes Pedro as "[i]gual que Durruti, pero de casa, nuestro" (Blanco Aguinaga, *Carretera* 23). The narrator and his friends are semi-ignorant of their own current events: "claro, no sabíamos cómo había empezado la Guerra" (Blanco Aguinaga, *Carretera* 19). But the reference to Buenaventura Durruti, a Republican soldier in the Spanish Civil War who became a martyr to the cause, as well as to "camiones pintados con letras que no entendíamos, sobre todo UGT, CNT y UHP" (Blanco Aguinaga, *Carretera* 21), referring to the three syndicate organizations active on the Republican side,[18] ground the story in history while emphasizing its irrelevance to children who cannot comprehend the complicated rumblings of war. To the boys in "El hermano mayor," Pedro's death at the front only confirms their lack of understanding. The narrator and his peers grasp history insofar as it relates to the clichés: they know that "los héroes, para serlo de verdad, siempre al final tienen que estar muertos, como en las películas" (Blanco Aguinaga, *Carretera* 23). The story's melding of history and childhood imagination, as in "El armario," stresses the perspective of war from the inner recesses of a child's mind, a place that no history book would enter. Blanco Aguinaga, no doubt from personal

Chapter Four

experience, understands that history is more myth than reality in the lives of young Spaniards during the war.

As the war intensifies, the mythical status of history dissipates. In "La desbandada," a conflict that has been smoldering in the background suddenly interrupts daily life. A young protagonist must cross the border from Spain to France, surrounded by families weighed down with suitcases and carts. The collective experience contradicts what the protagonist (whose gender remains unidentified) imagines should happen: "nadie piensa que las balas pueden desviarse, matarnos a nosotros: no somos sino espectadores de la Guerra porque siglos de vida fronteriza nos han enseñado que lo que ocurre en un país no tiene nada que ver con lo que ocurre en el país vecino" (Blanco Aguinaga, *Carretera* 29). This thought, of course, proves to be untrue. The bullets can hit the innocent, and the Spanish Civil War's threat will extend beyond the country's borders as it anticipates World War II. At this pivotal moment, a child begins to understand that what was once simply background noise has become the impetus for his or her own hurried removal from a familiar home. The child is no longer a spectator to history, but an active participant.

The stories in the second section of *Carretera de Cuernavaca* follow these naïve children from Spain and France to Mexico, where they slowly come to grips with the historical forces moving their lives away from their native country. This, too, was Blanco Aguinaga's experience as a child. He relates the sight of his grandfather crossing back into Spain from France, and of monitoring Mola's troops from Hendaye, portrayed in "Aquella casa" and "La desbandada," respectively, in an autobiography (*Por el mundo* 94–95 and 57). Like the author, the children in the first entries in *Carretera de Cuernavaca* look back on their lives from a removed adulthood. They are the sources of these stories, creating accounts of the past that conform to the vagaries of human memory. The narratives show second-generation exiles making their exit from Spain and beginning to cultivate an existence in Mexico in the second section of the book. On the ship crossing the ocean, they begin to learn about their new home.

"Información necesaria" acts as a thematic bridge between the theoretical approach to exile in Blanco Aguinaga's essays and his fictional stories. In these narratives, theory is transformed into praxis: it is contextualized and allowed to operate on characters set in different stages of exile. "Información necesaria" is less a linear narrative than a transitional piece that builds on the notion that the Spanish exiles' impending identity crisis has its roots in language. A child, among other Spaniards, travels by ship to Mexico alongside a Mexican woman who explains details of their destination to the passengers. Throughout the story, Mexico is spelled "Méjico," while in the last line, the young narrator explains: "También nos han dicho en el barco que Méjico se escribe con equis" (Blanco Aguinaga, *Carretera* 44). However, even in stating this information, the narrator does not spell the country's name with an x, continuing to identify Mexico with its Castilian spelling just as he continues to identify himself as a Spaniard. His awareness of the impending spelling change, however, will constitute a loss of innocence, as the boy must confront his own identity in something as seemingly banal as the spelling of his newly adopted country. In both "Sobre el exilio" and "Otros tiempos," Blanco Aguinaga emphasizes the linguistic proximity between Spain and Mexico, interpreting this as one of many causes for the exiles' relatively smooth transition to their adopted nation. Still, assimilation is not as simple as swapping *j* for *x*, as is clear when the author writes in his essay that "algo de español tiene la América que, mayoritariamente, habla castellano" (Blanco Aguinana, "Otros tiempos" 252). The second-generation exile who continues to interpret "American" Spanish as Castellano,[19] still influenced by Spain, views himself and his adopted country as a hybrid product composed of both Mexican and Spanish elements. That hybridity, as we have seen in Blanco Aguinaga's essays, is both the goal and the bane of the second-generation exiles' assimilation. How the exiles identify themselves and are identified in their host country is one of the themes around which Blanco Aguinaga structures his fiction and historiography.

    Once in Mexico, Blanco Aguinaga's fictional exiles take in the world around them. The young students in "El profesor de latín" try to grasp the life their Latin teacher leads as a first-generation Spanish exile. The students are vaguely aware that "nada sería ya como antes" (Blanco Aguinaga, *Carretera* 46). Their teacher was a professor aligned with the Republic in Spain. His wife was killed in a bombardment in Barcelona, leaving him to care for their four children and forcing his exit from his homeland. From the students' perspective, however, their Latin teacher is a distracted man with a past they don't understand: "no sabemos qué fue aquello de la primavera en España" (Blanco Aguinaga, *Carretera* 47). The historical and political circumstances that prompted the Latin teacher's exile are a mystery to the second generation. Their concerns are more for their immediate surroundings than for the past.

The difficulty second-generation exiles have in understanding the plight of the first generation is also apparent in "En el frente del Este, ya muy lejos," in which a return to memories of Spain has irreversible consequences. Raimon, an exile in his twenties, remembers fighting with the Republic as a teenage commissary. A group of younger Spanish exile friends listen to Raimon's stories on a balcony in the Azcapotzalco district of Mexico City. Raimon recounts the awful food, heat, and fleas at the front, as well as the day his comrade Pujol was shot in the face and killed. His mother told him to be brave, but at a certain point, Raimon says, "uno no puede ya con tanto muertos" (Blanco Aguinaga, *Carretera* 56). At dusk, the young friends descend to the sidewalk, only to find that Raimon has arrived first: he committed suicide, his lifeless body lying face down on the street. For the second-generation exiles left behind, Mexico begins to signify something more sinister than a safe haven. It is a space of uneven recuperation from the horrors of war witnessed in Spain. Raimon's death, moreover, is an acute reminder of the personal toll memories of the past can exact on the living.

Under different circumstances, Isabel gives her legal testimony in "Elogio de la destrucción, elogio de la belleza." She describes the turns her life took after witnessing the violence of Civil War–era Spain and exiling to Mexico. There, she encountered firsthand the "gachupines jóvenes" who thought that since they would not be able to return to Spain, they could "hacerse ricos a como diera lugar" (Blanco Aguinaga, *Carretera* 70–71). Given her beauty, her parents treated her as a commodity, marrying her off to another exile determined to exploit Mexico and Mexicans and make it rich in the new world. Ultimately, Isabel kills her violent husband, telling the lawyer that she needed to "defender [su] equilibrio frente a quien lo agredía" (Blanco Aguinaga, *Carretera* 73). In both Raimon's and Isabel's cases, the testimony they give about the brutality of war or the cruelty of exploitation causes an imbalance they feel they can only correct through violence. They can never regain the equilibrium of "before." The path to exile changes them dramatically. For the friends who witness Raimon's suicide and the lawyer who reads Isabel's testimony (not to mention the husband she kills), this instability in the exile's identity has a communal effect in his or her adopted country. Moreover, the theme of opportunism in "Elogio de la destrucción, elogio de la belleza" exemplifies the Spanish *gachupín*, putting faces on the labels Blanco Aguinaga analyzes in his essays.

"Primero de Octubre" tackles another key aspect of the second-generation exiles' assimilation that Blanco Aguinaga discusses in his essays: political involvement. Fernando and Sole are caught in a traffic jam caused by student protestors. The date is October 1, 1968, and the marchers are part of the uprising in Mexico that culminated with the deaths of numerous students at the hands of the police on the second of October. As Fernando complains about the traffic, Sole sympathizes with the protesters. She and Fernando are both second-generation Spanish exiles, but with divergent views on the place of their generation in Mexican society. While Fernando argues that the exiles have had every advantage and should stay out of Mexican politics, Sole thinks of her father's advice: "'O te aclimatas, o te aclimueres'" (Blanco Aguinaga, *Carretera* 77). Her father's comment betrays a difference in attitude between the first- and second-generation exiles. For Sole's father, there is no question that the exile must acclimate himself to the host country; Sole is not so sure she can or wants to assimilate. Frustrated that newspapers have exaggerated the participation of second-generation Spanish exiles in the protests, she argues that the few exiles who are involved are naturalized citizens and therefore "'son mexicanos y tienen derecho'" (Blanco Aguinaga, *Carretera* 79). She relates the student protests to the vague childhood memories she has of the left's struggle and defeat during the war: "La República, la Justicia, el Pueblo, Guernica y los males de la Guerra" (Blanco Aguinaga, *Carretera* 77). Trapped in the car, Sole is literally and figuratively caught between the passive assimilation of Fernando and the active participation of the student protestors, and she tentatively favors the students over her husband. The sense of being caught between two worlds and two national histories is overwhelming. Over the distant explosions of tear gas, Sole thinks about the next day not in terms of what it will bring for Mexico, but rather what it means for her hometown in Spain: "'Mañana es dos de octubre,' le dice, inmersa en sí, a Fernando. 'No sé qué san-to. Pero es el último día de las fiestas de mi pueblo'" (Blanco Aguinaga, *Carretera* 80). As Blanco Aguinaga knows, October 2 will be the definitive end of the exile's innocence as well. Sole's response to the student protests is to retreat to her memories of Spain, further demonstrating the unconscious impediment second-generation exiles face in wholly assimilating to Mexico and adapting their worldview to include Mexican politics as independent of Spanish politics.

Blanco Aguinaga also relates the events of October 2, 1968 in his "Sobre el exilio" essay. His interpretation of this historic day in Mexico's modern history highlights divisions among factions of Mexicans, exiles, and exiles who considered themselves Mexican in the long march to assimilation:

> [N]adie en su sano juicio puede pensar que no fue un movimiento *mexicano*. Sin embargo, puesto que algunos de los miembros del Comité de Huelga estudiantil... eran mexicanos hijos de refugiados españoles, no sólo la prensa, sino el gobierno de Díaz Ordaz acusaron insistentemente al movimiento de estar manipulado por lo que llamaban "extranjeros indeseables."... [A]quella propaganda... llevó a la deportación *ilegal* de varios mexicanos hijos de refugiados. A más de las muertes de aquellos meses y de la represión generalizada subsiguiente, aquellos hechos más o menos subterráneos sirvieron de aviso a los descendientes mexicanos de los exiliados, quienes por mucho tiempo se abstuvieron de toda política contestataria. ("Sobre el exilio" 33–34; emphasis in the original)

Blanco Aguinaga's description of the events that day are fraught with frustration and anger. He emphasizes the "*illegal* deportation" of second-generation exiles and the judgmental label of "undesirable foreigners." Although Blanco Aguinaga calls the exiles "Mexican children of Spanish refugees" he also defines the student protests as a "*Mexican* movement," a term that encompasses both the native Mexicans and the second-generation exiles who participated in the protests. But the Mexican government and press made a distinction between the children of Spanish exiles and the rest of the Mexicans participating in the march. Furthermore, these institutions blamed the second-generation exiles for the unrest, which protracted the exiles' assimilation into Mexican society. "Primero de Octubre" presents the perspective of an individual, Sole, who wants to belong, but who is unable to break down the barriers between native and transplanted Mexicans. In Fernando, the story also illustrates an exile who is more interested in coexistence than assimilation. These characters, as well as Blanco Aguinaga himself, for personal reasons coupled with outside forces, are trapped in an unending identity crisis. For the author, the student uprising of 1968 captures the personal and political obstacles that second-generation exiles faced in adapting to Mexico: "aunque mexicanos, los miembros de la primera generación hispano-mexicana rara vez sintieron que podían participar al cien por cien en la vida del país" (Blanco Aguinaga, "Sobre el exilio" 33). Through the lens of genre fusion, it becomes clear that the historical context in Blanco Aguinaga's essays enhances his story, lending a polyphonic account of the historical moment. The second-generation Spanish exile regains the voice denied him by Mexican authorities during the uprisings.

In two other stories from this second section of *Carretera de Cuernavaca*, Blanco Aguinaga returns to the relationships among three generations of exiles. Each generation approaches its experience and identity distinctly. As a mother talks to her child about the books she has read over her lifetime, or a grandfather explains to his grandson how American cars could never have traversed narrow European streets, both reader and narrator listen to the testimony of first-generation exiles, who have their own set of memories and concerns. These characters present a point of reference that forms the basis from which successive generations will differentiate themselves and their exile experience. The mother in "Libros que leía mi madre" compares "la gran matanza del 2 de octubre" with the conflicts between Nationalists and Republicans in the Spanish Civil War. Her assessment that it was "'[i]gual, diferente pero igual que lo que nos hicieron a nosotros'" (Blanco Aguinaga, *Carretera* 100) simplifies a Mexican conflict that, as is evident in "Primero de octubre," introduces new struggles between emerging populations in a world much different from Spain in the late '30s. The fundamental historical points of reference for first-generation exiles are virtually incoherent for later generations. The grandson in "Hizo la maleta y se fue a Chiapas" reveals that he was "muy niño y claro está que no entendía el sentido real de aquellas referencias, alusiones, reticencias" (Blanco Aguinaga, *Carretera* 102) that his grandfather makes about Spain and Europe. There is a sense of disconnect between generations of Spanish exiles,

Chapter Four

between the cultures and shared experiences of Mexicans versus Spaniards, between historical antecedents that mark the course of one generation versus another, and between the aspirations of some to go home and others to assimilate. Conversely, this disconnection binds the stories in *Carretera de Cuernavaca* together and introduces the thematic elements central to the book's third section, consisting of the story that gives its name to the collection.

* * *

Blanco Aguinaga makes his presence felt obliquely throughout the stories in *Carretera de Cuernavaca*, representing aspects of his childhood, his historical concerns, and his exile life in Mexico. However, in the collection's final narrative, "Carretera de Cuernavaca," he patterns his protagonist on himself while touching on most of the salient themes in his two essays. This novella-length story examines modern day Mexico through the eyes of Antonio, a middle-aged writer and second-generation Spanish exile, and his *Rayuela*-esque group of intellectual friends. Like Julio Cortázar's cast of characters, all are exiles who gather for dinner parties in their adopted city to analyze the effects exile has had on them.[20] Antonio struggles to write a historical novel about the exile passage to Mexico based on firsthand testimony. This novel is also his attempt to make sense of his own life. As the story opens, he wonders "¿para quién escribo? Y, por lo tanto, ¿para qué?" (Blanco Aguinaga, *Carretera* 111). Antonio's recurring reflections and doubts about the writing process recall Ugarte and Blanco Aguinaga's arguments that, through writing, the exile delves into a deeper understanding of the personal and universal nature of his experience. In "Carretera de Cuernavaca," Blanco Aguinaga channels his auto-examination of the exile writing process through Antonio's reflections on his writing.

Antonio and his friends discuss the question of their own displacement constantly. A friend's son, passing through the group deep in conversation, comments: "'¿Qué pasó, los inseparables? ¿Hablando siempre de sus cosas?'" (Blanco Aguinaga, *Carretera* 116). This offhand remark from a third-generation exile—who, in the eyes of the second-generation exiles is no longer an exile—depresses everyone. One of the friends considers their generation so removed from other generations of exiles that "'nuestras cosas ya no son para él reales, no son reales para nadie'" (Blanco Aguinaga, *Carretera* 116), and therefore they do not represent a universal experience of exile at all. Antonio worries about writing an objective historical tale, which he hopes "[e]n el peor de los casos puede servir de terapia" (Blanco Aguinaga, *Carretera* 116). He has greater aspirations that the story he tells can still represent a collective experience: "en el mundo en que vivimos cualquier historia, sea de donde sea, puede ser de todos" (Blanco Aguinaga, *Carretera* 117).

The fact that Antonio has a Mexican girlfriend both exaggerates and contradicts his sense of isolation. He alternates between feeling that she is his entrée into Mexican society and thinking she fails to understand him and distances him from his exile peers.[21] Antonio and his friends see themselves as "refugiados, o desterrados, o trasterrados, o exilados (o, peor aún, exiliados, insoportable vocal sobrante)" (Blanco Aguinaga, *Carretera* 157), referencing the same distance between signifier and signified that Blanco Aguinaga examines in "Otros tiempos" and "Sobre el exilio." This repetition of the debate on terminology pinpoints a central problem for Blanco Aguinaga: the inability to agree on a name for the second-generation exiles, which only aggravates their growing identity confusion. The linguistic issue exposes the advantage of a genre fusion approach to the author's historiography and fiction by bringing the arguments he makes in his essays to bear on the plot of his story. As for Roig, Martín Gaite, and Marías, genre fusion demonstrates how Blanco Aguinaga balances his duties as historian and short story writer using his research and collection of personal memories as the source material for his essays and his fiction.

Spurred by the naming debate, Antonio's friends identify a lack of personal and national connection that radiates through the second-generation exiles' experiences in Spain and Mexico. One of Antonio's friends argues that their generation has never belonged to any country, since they do not remember anything about Spain and they are not permitted to assimilate to Mexico:

> Ni provocamos la Guerra, ni luchamos en ella. Luego, nos trajeron. Nos metieron enseguida en aquellas escuelas, las vuestras y la mía, en las que no hacían sino hablarnos de España, directa o indirectamente, de una España que no conocíamos, que era la de ellos y que, sólo por eso, se suponía que tenía que ser nuestra. (Blanco Aguinaga, *Carretera* 148–49)

Chapter Four

Expanding on Blanco Aguinaga's descriptions of Mexican children deriding young Spanish exiles in "Sobre el exilio," this fictional passage exposes the raw frustration of the second generation. They were educated with left-leaning Spanish rhetoric in schools and at home. How were they to assimilate easily to a more conservative Mexican culture while still educated as though they were Republicans fighting in the Spanish Civil War?

Antonio's ruminations on the second-generation exiles' relationship to their native country and to their adopted country, on the other hand, do take into account how the exiles have been educated by two different discourses. The end result, however, is that neither discourse leaves its mark:

> Lo nuestro no es sino un hablar de lo nuestro. No somos ya sino lenguaje, repetición mecánica de palabras que se dicen solas a sí mismas. Lo cual resulta especialmente grave, especialmente lamentable cuando pretendemos acercarnos a lo que nos rodea, cuando intentamos encontrarnos en la otredad de un discurso ajeno que también llevamos dentro y que, sin embargo, es radicalmente imposible, inalcanzable en nosotros. ¿Cuántas veces al día decimos cuánto queremos a este país, cómo sin él no seríamos nada, cuánto nos importa lo que aquí pasa? Pero al decir eso, que es verdad, que es la pura verdad, suena siempre a mentira porque no acabamos de decirlo desde el interior del discurso al que queremos y no queremos acercarnos. Sólo que tampoco estamos en el discurso que aquí nos trajo. El nuestro es un lenguaje como de anfibios. (Blanco Aguinaga, *Carretera* 150)

Language is the exile's only recourse, and yet it traps him in an endless cycle. This "amphibian" discourse reveals the second generation's inner struggle: they both fight to adopt their new Mexican discourse and fight to remember their old Spanish discourse. Theirs is a taut internal debate. They reach to internalize Spain, which is a country they know only by memory (their childhood memories and the memories of their elders), and that therefore remains foreign to them. At the same time they reach to internalize Mexico, which is both physically near them yet emotionally distant from them. As they are forced by circumstance to shed their Spanish skin, they are left with a Mexican skin that does not feel entirely their own. Nationality becomes a figurative struggle between two nations to inhabit the individual. The second-generation exile is left void of either nation, imprisoned instead in a life-long identity crisis, an "otredad" that seemingly can never be resolved.

Language and literature's role in representing the "emptiness" of the exiles' inner life is clear in Blanco Aguinaga's two essays, as we have seen. In "Carretera de Cuernavaca" Antonio imagines poetry as "estrictamente personal y, por tanto, absolutamente abstracto," whereas in narrative, "[t]odavía, a pesar de todo, parece ser que hay que contar cosas. ... Es decir, algún pie hay que tener en la tierra de cuyas cosas tendrías que hablar" (Blanco Aguinaga, *Carretera* 130). Blanco Aguinaga's essays concentrate primarily on the ability of poetry to express the ineffable emotions of exile. In this story, however, it is narrative that best, and more concretely, represents the exiles' void. Although Antonio levies this judgment explicitly, it is also implied by the narrative itself. In writing "Carretera de Cuernavaca," Blanco Aguinaga's choice of genre makes an implicit value judgment on the relative merits of narrative in expressing the exile identity crisis. In "Sobre el exilio" Blance Aguinaga writes that "la poesía del exilio, al igual que el conocimiento de los interiores de la vida cotidiana de ese exilio, nos revela que, en el centro de tanta actividad y de tanta asimilación inevitable y positiva, siempre hubo un vacío" (33). Juxtaposing Blanco Aguinaga's determination with Antonio's assertion in "Carretera de Cuernavaca" that poetry, although personal, lacks the detail and context that prose provides to the exile experience, we arrive at a schism in the artistic lives of the Spanish exiles. Blanco Aguinaga has studied the exile poet Prados extensively and bases his novel *Esperando la lluvia de la tarde: fábula de exilios* on Prados's life story. In practice, however, by vehemently defending the merits of exile poetry while representing even the exile experience of a poet through narrative, Blanco Aguinaga argues both sides of the debate about which genre more effectively portrays the ephemeral qualities of exile. Moreover, this internal disagreement is an apt echo of the unstable Spanish/Mexican exile identity around which the author's writing revolves. Just as exiles are destined to inhabit the space between nationalities, so too is writing about exile located in the space between genres: between poetry and prose, and between fiction and history. Blanco Aguinaga's choice of narrative in his own writing, rather than a value judgment against the expressive and representative qualities of verse, indicates a desire to represent the exile experience through the kind of detailed storytelling antithetical to poetry but at home in prose and narrative historiography.

Blanco Aguinaga and his fictional protagonist write about themselves and their generation of exiles with a stake in their subject matter. Antonio maintains another Unamunian commonality with his creator: he is writing a novel that crosses the boundaries between fiction and history. His in-progress tome about two ships that brought refugees and Republican fortunes to Mexico, the *Vita* and the *Tramontana*, is based on the account of a witness to the events, who narrated his story to Antonio.[22] However, Antonio's memory has failed him in parts, and so he embellishes the gaps with his own created details, in the hopes that they will enliven the adventure. Antonio's method in writing this pseudo-historical novel captures the essence of his generation's recording of its life history. When a life depends on memory, and the mind cannot recall those crucial first years, the life story must be at least partially invented.

The second-generation exiles in Mexico only hazily remember their childhoods in Spain; their memories encompass instead the life invented for them in Mexico. Ugarte asserts that autobiography and testimony are frequent creative outlets for the exile writer, but that the "I of exile needs evidence for having experienced something, and it is the nebulous nature of this evidence, the fact that it is a linguistic creation, that gives exile literature its characteristic tension" (20). For both Antonio and Blanco Aguinaga, Spain and their childhoods are limited in substance; their life-writing is thus based on a linguistic creation. It can be argued that life writing is always based on invention, in that adults never remember their childhoods with the utmost fidelity. But the second-generation exiles suffer from a lost childhood re-created for them by their elders, then diluted again by a cross-cultural tension. In the end, this tension marks the universality of exile and its characteristic identity crisis. Antonio asks a friend: "'Porque si tú y yo, por ejemplo... nos adentramos seriamente en lo estrictamente personal, marcado o definido históricamente por el exilio infantil, ¿por qué no vamos a poder representarlo como general, o universal?'" (Blanco Aguinaga, *Carretera* 134). Blanco Aguinaga agrees with his protagonist on the ultimate universality of the exile experience. In one of his essays, he writes: "bien podríamos llegar a sospechar que el mestizaje cultural, como el racial," that is, the blending of cultures inherent in exile, "está en la naturaleza de las cosas, es decir, de la Historia" ("Sobre el exilio" 37–38). The universal history inherent in the exile experience is founded on the collective memory of the exiles themselves.

Antonio's novel and its ambiguous relationship to history is another example of the dialectic between fiction and history. While based on a historical account, his embellished or created details and subjective reliance on memory move the text to the realm of historical fiction or memoir. Antonio's novel begs the question of whether there is any form of historical writing that is an "accurate" account of the events. Hayden White asserts that narrative, as one among many different discourses from which the historian can choose to express the chronology of history, cannot escape imposing meaning on the historical content it approximates. Indeed, White writes that "all representations of reality are ideological in nature" (*Content* 148). In essence, historiography is embellished by narrative forms just as fiction is embellished by historical material. Both genres are influenced by the desire to represent history accurately, based on the author's and reader's judgment of accuracy. But historical fiction and narrative historiography are also mitigated by imagination and subjectivity, resulting in a form of writing that presents an individualized representation of reality. Still, this "individual" history, in that it captures a shared experience, reproduces a collective notion of history. In writing about his own experiences as an exile, Blanco Aguinaga also writes for second-generation Spanish exiles as a marginalized collective.

The ending of "Carretera de Cuernavaca" brings us squarely back to Blanco Aguinaga's essays, reminding us again of the utility of applying genre fusion to the author's work. He argues in "Otros tiempos" that "la relación entre América y los españoles que llegaron a ella huyendo del fascismo no se resuelve en un *happy ending* del trastierro" (Blanco Aguinaga, *Carretera* 251; emphasis in the original).[23] The exiles cannot hope for a fairytale resolution. Each successive generation will face its own distinct and complex identity problems that will not result in a definitive "happily ever after" ending to their lives. "Carretera de Cuernavaca" ends with the ambiguous death/suicide of two of Antonio's friends in a traffic accident, an event Antonio cannot separate from his own experience nor from the novel he is writing. Sitting in a taxicab, he thinks about the ship full of passengers seeking a port in his

Chapter Four

novel: "Todos navegando con la radio desenchufada entre las grandes nieblas, todo ya fantasmal silencio, todo convertido en literatura, palabras vacías que digo hacia adentro mientras corre el taxi por el Periférico, palabras que no escribo" (Blanco Aguinaga, *Carretera* 177). The ship adrift from the world and forced into silence is analogous to the exile's emptiness. This void is only truly expressed in literature, but normally remains hidden at the core of the exile's identity crisis. Yet Antonio does not record the words he thinks to himself, and thus fails to combat the great void of exile through literature. The unwritten words leave the story, Antonio's fate, and the future of the second-generation exiles in limbo, just where they began. Blanco Aguinaga's essays and the trajectory of his life constitute a rounded and personalized interpretation of the second-generation exile experience when read in tandem with the stories in *Carretera de Cuernavaca*. As a whole, the points of intersection between the author's life, his essays, and his collection of short stories read through genre fusion levy a singular judgment: the identity crisis of second-generation Spanish exiles in Mexico is a unique phenomenon that nevertheless reflects the universal experience of exile.

In *Shifting Ground*, Ugarte argues that exile essayists struggle with the task of reconciling the abstract political and historical consequences of exile with their personal, individual experiences of exile. Blanco Aguinaga's role as both essayist and novelist dovetails with Ugarte's notion of reckoning with history and personal reflection. Blanco Aguinaga's individual experience of exile is evident in the two essays and the fictional work discussed in this chapter. All three contain elements of the major events in the author's life: his upbringing in the Basque Country, his passage to Mexico, and his struggles with assimilation in the Americas. Ugarte affirms that "[t]he literature of exile brings into play a variety of texts; those of literature and criticism, of fiction and reality, of history and the recording of history. And in many ways it is this intertextual weaving which is the mainstay of literature, whether in exile or not" (68). Indeed, we see Blanco Aguinaga's body of work, with its incorporation of a variety of texts and genres around a central theme of exile, fitting neatly into Ugarte's analysis and the genre fusion model.

Blanco Aguinaga's concrete examples of the interweaving of historiography and fiction constitute novel ways of looking at the exile experience in Spain, situated among historical context, memory, testimony, narrativity, identity, and nationality. A single voice becomes eminently clear in these texts: that of Blanco Aguinaga, filtering his own experiences through the recording of history and the representation of fiction. This individual voice rendering a story of a collective exile experience bestows an authority and resonance on Blanco Aguinaga's texts that encourages the reader to trust its historical accuracy. Consequently, a community of second-generation exiles combats its marginalization through the genre fusion of the author's rewritten history.

Chapter Five

Javier Marías
Genre Fusion in the New Millennium

> *Para que un personaje histórico y real*
> *permanezca en la memoria de las gentes,*
> *le es necesario revestirse de una dimensión imaginaria,*
> *o de ficción, que es lo que, por otra parte,*
> *va a acabar por falsearlo, difuminarlo y*
> *finalmente borrarlo en tanto que*
> *verdadero personaje histórico.*
> Javier Marías
> *Sobre la dificultad de contar*

The Past in the Present in Twenty-first-century Spain

The Spanish daily newspaper *El País* published an editorial by Javier Marías one day after the terrorist attacks at Madrid's Atocha train station in 2004. Marías located this brutal act in the context of a well-worn routine:

> Cada vez que ETA asesina —y casi siempre lo hace de buena mañana, los terroristas madrugan, o quizá es que no duerman la noche previa—, existe la costumbre de que, hacia el mediodía, los responsables de los ayuntamientos de las ciudades salgan a la puerta de sus edificios, con calor, frío o lluvia, y guarden uno o dos minutos de silencio. ("De buena mañana" 45)

Marías's editorial occupies the lower half of a page of the March 12, 2004 edition of *El País* dedicated to the attacks, sharing the broadsheet with a prominent article above the fold on Mariano Rajoy's reaction to the event. In that article, Rajoy, the Popular Party (PP) presidential candidate in the general elections that would be held two days later, unequivocally attributes the attacks to the Basque terrorist group ETA. Rajoy declares: "'A ETA, sólo hay que decirle una cosa: 'Vamos a por ellos.' Nada más'" (Marcos 45). But questions as to who was to blame for the attacks were already in the air.

By the time Marías's editorial was published in the United States, later that same day, there was doubt as to the definitive identity of the perpetrators. This prompted a more ambiguous start to the author's translated observations: "The terrorist attacks almost always happen in the early morning. Whether it turns out that yesterday's train-station bombings were the work of the usual suspects—the Basque terrorist group ETA—or of Al Qaeda or another group altogether, the murderers stuck to the usual timetable" ("Another Silent Noon in Madrid"). The confusion and duplicity that reigned over these three days in Spain is one of the root causes of the subtle change to Marías's article. Marías responds to the confusion over his editorial in "Informe no solicitado sobre el jueves negro," published in *El País Semanal* a few months later. He cites the Spanish government's refusal to consider publicly other possible perpetrators of the attacks and the American press' questioning of this party line as the reason why "apareció mi leve incertidumbre sobre la responsabilidad de las matanzas, insertada de mala manera a última hora" (*El oficio de oír llover* 239). The immediacy with which Marías places himself at the center of a public dialogue about terrorism within Spain and abroad following the attacks is a testament to the author's commitment to exploring the threads that are or will form part of the country's historical memory. This commitment has been integral to his recent journalism and works of fiction.

On the third anniversary of the September 11th terrorist attacks in New York, also in 2004, Marías returned to the editorial pages of the *The New York Times*, writing about memory and forgetting in an age of traumatic catastrophes. Only a few months after the Atocha attacks, Marías observes that "[o]ur perception of time is all too variable, and there are many factors that can strangely affect it, breaking the thread of continuity" ("How to Remember"). This temporal perception, he opines, has contributed to the uneasy sensation of a Spanish population consumed by the calamity of a terrorist attack while it returns to its everyday activities. He observes that "six months later, [Spain] seems already to have overcome the trauma of the railway bombings. ... Our habits seem as unchanging as the streets, the bars, the restaurants, the stadiums, the airports and the train stations, all just as crowded as ever—and as lively and buoyant" (Marías, "How to Remember"). The enemy, Marías argues, is too disperse. Although Spanish soldiers were at this moment fighting in Afghanistan and Iraq, in Marías's opinion, "[h]ere in Spain, we don't feel as if we are at war, because we aren't" ("How to Remember"). War in Spain is a known entity: it is the devastating bloodshed of brother fighting brother in a country divided by the Civil War. In 2004, unlike for "[t]he Madrilenians who lived through the siege of their city from 1936 to 1939," there is no war at home, no disruption of daily life (Marías, "How to Remember"). In order to decipher an event that had no antecedent, Marías cloaks the aftermath of the Atocha attacks in the context of the more familiar Spanish Civil War. It is not a coincidence that the protagonist of Marías's *Tu rostro mañana* trilogy, Jaime Deza, echoes Marías's observations about the atmosphere in Madrid after March 11. Deza describes that "'[e]n Madrid nada ha cambiado mucho... Es ya como si no hubieran ocurrido [los ataques]'" (Marías, *Tu rostro mañana. 3* 159). The Spanish Civil War is a prominent point of reference for the current state of Spain in Marías's synthesis of fiction and nonfiction. Comparing Deza's and Marías's assessments of Madrid through genre fusion illuminates the author's goal of making Spanish history personal.

In the first decade of the twenty-first century, Spain has become yet another nation facing global terrorism on local soil. As the country tries to navigate the threat of terrorism from afar, it has also begun to re-evaluate its own past in a public forum. By folding the stories of individuals on the margins of postwar Spanish society into an open dialogue about the country's history, Marías continues the aims of Montserrat Roig, Carmen Martín Gaite, and Carlos Blanco Aguinaga. Like his predecessors, Marías applies a familiar narrative framework to questions of history and memory. As a man from Castilla la Mancha, a best-selling international author, and a member of the Real Academia Española, however, Marías is not on the fringe of Spanish society. Nevertheless, the historical focus in his recent journalism and novels is on the *vencidos*, the losers of the Spanish Civil War. He employs multiple vantage points to capture the experience of this marginalized population, including his own. Marías counts himself as part of the legacy of the *vencidos*, in that his father was ostracized during the dictatorship for his political loyalties. Similar conflicts between the government and the people continue to exist in present-day Spain, in Marías's view.

The author's *Tu rostro mañana* trilogy, published between 2002 and 2007, incorporates the pursuits of historiography into a fictional narration that skirts the boundaries between the real and the imagined. As a columnist during the same time period, Marías produces a by-product of narrative historiography combined with editorial, autobiography, and cultural commentary. He operates on both sides of the history/fiction divide, combining the two genres around his attempts to understand the impacts of Spain's changing cultural and political tides on the country's historical memory in his journalism, and around his intermingling of Spanish Civil War historiography with fictional narrative in his novels. Roig, Martín Gaite, and Blanco Aguinaga, liberated by Spain's transition to democracy, merged history and fiction into intimate views of the individual's and the collective's place in the Spanish historical imagination of the late 1970s and early 1980s. Thirty years later, Spain has officially begun to grapple with its past while facing the challenges and opportunities of globalization. Marías is part of a new generation of writers working in the spaces between genres, continuing a tradition of highlighting the role of those on the margins of postwar Spanish society and culture in a newly central discourse on Spain's history.

The *Tu rostro mañana* trilogy joins an on-going resurgence of historically committed cultural production in Spain that has been building since the dictator's death in 1975. Unburdened by censorship, early post-Franco narratives were at liberty to mix historical context culled from actual events with fictionalized settings. Consequently, a variety of historical literature was published in the late 1970s and 1980s, from novelized autobiographical accounts to historiography reexamining previously censored aspects of Spain's Civil War and postwar. By the late 1980s, this sustained desire to render a faithful representation of the recent past gave way to either a rejection of the historical in Spanish literature or an incorporation of the historical into a host of diverse literary genres, from detective novels to experimental fiction. Though it never completely disappeared, this historical push waned through the 1990s, which can be interpreted as a reaction to the near-saturation of historical fiction during the late Transition period. Spain's entry into the twenty-first century, however, has yielded a renewed interest in resurrecting historical memory in all its forms. The country has emerged from an era of government-sanctioned amnesia characterized by the Pact of Silence. Films, literature, and historiography have become, as Carmen Moreno-Nuño notes, "los encargados de construir esa nueva memoria en la etapa democrática" (55). They have opened the public's consciousness to a topic that was once officially and socially taboo, becoming the medium through which Spain would begin to envision itself as a product of its past conflicts, a task the Spanish government was uninterested in shouldering.

Spain's assimilation into the eurozone, as it traded *pesetas* for euros from 1999 to 2002, paralleled a series of alterations to the cultural and political landscape. In 2001, the year before Marías published his first *Tu rostro mañana* installment, Spain was at a crossroads in historical memory. The ruling conservative party was content to continue an official Pact of Silence on matters regarding the Civil War and its aftermath. Nevertheless, a popular tide of historical re-examination in novels, television shows, films, and periodicals was beginning to materialize.[1] The Spanish judge Baltasar Garzón's quest to extradite Chilean dictator Augusto Pinochet for war crimes in 2000 became significant for its symbolic ushering in of a new era of historical accountability. It heralded, for example, the exhumation of Emilio Silva's grandfather in Priaranza del Bierzo and Silva's foundation of the Asociación para la Recuperación de la Memoria Histórica that same year. The disinterring of Silva's grandfather would be the first of many investigations of Civil War–era mass graves in Spain in the decade to come.[2]

The country also felt the reverberations of the attack on the World Trade Center in its rapid inclusion among nations battling global terrorism. Spain joined United Nations and American military forces fighting in Afghanistan in 2001. That same year, the European Union officially recognized the Basque terrorist group ETA as a terrorist threat. Subsequently, hundreds of thousands of Spaniards across the country participated in silent demonstrations against ETA. These events gave Spain global recognition at the turn of the century. They served as a dividing line between a country manipulated by silence as a political tool (as in the Pact of

Silence) and a country using silence or its rupture (as in the case of the ETA protests) to reinforce its international presence.

The Atocha attacks left no doubt that Spain had entered a new historical era, one in which the concept of an isolated peninsula, without any bearing on world affairs, simply no longer applied.[3] The attacks marked a turning point in Spain's break with its past culture of silence. Mass public demonstrations followed the PP's insistence that the violence was the work of ETA and not jihadist terrorists. Three days after the attacks, Spanish voters rejected the claims of the PP, voting in a Socialist government. Other watershed moments of historical reconciliation in the first decade of the twenty-first century, from the negotiations over exhuming the body of the poet Federico García Lorca to a groundbreaking 2006 national conference in Madrid that gathered hundreds of historians from Spain and abroad to re-examine the Spanish Civil War and its historical impacts ("Madrid acoge el congreso más ambicioso sobre la Guerra Civil"), culminated in the 2007 passage of a law specifically designed to fold historical memory into legal precedent. The Law of Historical Memory provided for a state-sanctioned entry point to the public debate over how Spain should approach an overarching conception of its history. It prompted more specific discussions as well, ranging from what constitutes a cultural icon promoting the victors of the Civil War, to how much the families of the vanquished should be compensated for their pain and suffering and whether that compensation should be extended to the families of the fallen victors as well.

The draw toward historical re-examination evident in these movements, laws, and conferences has also trickled down to literature. There is a growing interest in imbedding a historical narrative inside a fictional framework in recent Spanish novels such as Javier Cercas's *Soldados de Salamina*, Josefina Aldecoa's *Historia de una maestra* trilogy, and Almudena Grandes's *El corazón helado*. These postmodern historical narratives share common traits with the dynamic and contentious historiography of twenty-first-century authors such as Silva, Pío Moa, Reyes Mate, and Santos Juliá. These new historical novels and contemporary narrative historiography incorporate chronology, testimony, historical documents, and the author's own subjectivity as source material in the process of recording and crafting a narrative. Both genres, furthermore, seek to allow the voices of a few to speak for the experiences of many.

Marías's latest trilogy extends the author's work into a similar territory that can be interpreted through genre fusion.

As with his editorials on the Atocha attacks, Marías has not hesitated to join the debate on Spain's engagement with its past. In his columns in *El País Semanal,* throughout his *Tu rostro mañana* trilogy, and in his published speech to the Real Academia Española, Marías confronts the rapid changes Spanish society is undergoing as it re-envisions its past. In publications, Marías reflects on how and why he intermingles fiction and history, thus theorizing his own practice of what we have come to identify as genre fusion. By interpreting the Spanish zeitgeist on a weekly basis in his columns and maintaining a strong personal connection to the divisions brought about by the Civil War, Marías manipulates the connections that bind his fictional narrative to Spanish history as well as to his own life story and criticism. In the process, he creates a body of narrative work that both inhabits and attempts to understand an intermediate space between fiction and history for the new century.

As a columnist and novelist, Marías presents a contemporary counterpart to the blurred genres evident in the works of Roig, Martín Gaite, and Blanco Aguinaga during the Spanish transition to democracy. He reworks his predecessors' approaches to history and fiction through his own subjectivity. Like Roig, he explicitly interweaves material from his nonfiction writing into his novels. Like Martín Gaite, he theorizes about the craft of the novelist and cultural observer, and sees historical significance in their overlap. Like Blanco Aguinaga, he mines his and his family's personal experience as relevant to the overall historical narrative in his fiction and nonfiction. Like all three of his counterparts, Marías is both reader and subject of his texts. This self-referentiality is especially evident in the moments when the author or his characters step away from the page to consider their impact on the text itself. Still, Marías deviates from the pattern of fused fiction and historiography these three Transition-era authors have established. Instead of self-consciously borrowing from one genre to feed the other, in a manner discernible to the astute reader, Marías's practice results in seamless historical and narrative texts, halfway between fiction and nonfiction. While continuing to capture the essence of narrative historiography and historical fiction, the author transforms both genres into hybrid texts concerned, in one fashion or another, with Spanish history. As both a product and a point of rupture with the practice of melding genres during the Transition, Marías's unique approach writes the next chapter in Spain's understanding of its past as it enters into a global era. Marías assumes a dual role as a commentator on Spain's global politics, terrorism, and the recuperation of its historical memory, and as a novelist who incorporates a narrative historiography into his fiction. Analyzed through the lens of genre fusion, this tactic foretells how Spanish letters will treat history and fiction in the future. Marías's critical commentary, moreover, lends a distinctive voice to Spain's continued contemporary struggle to map its history.

Editorializing History: Marías as Witness to a Global Spain

Javier Marías entered the literary mainstream at the age of 19 with his first novel, *Dominios del lobo* (1971).[4] Over the course of his career, the author has joined Spain's literary elite, culminating in a prized seat with the Real Academia Española in 2007.[5] Marías is the rare literary phenomenon who has enjoyed both local and international success. Through his prolific contributions to the Spanish press, he is a highly visible public figure in contemporary Spanish culture. Since 1994, Marías has written a weekly column for the Sunday supplement to *El País*. In these essays he reacts to, critiques, humors, assails, complains about, contemplates, and parodies current events and trends related in some form or another to contemporary Spanish society.[6] A perusal of his columns makes clear a number of Marías's tropes and positions. He eschews email, cell phones, and computers in favor of the post office, being unreachable, and his typewriter. As a voracious reader and viewer of films, Marías peppers his writing with references to cultural material from a variety of national and international sources. He relishes a witty repartee with his frequent "compañero de página," Arturo Pérez-Reverte. Marías and Pérez-Reverte are two among a number of contemporary Spanish authors who moonlight as columnists for *El País* or another Spanish media outlet.[7] Above all, Marías is an astute observer of his native city, Madrid, and dedicates countless column inches to critiquing it, its inhabitants, and its city government. These everyday concerns feed

Marías's imagination and highlight his narrative acumen in essays written as engaging nonfiction stories.

Marías's preoccupation with Spain's position in world affairs, however, is never so clear as during the period surrounding the September 11, 2001 terrorist attacks in New York and the March 11, 2004 terrorist attacks in Madrid. Marías published nearly 200 columns between 2001 and 2005, many of which directly address the changing political climate in Spain and its emergence on a global stage. Yet at the same time, Marías does not stray far from a relevant issue that has preoccupied him for decades, inside and outside of his novels: his father's treatment during and after the Spanish Civil War. The four years between these two attacks also coincide with the publication of the first two volumes of *Tu rostro mañana* and presumably the composition of the entire trilogy. These columns provide a unique avenue to explore the overlap among Marías's novelistic threads, his preoccupations with current events, and the ways that both relate to his family history.

While Marías's contributions to *El País Semanal* are often mentioned in overviews of his work, few scholars have examined the overlap between his columns and his novels.[8] One exception is Maarten Steenmeijer's exploration of the disconnect between Marías as an autonomous author and individual, and as the narrator in many of his novels. Steenmeijer questions the assumption that Marías writes "as himself" in his columns, when the ways he navigates anonymity and autobiography in his novels are fairly well established. Marías has described his autobiographical doubling in his narrators, particularly in his novel *Todas las almas*, as representing a character "'quien yo pude ser pero no fui'" (*Literatura y fantasma* 95). The notion that one of the author's novelistic characters could be him but is not mirrors Martín Gaite's identification with but carefully crafted distance from "C." in *El cuarto de atrás*. It is a postmodern game that Marías will continue to play in the *Tu rostro mañana* series.

But one particular aside in a Marías column—"los novelistas no somos muy de fiar cuando no hablamos ficticiamente"—caused an uproar among the author's reading public, Steenmeijer reports (265). Marías's suggestion that novelists are more trustworthy within the pages of their fiction than in their journalism is intentional. This comment questions whether a novelist is held to

Chapter Five

a standard of veracity in the press not only when he documents events, but also when he inserts himself or his persona into his journalism. Steenmeijer argues that Marías as a columnist is as fictional an invention as the various self-reflexive narrators the author has created in his novels. At the same time, Steenmeijer interprets the presentation of reality in Marías's columns as "más bien concretos, contundentes y directos," while the references to reality in his novels are "inciertos, indagadores y circunspectos" (269). A detailed examination of the *Tu rostro mañana* trilogy in comparison to the columns Marías wrote during the same period contradicts Steenmeijer's assertion. Marías is more direct and concrete when referencing historical reality in his novels than in his columns. In his trilogy, he cites previous works of Spanish historiography, illustrates history with posters and photographs, and includes personal recollections of events that contextualize his fiction within Spain's past. In his columns, on the other hand, Marías is more interested in his own reflections on history and current events, held to a looser standard of historical documentation. He draws comparisons between Spain's past and today, and highlights the themes of betrayal, the dangers of telling, and the ability to read history and current events as precursors to future actions in his nonfiction columns. Although these themes run throughout the three volumes of *Tu rostro mañana* as well, they are bolstered by more concrete historical details in his trilogy than in his columns. The reader's anticipation of journalistic standards of documentation is compromised because Marías is an editorial columnist, not a reporter or historiographer. Yet in the pages of his trilogy, Marías adheres more closely to this standard of veracity. He conspicuously embodies a hybrid between novelist and historian (or journalist) throughout his texts.

El oficio de oír llover collects Marías's weekly columns from February 16, 2003 to February 6, 2005. It is a highly political and critical collection that spares no kind words for George W. Bush or José María Aznar during a time when both leaders were immersed in the war in Iraq. In "Época de leyendas" from March 2003, Marías touches on the process of altering history by making it out to be what we want to believe happened, instead of what actually happened. He calls the current moment an "época ávida de leyendas y desdeñosa de las certidumbres y de la verificación" (*El oficio* 26). Marías's immediate focus is on the lack of verification of the existence of weapons of mass destruction in Iraq, which, to the author, would be the sole justification for the war Spain is fighting. However, Marías criticizes this process of seeking proof when mitigated by human memory and emotion: "a medida que se perfeccionan y amplían los medios y las técnicas para averiguar lo ocurrido, mayor es la capacidad humana para negar hechos, o borrarlos, u ocultarlos, o tergiversarlos, o inventarlos, o añadirlos: para escribir historia-ficción, tanto a nivel colectivo como personal" (*El oficio* 26). Marías's dismissal of "historia-ficción" as more invention or manipulation than actuality is a topic to which he will return as he negotiates his own intermingling of history and fiction. The contemporary "era of legends" Marías identifies recalls the creation and imposition of a mythic Francoist historiography during the dictatorship. Marías makes implicit and explicit comparisons between Spain's politically contentious present and its divided past in order to draw out the dangers of repeating past mistakes.

The theme of denial and obviation to which Marías returns throughout the two years of columns collected in *El oficio de oír llover* will culminate in the false accusations the Popular Party and Aznar disseminated about the perpetrators of the Atocha attacks. Marías ponders the same issue regarding his personal life: the author returns again and again in his essays, interviews, and commentaries to the false accusations his father endured during the Spanish Civil War. In "Crímines por anticipado," written before the Atocha bombings, Marías makes a clear allusion to his father's plight. He identifies a similarity between false accusations in Spain's wartime history and a lack of verification of weapons of mass destruction in Iraq: "después de la Guerra Civil, y durante largos años, casi siempre bastaba con acusar a alguien para que en la farsa de juicio que se seguía fuera condenado ese alguien" (*El oficio* 32). The 2005 column "'Pero me acuerdo'" offers another example of Marías's preoccupation with his father's legacy. Marías revisits an article he wrote a decade earlier for *El País* in which he outlined his father's life story and aired his continued rancor toward his father's treatment in postwar Spain (*El oficio* 224–25; Marías, "El padre"). These repeated preoccupations underline Marías's identification with his father's marginalization during the dictatorship. In the contemporary era, Marías is angry at the Spanish government's duplicity, which he associates with a general disregard for historical verification in the country. The author's indignation over his father's treatment extends to his own and the Spanish population's treatment as conscientious objectors to war in a country embroiled in a diffuse terrorist threat.[9] For father and son, the truth is necessary but illusory.

Read with the benefit of hindsight, there is a sense in "Época de leyendas" that Marías can see toward the future misconduct of Spain's government after the Atocha attacks. He will ascribe this ability to be able to read "tu rostro mañana" to Jaime Deza, the protagonist and narrator of *Tu rostro mañana*. Beyond Marías's prescient abilities, however, he maintains a critical approach to the politics of truth in these columns, especially as they relate to the government's role in representing history and actuality to the Spanish populace. The author mourns the fact that readers pass over the tomes of "historiadores documentados y responsables" (*El oficio* 26) in favor of fleeting and inaccurate images in the press and on television. To Marías's mind, mass media creates "una memoria difusa y nada fiable" (*El oficio* 26) of Spanish history. It stands to reason that Marías is not interested in feeding these inaccuracies. As he dives in and out of historical context in these columns, however, it is clear that he contributes to a popular historical imagination in Spain.

Marías continues his comparisons of contemporary Spanish politics with the politics of the Civil War in the January 2004 two-part column "El país antipático" and "Y tan antipático." An American student who uncovered copies of censors' reports on Marías's first two novels, published during Franco's regime, sends them to the author. Marías interprets these reports, which bring the past to bear heavily on his own work and career, as the markers of an unfriendly—"antipático" and "tan antipático"—country. He responds to the student's inquiry by emphasizing that he was at the time ignorant of the apparatus of censorship. Yet Marías admits that, had he been privy to it, he would have despised the censorship office and all it stood for: "El régimen entero, desde Franco hasta su último censor, me parecía despreciable" (*El oficio* 159). The schism that Marías felt between himself as a young novelist and the governing forces of the dictatorship during the end of the Franco regime has arisen, once again, under Aznar's presidency. This antipathy, moreover, is based on a historical antecedent, according to Marías: "hay un poso de antipatía histórica que es fácil remover y hacer salir a la superficie" (*El oficio* 162). Marías writes that Aznar declared, when Spain entered the war in Iraq, a statement to the effect of "'España tiene que dejar de ser un país simpático'" (*El oficio* 158). Marías responds, contextualizing the present moment with the past, that "[l]os futuros gobernantes deberían recordar, además, lo peligroso que este país se torna cuando se pone de verdad antipático. Se lo puso mucho en 1936, y la odiosidad nos duró casi cuarenta años" (*El oficio* 163). The concept of the past repeating itself is clear in "Crímenes por anticipado" about false accusations, and in "Y tan antipático" when Marías applies the same idea directly to how the power divisions during and after the Spanish Civil War resonate in contemporary Spanish society. Unlike Blanco Aguinaga and Martín Gaite, Marías did not experience the war firsthand. He is thus, like Roig and others of their generation, limited to the testimony and reports of others in compiling an understanding of the war. He does so in part by reconfiguring Spain's past to explain the country's present situation.

The dividing line in the columns collected in *El oficio de oír llover* is the 2004 terrorist attacks on the Atocha train station in Madrid. This event effectively redirects Marías's general discord with the contemporary Spanish political situation to a finite moment in time: the days between March 11 and the elections on March 14. Over the course of these four days, the Spanish Minister of the Interior under the Aznar administration, Ángel Acebes, repeatedly and publicly drew suspicion toward ETA as the perpetrators of the attacks. In the weeks following the general elections on March 14, it became increasingly clear that the attacks were carried out by an Al Queda-inspired Islamic extremist terrorist cell. As we have seen, the author's initial response is as confused and inaccurate as the government's own. In a column written on March 15 and published two weeks later, Marías admits to his inability to predict the changes to his country that are bound to arise in the intervening weeks: "[E]n estos días me resulta imposible 'instalarme' en tiempo futuro tan lejano como el 28 de marzo" (*El oficio* 191). Four months later, in "Informe no solicitado sobre el jueves negro," Marías clarifies the events that transpired as he wrote the contradictory editorials for *The New York Times* and other international newspapers. By July 11, 2004, Marías had decided that he was, indeed, prescient in his assessment of the Spanish government in his March 14 column: "Lo cierto es que sólo diez días antes había yo escrito la columna... titulada 'Noventa y ocho patadas,' en la que decía del Partido Popular lo que sigue: 'Ya sabemos de qué es capaz y de qué no (lo es de mentir y despreciar a los ciudadanos, ilimitadamente)'" (*El oficio* 238). Marías's self-proclaimed ability to predict the Spanish government's future deceptions suggests that the protagonist of *Tu rostro mañana*, whose profession is, in fact, to predict the future actions of persons of interest to the British government, is an extension of the author himself. The self-referentiality in Marías's columns and novels is a connection that allows them to be read through the lens of genre fusion.

El oficio de oír llover traces the author's thought process on the nature of veracity, especially regarding Spain's political history. In a number of columns, Marías explores false accusations, political misinformation, and past atrocities doomed to repeat themselves for lack of a reliable memory, themes he will resurrect within a fictional construct in *Tu rostro mañana*. In "Época de leyendas," Marías sees historical reality pass through a series of twists and alterations before it arrives at its ultimate destination: historical fiction. But the role of the novelist who dabbles in the historical is complicated for Marías. In his column "Asesinos memos" he identifies the fiction writer as an antidote to reality, especially if that reality is an inescapable and irrational horror that consumes a nation, like the Atocha attacks: "En las temporadas trágicas uno cree entrever una razón añadida para la existencia de las ficciones: han de ser para compensar un poco la grosería y la idiotez de las realidades" (*El oficio* 203). There is fiction that provides an escape from reality, and there is fiction that tackles reality head-on. Marías, in the *Tu rostro mañana* trilogy, proves himself to be an author who writes fiction firmly located in the middle.

The doubts and digressions Marías airs in his columns and editorials spanning the Atocha attacks find their way into the thematic thread of his trilogy, as do his recurring concerns with the lingering effects of the social implications of the Spanish Civil War. The reliability of memory and the truth value afforded historical representation are also repeated thematic elements in these texts. Roig, Martín Gaite, and Blanco Aguinaga concern themselves with exacting historical details and events in their works. In his twenty-first-century blend of history and fiction, Marías utilizes an at-times abstract notion of Spain's past, through his own personal experiences and those of his characters, to understand its consequences on the Spain of today. Nevertheless, Marías proves his commitment to history in his columns. In that he self-consciously exhibits the same commitment in his fiction, these texts conjoin when analyzed through genre fusion.

Tu rostro mañana: Facing the Past

Jaime Deza[10] opens volume one of *Tu rostro mañana* by sounding an alarm to the dangers of telling: "No debería uno contar nunca nada, ni dar datos ni aportar historias ni hacer que la gente recuerde a seres que jamás han existido ni pisado la tierra o cruzado el mundo, o que sí pasaron pero estaban ya medio a salvo en el tuerto e inseguro olvido" (Marías, *Tu rostro mañana. 1* 13). Through three volumes of Deza's encounters with the risks involved in sharing experiences and revisiting the past in order to shed light on the present and the future, he arrives, at the end of the final volume of the trilogy, at the same conclusion. It turns out, however, that his mentor Peter Wheeler originally gave him this advice, and now repeats it with a caveat: "'Así es, Jacobo, uno no debería contar nunca nada… hasta que uno mismo es pasado, hasta su final'" (Marías, *Tu rostro mañana. 3* 687). Readers learn at the end of the trilogy that Deza recounts his story only once it is behind him, having moved on to another stage of his life, in a sense following his mentor's advice. Despite the risks of telling his tale, Deza does it anyway. This trilogy and the personalized account of Spanish history it provides is the result.

Recounting the untold stories or histories of people invented and real is a task that falls to both novelist and historian. These roles are often intermingled until the borders that separate them—and consequently that separate fact from fiction—become blurred. From the first lines of the novel Deza airs his ambivalence about the complicated task of historiography. Nevertheless, he will take on the role of active historiographer in the trilogy. Marías's character faces the consequences of telling—among them, treason and trauma—while at the same time combating the unstable forgetting that is a natural consequence of staying silent. In the *Tu rostro mañana* trilogy, Marías shows his commitment to Spanish history through a narrative method that self-consciously fuses historiography and fiction. He also delves into the methodology behind both genres and their reception by readers and listeners. These works, contextualized amid a contemporary urgency to recuperate and renew a collective memory of the Spanish Civil War, reveal an innovative and interdisciplinary movement toward historical engagement in twenty-first-century narrative. Examined through genre fusion, the volumes of Marías's *Tu rostro mañana* trilogy, coupled with the essays and editorials that inform them, display the urgency of a dialogue between history and fiction that attempts to negotiate historical understanding in contemporary Spain.

Marías's body of fiction has only recently begun to elicit monographic studies. Isabel Cuñado's 2004 panorama of the author's work describes Marías's recent novels as characterized by the "recuerdo explícito de la guerra civil y de la dictadura junto con el reconocimiento articulado de sus efectos en el presente" (4). The *Tu rostro mañana* trilogy goes above and beyond this "explicit memory," extending into territory normally inhabited by contemporary historiographers who seek to interpret and report on history. Deza is a Spaniard working as a translator in England while moonlighting for the clandestine forces of the MI6 overseas British intelligence agency. He has been hired to predict the future actions of suspects under surveillance. By virtue of this role, in addition to his personal drive to understand his own past and by extension his country's past, he spends the better part of *Tu rostro mañana. 1 Fiebre y lanza* amassing source material. In the context of the novel this material serves his own curiosity, but in the larger frame of Marías's trilogy it is how the reader orders scattered pieces of Spanish postwar history. Deza, as an armchair historiographer, operates within the framework of a postmodern novel to explore Spain's modern historical saga from a new vantage point. Marías, in turn, has self-consciously crossed the divide between fiction and history.

Deza's previous self-imposed exile in England, as an Oxford student, led him to his mentor, the renowned Hispanist Peter Wheeler. Years later, Wheeler spots Deza's particular gift for knowing today what "your face tomorrow" will reveal. Conversing with his mentor early in the first volume, Deza learns that Wheeler was in Spain at the time of the Spanish Civil War, and participated in the conflict. Wheeler is reluctant to reveal any more information, however. Deza, clue in hand, spends a night in Wheeler's home library, investigating his mentor's role in an event that holds a deep personal significance for Deza. Periodicals and books spread before him, Deza peruses notes Wheeler has scrawled in the margins of texts and connects the strands of history that fuse his life to his mentor's. The reader looks over Deza's shoulder as he investigates, also participating in the reordering of these historical clues.

Deza pours through historical accounts of the Spanish Civil War, examining the indices of specific volumes for mentions of Wheeler. Marías references Hugh Thomas, George Orwell, Stanley Payne, and a dozen other Civil War historians in the narration, but not Wheeler.[11] Defeated, Deza turns to another historical figure mentioned earlier in the evening's conversation: Andrés Nin. In reality, Nin was a Catalan leader of the Partido Obrero de Unificación Marxista (POUM) in Barcelona who disappeared and was presumably shot in 1937 for his anti-Stalinist involvement. Deza's research into Nin comprises over ten pages of Marías's narrative, and includes a meandering investigation into other seemingly tangential sources. For example, Deza finds a copy of Ian Fleming's James Bond novel *From Russia with Love*, with a handwritten dedication to Wheeler and more references to the POUM and Nin.[12] In a structure reminiscent of Roig's inclusion of unattributed quotations from her own historiographic work in her novel *L'hora violeta*, Marías quotes directly from Thomas. Deza reads in the historian's book: "'Así que una noche oscura... probablemente el 22 o el 23 de junio, diez miembros alemanes de las Brigadas Internacionales asaltaron la casa de Alcalá en que se hallaba retenido Nin'" (*Tu rostro mañana. 1* 148). This closely matches a sentence from Thomas's 1976 Spanish edition of *La guerra civil española*, but a reference to the original source is omitted from the narrative.[13] The novel retains its essential storytelling quality, which footnotes might interrupt with the documentary referentiality of historiography.

The Borgesian scene Marías creates in Wheeler's library is a heady collision of history and fiction. Marías sets accurate references to names, places, dates, and events that are unquestionably touchstones of the Spanish Civil War against the fictionalized figures of Wheeler and Deza, both led into labyrinthine pursuits of historical knowledge. Marías's narrative play between the two poles of reality and invention mitigates the way the reader absorbs Spanish history in the novel. At once flooded with information and sources on the Spanish Civil War, the reader is at the same

Chapter Five

time denied clear references to source material. Moreover, the novel is presented as a work of fiction. Thus it is left up to the reader to differentiate between the novel's imaginative and historical elements, a test of his or her knowledge of Spanish history. In Marías's trilogy, history and fiction do not reside in opposing poles, rather they work in conjunction to construct an intimately personal representation of historical consciousness.

Professor Sir Peter Russell dropped the surname of his father, Wheeler, after his parents' divorce. He was a renowned Hispanist at Oxford who died in 2006, and a close friend of Marías's. The author leaves little doubt that Wheeler is a fictionalized Russell, openly intercalating elements of Russell's life story into Wheeler's. Marías even includes a photograph of Russell, which Deza presents as a photograph of Wheeler, in the trilogy's third volume. Marías worked under Russell at Oxford in the mid-1980s. In Russell's obituary Alan Deyermond cautions that Russell, "like other Oxford Hispanists, is portrayed—for the most part quite unfairly—in the novels of Javier Marías, published in the 1990s (an awful warning to professors who think of appointing novelists as language assistants)" (Deyermond and Michael). Although Russell appears fictionalized in other novels by Marías, Russell's presence in *Tu rostro mañana* is, with one notable exception, more faithfully matched to his varied life experiences than in Marías's earlier novels. In response to Deyermond's critique of Marías, Ian Michael writes that Russell "was not at all displeased at being the inspiration for the leading character in four of the novels of Javier Marías" (Deyermond and Michael).[14] In fact, Michael continues, Russell "considered that Javier (elected to the Royal Spanish Academy seven days after Peter's death) had offered him literary immortality" (Deyermond and Michael). The two reactions to Russell's fictionalization in Marías's novels reflect the multiple ways the author self-consciously confuses reality and invention throughout the trilogy. Readers of *Tu rostro mañana*, including the real-life versions of those present in the novel as pseudo-fictional characters, must come to their own conclusions about where fact leaves off and fiction begins. One of these pseudo-characters is the author himself, who will also make these "fact or fiction" determinations when he theorizes about his work.

As the trilogy progresses, Wheeler's and Russell's life stories continue to run parallel to each other, though it is impossible for the reader to discern to what extent the conversations between Deza and Wheeler are invented or real. Still, in the context of a fictional novel, Marías takes liberties with such a well-known persona as Russell. In the trilogy, Wheeler has been married twice, and both wives figure prominently in Deza's narrative. In real life, however, Russell was never married. Marías has also never married, nor does he have any children. These are relevant details given the autobiographical connection between Marías and the Deza character, who is estranged from his wife, Luisa, and separated from his children. Marías is no stranger to autobiographical games between himself and his narrators. His previous novels, Manuel Alberca describes, leave readers "perplejos y vacilantes" ("Las vueltas autobiográficas" 52) as to the autobiographical identification between author and narrator. These self-referential threads, especially in the paternal relationships Deza maintains with both his father and Wheeler, are firmly rooted in a personal account of Spain's history. The intimate account of Spanish history it affords is another advantage of applying genre fusion to Marías's texts.

After Deza's digression into Andrés Nin's biography in *Tu rostro mañana. 1*, the protagonist begins to page through articles in the volumes of wartime Spanish newspapers on Wheeler's shelves. His gaze leads from references to Nin to articles his father authored. Juan Deza worked in Republican-controlled cities as a reporter, covering topics such as the renaming of Madrid's Castellana Boulevard to the "Avenue of the Proletariat Union" (Marías, *Tu rostro mañana. 1* 192). In that both are interpreters of history, there is an implicit correspondence between Deza and his father. Juan Deza observes and reports on his wartime surroundings. Jaime Deza, with the benefit of historical hindsight, contextualizes this diverse historical material (from Andrés Nin to Ian Flemming to his father's reporting), filtering it through his own personal outlook on a war he did not witness. Deza's father was witness to and victim of the war, falsely accused of running a communist newspaper by a friend whose betrayal caused Juan Deza's imprisonment. In asking his father if he had any indication that his friend was going to betray him, Jaime Deza wonders: "¿Cómo puedo no conocer hoy tu rostro mañana, el que ya está o se fragua bajo la cara que enseñas o bajo la careta que llevas, y que me mostrarás tan sólo cuando no lo espere?" (Marías, *Tu rostro mañana. 1* 199). By keeping the identity of the man who betrayed him secret and hiding his inner pain,

Juan Deza demonstrates his concern for keeping up appearances. He also draws a connection to his son who, as a prognosticator, is assigned the task of knowing today what will happen tomorrow.

Readers familiar with Marías's own family background cannot be faulted for drawing a connection from Jaime and Juan Deza to Javier Marías and his father. Julián Marías was a newspaper reporter during the Spanish Civil War. He was betrayed by a friend who falsely accused him of writing for a communist newspaper. Lucky not to have been killed for the offense, Julián was imprisoned and, once released, was unable to establish himself professionally under the Franco regime. Julián Marías eventually published again in Spain, and became a prolific author of works on Spanish philology. Nevertheless, this family trauma left an indelible mark on his son, Javier. As we have seen in his columns, Marías's sense of injustice and resentment toward his father's marginalization during the dictatorship is ever-present. In *El oficio de oír llover* he compares the false accusations that led to his father's imprisonment to the false claims of weapons of mass destruction that led to the war in Iraq (32–33). In *Tu rostro mañana* this episode of betrayal is a motivating force and thematic thread throughout the trilogy. Deza's thoughts regularly return to the treason perpetrated on his father until Juan Deza's death at the end of the third volume.[15] The autobiographical and biographical elements of *Tu rostro mañana* serve to ground the novel in historical consciousness. The stories of these "true life" characters represent Spain's contemporary movement not only to recover its past, but also to understand history as a collective personal experience, formed by memory and revealed by bearing witness.

Deza's tireless investigation into Wheeler's and his own past in *Tu rostro mañana. 1* contextualizes the return to Juan Deza's personal history in the second volume. In volume 1, Deza describes a photograph of his uncle Alfonso as a young man, which his mother kept neatly wrapped in a Republican poem. Alfonso was later killed for his involvement with the Republic. Both the photograph and a facsimile of the poem are reproduced in the novel, providing the reader with another point of confusion between the real and the invented. Elide Pittarello interprets the narrator's thoughts about the photos of his uncle as a way to "pone[r] en marcha metonímicamente una memoria autobiográfica que se descubre carente de datos" ("Haciendo tiempo" 40). Pittarello confirms that the man in the photo is Marías's uncle, "Emilio Franco, muerto en circunstancias análogas a las que se cuentan en la novela" ("Haciendo tiempo" 41).

Marías draws inspiration from his "autobiographic memory" by steeping his narrative in a prolonged intermingling of fact and fiction. The photos, artwork, and posters of political propaganda that appear in the first and third volumes of the trilogy are realia included as an integral part of the text. These artifacts ground the novels in a historical reality indistinguishable from the fictional story Marías has composed. Reproductions of political posters from the Spanish Civil War and World War II, photos of Marías's uncle and Sir Peter Russell, and a facsimile of a painting by Parmigianino hanging in the Prado Museum in Madrid are as much a part of the story as the narrative itself. They definitively connect the novels to reality, though without citations to aid the reader in making those connections. To that extent, they again recall Roig's unattributed quotations in *L'hora violeta*, while also suggesting the pages of photos, maps, and lists provided as historical evidence in *Els catalans als camps nazis*. Indeed, Marías is interested in making historical evidence work in conjunction with a fictional framework to produce a historical retelling. The author's intentionality in combining source material—real and invented, national and personal—in his text is suggestive of a drive to reinterpret history. Deza's role as historiographer to his own family history correlates with the investigations families have performed into their own past traumas in contemporary Spain. As viewed through genre fusion, Marías's texts arrive at a historical consciousness that represents an event-driven History alongside *historia*: the personal, collective history of generations of Spaniards that was omitted from Spain's official postwar history.

* * *

The historical elements of Marías's first volume, although explicit, are buried within a larger tale of intrigue and mysteriously interconnected characters. *Tu rostro mañana. 2 Baile y sueño* continues this interred history. Under layers of Deza's interrelated but chronologically disperse movements through the shadowy world of British intelligence, the protagonist's thoughts return to Wheeler and his own father. Both men, as witnesses to history, have suffered

Chapter Five

internal divisions over the act of telling that forms the conceptual base of the trilogy. Wheeler, reluctant to recount his experiences in the Spanish Civil War in the first volume, continues to fight against revealing personal memory in the second volume. He tells Deza that "'[l]a vida no es contable, y resulta extraordinario tanto empeño en relatarla… A veces pienso que más valdría abandonar la costumbre y dejar que las cosas sólo pasen" (Marías, *Tu rostro mañana. 2* 170). Juan Deza counters Wheeler's argument for abandoning the pursuit of historical consciousness, a reminder of Deza's initial warning against telling in volume 1, by finally revealing to his son the remnants of the historical memories that still plague him.

In the first volume, Jaime Deza is an amateur historiographer investigating his national and personal history. In the second volume, Deza becomes an active interpreter of his father's past. It is not, however, what Juan Deza directly witnessed that causes him pain in the present. Instead, secondhand accounts of history have deeply affected him. Juan Deza recalls to his son the violent episodes described to him or that he overheard during and just after the war. In one instance, he listens as a woman tells her friend about her role in a Republican mob that killed a wealthy couple at the outbreak of the war. The woman coldly describes having swung the couple's child against a wall like a rag doll, until she killed him (Marías, *Tu rostro mañana. 2* 300). In another example, after the war Juan Deza finds himself among a group of Francoist-sympathizer colleagues. One of them blithely brags of leading a group of Nationalist soldiers to capture a proud university student who repeatedly told them: "a él lo matábamos, y a golpes si nos venía en gana, pero que torearlo, no. 'Como que me llamo Emilio Marés, a mí no me toreáis,' insistió" (Marías, *Tu rostro mañana. 2* 318). To spite the student, this man and his fellow soldiers impaled him with banderillas as they forced other prisoners to watch and yell "olé." As Juan Deza listens in mute horror, the man describes stabbing the prisoner, shooting him, and mutilating him by cutting off one of his ears as though he were a bull. The man who participated in and then related this violent scene to Deza's father was a famous writer in Spain. Juan refuses to reveal the writer's name to Jaime, however, not wanting to defame the man's family, although decades have passed since the episode occurred. The dangers of telling in this case are personal as well as practical. Juan Deza guards the man's identity as his was left unguarded when he was betrayed. He protects himself during the dictatorship, when revealing the man's name would have been to his detriment.

Jaime Deza's interpretation of his father's lingering traumatic reaction to this secondhand testimony, which has now been passed on to his son, is that "no se recibe, no se encaja igual la información de primera mano de un desconocido—un cronista, un testigo, un locutor, un historiador—que la de quien uno lleva tratando desde que nació" (Marías, *Tu rostro mañana. 2* 313). To Jaime Deza there is a greater depth of emotion emanating from such a vivid and horrific retelling from the archives of his own family history than what he might have gleaned from reading the account in a history book or hearing it from an acquaintance. By listening to his father's traumatic past, Jaime also shares in it. Dori Laub explains that "the listener to trauma comes to be a participant and a co-owner of the traumatic event: through his very listening, he comes to partially experience trauma in himself. ... The listener, therefore, by definition partakes of the struggle of the victim with the memories and residues of his or her traumatic past" (Felman and Laub 57–58). The chain of witnesses and listeners all become co-owners of past events. Together, they compile the collective memory of silenced traumas in Spain's history.

His father warned Jaime that he'd kept these stories to himself for so long so as not to infect his son with their horrific images. Deza considers that faulting his father for recounting these experiences "'sería como reprochar a los historiadores que escriban lo que averiguan o lo que conocen de primera mano'" (Marías, *Tu rostro mañana. 2* 308–09). Indeed, the main difference between the historical imprint that characterizes these first two volumes of *Tu rostro mañana* is that volume 1 includes explicit references to historical data. Volume 2, on the other hand, relies on anecdotal evidence, what Deza and his father gain from personal discovery. Both, however, are considered source material in the kind of dynamic historiography that seeks to position historical data in the context of personal experience and testimony to construct a larger view of the historical consciousness of a population. And Deza, as his assessments of his father's testimony reveals, actively interprets both forms of historical representation throughout Marías's trilogy.

The participants, witnesses, listeners, re-tellers, and writers in volumes 1 and 2 of *Tu rostro mañana* demonstrate the process of creating historiography from multiple vantage points. These

Chapter Five

characters attempt to capture the original event as well as its representation filtered through the limits of memory and narrative reconstruction. Deza uncovers the scars the Spanish Civil War left on his family in volume 1. His role as interpreter of his father's experiences, and even of his father's once-removed interpretations of the experiences of others in volume 2, underlines the dynamic interplay between experiencing and understanding history. Marías captures this exchange in his characters' thoughts on the meanings imposed by history and their reception. These moments of historical consciousness—invented, real, and part-invention/part-reality—are embedded in a larger fictional framework. David Herzberger has commented that in *Tu rostro mañana. 1,* "Deza's task is to tell a story with an end that has yet to occur, analogous but ultimately opposed to the historian's task of emplotting time that has already passed" ("Javier Marías's *Tu rostro*" 217). However, it is clear that Deza's self-imposed task throughout the first and second volumes is, in fact, analogous to the historiographer's task of emplotting history to construct a narrative.[16]

Deza's job as a prognosticator for British intelligence and his quest to fill in historical gaps in his country's and his family's history remind us that historical representation is ever-evolving. It merges the past with how it is remembered in the present and will be told in the future. The fact that Deza is a fictional entity in a novel does not diminish the contributions of Marías's fiction to the disinterring of history. This history is located in the realm of memory and personal experience. Its authenticity, even in a fictional narrative, is left to the reader to determine. The application of genre fusion has demonstrated that both literary and historical narrative interpret the movements to recuperate and renovate a collective historical consciousness in twentieth- and twenty-first-century Spain. This process continues as Marías at last weaves together the threads begun in volumes 1 and 2 toward a conclusion in the third volume of *Tu rostro mañana.*

* * *

Ultimately, Deza's work for British intelligence becomes complicated beyond his initial function as translator and prognosticator. At the end of *Tu rostro mañana. 2,* he watches as his boss, Tupra, wields a sword to threaten and nearly behead a man for a perceived transgression. Witnessing this act of violence, Deza's tranquility and the seemingly innocent notions he held about his line of work are shattered. As *Tu rostro mañana. 3 Veneno y sombra y adiós* opens, Deza is even more embroiled in the underbelly of the MI6, forced by Tupra to watch video clips of violent scenes involving his colleagues. Paralleling the scenes of violence his father witnessed or heard in volume 1, Deza's experiences watching Tupra's actions and the violence of others on the television screen have an adverse effect on Deza's own state of being. His work with the MI6 was once grounded in abstract notions of future actions, but is now grounded in visceral and actual violent experiences. This change leads him to harbor violent thoughts that would have been foreign to Deza in the first two volumes of the trilogy. On a return trip to Madrid, he confronts his wife's lover, Custardoy,[17] who has attacked Deza's wife. He threatens Custardoy with a Civil War–era pistol, then cuts and crushes one of the man's hands with a fireplace utensil. The pistol's origin in the Civil War and Deza's disfiguring attack on Custardoy draw a direct comparison with the violent episode between Emilio Marés and his would-be *torero* attackers narrated in volume 2. Much as Marías emphasizes in his columns, these details underline an unchecked history doomed to repeat itself. The Spanish Civil War has become the original trauma through which Spain's present social and political ills are read.

As Deza narrates this series of incidents, he builds the interconnections that will lead to the trilogy's climax. Yet another occurrence will turn Wheeler's warning about the dangers of telling into a core reason why Deza leaves the MI6 intelligence group. Deza is tasked with predicting the future actions of a fame-obsessed rock star, whom Deza identifies by the pseudonym Dick Dearlove. Deza marks Dearlove as someone who "a lo mejor cometería un día una barbaridad para que al menos se lo recordase por ella" (Marías, *Tu rostro mañana. 3* 259). When the news reaches Deza on his return from Madrid that Dearlove has killed a young man under suspicious circumstances, Deza fears that the scenario he predicted has comes to pass. However, given what he has witnessed of Tupra's violent tendencies, Deza suspects that his intelligence group is involved, and most likely organized the homicide. His father, steadily declining in health when Deza visits him for what will be the last time in Madrid, told him: "de lo que estoy más contento, Jacobo, es de que nadie haya muerto nunca por lo

Chapter Five

que yo haya dicho o contado" (Marías, *Tu rostro mañana. 3* 521). Deza considers himself at fault for the death of the young man. He looks to his father as his role model, and realizes that his legacy is in jeopardy if he remains with MI6. In a sense, Deza has betrayed himself the way his father was betrayed.

As he contemplates his tenure with British intelligence, Deza relates his profession to that of a novelist who controls his characters. His time with the group is absorbed:

> [D]iciendo quién era de fiar y quién no, quién mataría y quién se dejaría matar y por qué, quién traicionaría y quién sería leal, quién mentía y a quién le iba a ir mal o regular en la vida, quién me reventaba o me daba lástima, quién fingía o me caía en gracia, y qué probabilidades llevaba cada individuo en el interior de sus venas, igual que un novelista que sabe que lo que diga o cuente de sus personajes, o les atribuya o les haga hacer, no saldrá de su novela y no hará daño a nadie, porque por mucho que se los sienta vivos seguirán siendo ficción y nunca interferirán con ningún ser real. ... Pero no era este mi caso, no escribía yo nada con tinta y papel sobre quienes jamás han existido ni pisado la tierra o cruzado el mundo, sino que describía y desciframa a personas de carne y hueso… (Marías, *Tu rostro mañana. 3* 550)

The essential difference between Deza's work and that of a novelist hinges on control. According to Deza, the novelist controls the actions of his characters, and those actions do not cross the boundary between the invented and the real. As a prognosticator, however, Deza's work for British intelligence denies him any control over the past, present, or future actions of his subjects. Still, there is a strong identification between Deza and Marías throughout the trilogy, with Deza's trajectory in part following Marías's in a fictional setting, much like "C." and Martín Gaite in *El cuarto de atrás*. Within this identification between author and character lies the inherent contradiction evident in Deza's assertion that he, unlike a novelist, describes people of flesh and blood: Marías includes actual figures in his trilogy. Some are stand-ins for real people, like Jaime Deza as a surrogate for Marías's father, Julián. Others have been altered ever-so-slightly from their real-life counterparts, like Peter Wheeler. Still others are alive and well, and included without pseudonyms as characters in the novels. The imposing figure of the Spanish philologist Francisco Rico, for instance, makes an appearance as himself in *Tu rostro mañana. 3*. To this end, the real is very much alive in the pages of Marías's trilogy, though, as Deza points out, even characters based on real people have a limited capacity to influence the world outside the novel. This hybridization of the real and the invented pulls Marías's blurring of fiction and history into new realms. Not only do his works of fiction overlap with his nonfiction columns thematically, he also expressly blends fiction and historiography in his trilogy.

* * *

Marías wonders, in a lecture given at his induction into the Real Academia Española, about the effect of including representations of the real in a novel—and especially of real individuals—on the reading public's perception of history. Will a fictionalized representation, over the course of time, come to supplant a real person? In his speech, Marías admits to having fictionalized his father, Peter Russell, and Francisco Rico in *Tu rostro mañana*. He questions the effect that a character based on his father will have for his actual father's legacy:

> El recuerdo de mi padre está aún fresco en la memoria de cuantos lo tratamos, incluidos ustedes en su mayoría. Pero alguno de mis hermanos ya prevé, o no sé si teme, que tal vez, de aquí a unos años…, para quienes no lo han conocido lo que más quede de él no sea él, sino su trasunto literario, con el que, de suceder así, ya no sé si le habría hecho un favor o causado un perjuicio. ("Sobre la dificultad de contar" 35)

The concern Marías and Deza have for the deleterious effect of fictionalizing actual figures on their standing in the historical record is only one of the ways Marías plays with history and fiction. The author questions the divide between the two genres, and therefore between what can be predicted, versus what is based on pure invention composed to mimic the real. However, the real Francisco Rico gets his opportunity to reply to Marías's doubts when he gives the response to the author's induction lecture. Discussing the relationship of the author's fiction to reality, Rico contends that it is possible that "el ficticio narrador de [Javier Marías] acabaría por ser más verdadero que el [Javier Marías] real, hasta transfigurar la biografía del [Javier Marías] real, reteniendo los datos del narrador

Chapter Five

que lo muestran a una luz más favorable" (Marías "Sobre la dificultad" 51). Rico identifies this *esperpéntico* outcome of character/narrator overtaking author as a consequence of Marías's manipulation of reality. Nevertheless, in Rico's opinion, Marías's novels "se nutre[n] de hechos que inevitablemente remiten a una cierta especie de realidad" (Marías, "Sobre la dificultad" 52), even as Marías labors to confuse the borders between invention and actuality or ignore their mutual influence.

This divide between the real and the invented arises again in *Tu rostro mañana. 3* when Deza speaks with a colleague who has advised him in the past. She tells him that "preocuparse por lo que pasaba con nuestros informes era como si un novelista se preocupara por los compradores y lectores posibles de su libro, por lo que entendieran y sacaran de él" (Marías, *Tu rostro mañana. 3* 560). Deza rejects the comparison between intelligence agent and novelista, arguing that "el novelista, en todo caso, podría preocuparse por lo que mete en su libro, ¿no?" (Marías, *Tu rostro mañana. 3* 560). Deza has little control over the "characters" he examines in his intelligence reports. Furthermore, as is evident in his speech to the Real Academia Española, Marías is an author concerned with how his readers will interpret his novel. Will they come to know his father as a partially invented character instead of the man he really was? This multifaceted debate in the pages of *Tu rostro mañana* and in Marías's editorials, columns, and speech, serves to prove the self-conscious blurring of history and fiction the author incorporates into and then questions in his work. The reader attempts to predict what Deza and Marías are capable of: what are their intentions, what are the meanings behind their actions, what will they do next, are they telling the truth? But, as Deza knows all too well, these predictions can be both accurate and dangerous. The muddling of reality and fiction is well ingrained not only in the texts themselves, but also in the underlying theme behind them. The reader will never know "your face tomorrow," that is, what is true and what is invented. In this sense Marías picks up an issue one of the deportees in Roig's work on Catalans in Nazi camps raised, as discussed in Chapter 2. The man who told Roig that she would never know the truth seems to share a belief with Marías that the historical cannot be distilled to an absolute truth, and certainly not in an atmosphere characterized by genre fusion in which both history and fiction together function to fill in gaps in collective memory.

Marías brings his trilogy full circle with Deza's final visit with Wheeler before the latter's death. As in volume 1, Deza's interactions with Wheeler raise historical questions for both character and reader. Marías splices together the real and invented sources of this seemingly fictional interaction to arrive at a disorienting blend of fiction and history. The astute reader's first indication that Deza has returned to his role as popular historiographer is the book he gives Wheeler: *La Guerra Civil en dos mil carteles*. In reality, this is a two-volume work published in 1997 containing Spanish Civil War posters along with some examples of British propaganda posters from World War II (Carulla and Carulla). The posters Deza and Wheeler discuss treat the message of "careless talk," the focus of the conversation Wheeler and Deza had in the first volume of the trilogy, and are reproduced in the novel. Unlike the conversations between Wheeler and Deza in the first two volumes, however, in this third volume, when Deza presses Wheeler on the details of his time in Spain during the Civil War, Wheeler finally relents. He speaks about the intersections between his life story and the history of Spain in great detail. His confessions confirm the identification between Sir Peter Russell and his alter-ego, Sir Peter Wheeler, and also demonstrate a commonality between Wheeler and Deza's father. Wheeler describes going to Spain in the late-1930s with "the Red Dean" or "el bandido Deán de Canterbury" (Marías, *Tu rostro mañana. 3* 588). Deza realizes this was one of the people with whom his father was accused of associating, resulting in his denunciation and imprisonment in 1939. Acting as a spy for British intelligence, Wheeler passed through Spain twice during the war. While taking photos of one of the Spanish armada ships, he was captured by Francoist troops who accused him of espionage. Had it not been for Franco's intervention, he might have been executed. Wheeler demonstrates his supposed loyalty to the dictator by recalling that he attended a Hitler Youth Camp in Bavaria in 1935, which saves him from imprisonment. He tells Deza: "'Así que ya ves, pese a lo nefasto que fue para la historia de tu país y de tantísima gente, para la mía personal Franco resultó decisivo'" (Marías, *Tu rostro mañana. 3* 594). Wheeler's story shows the interpretive process of history, how it changes depending on personal vantage point. A man who caused the forty-year oppression of an entire society is, for one individual, a savior. This minute detail expands the reader's historical perspective, even as it is represented in a work of fiction.

Chapter Five

Wheeler was, however, expelled from Spain. Considering his unlikely salvation at the hands of Franco, he thinks aloud to Deza: "'a mí mismo me parecen ficticios, o casi fantasiosos, episodios que yo he vivido'" (Marías, *Tu rostro mañana. 3* 594). The tales Wheeler relates to Deza in the final moments of the third volume of *Tu rostro mañana* are anything but fictitious. They do, however, reveal the proximity between history and fiction in Marías's novel. Wheeler continues to disclose details that connect him to touchstone historical moments and to his real-life alter-ego, consequently connecting the novel to the specifics of history. Wheeler's experience at the bombardment of Durango, accompanying the British Naval officer Alan Hillgarth across Spain, providing safe passage for the Dukes of Windsor, and his possession of Ian Flemming's passport from 1941 that finally explains why Flemming dedicated a book to Wheeler in volume 1, all serve to ground *Tu rostro mañana* in an unmistakable historical reality. There is no question that Wheeler is a representation of Sir Peter Russell, down to the telltale scar on Russell's chin in the reproduced photograph (Marías, *Tu rostro mañana. 3* 686), and the shared biography from which Wheeler's accounts clearly derive.[18] Marías intentionally confuses the real and the fictional in the novel, leaving it up to the reader to judge which is which.

Wheeler has warned Deza consistently since volume 1 about the consequence of telling. In the last volume, Wheeler relates a harrowing tale of betrayal involving his first wife, Valerie, and her work with the Political Warfare Executive (PWE), a British intelligence group during World War II. As in other accounts attributed to Wheeler, Marías flashes between fact and fiction. He draws out a story in which Valerie revealed a German friend's Jewish ancestry to the PWE. This information found its way to the Germans and led to the extermination of the majority of the friend's family and, ultimately, to Valerie's guilt-ridden suicide. In the opening pages of the first volume of *Tu rostro mañana*, well before Deza tells any of his convoluted tale, he concludes: "No, yo no debería contar ni oír nada, porque nunca estará en mi mano que no se repita y se afee en mi contra, para perderme, o aún peor, que no se repita y se afee en contra de quienes yo bien quiero, para condenarlos" (Marías, *Tu rostro mañana. 1* 15). The consequences of telling cause a chain reaction effect on characters well removed from the individual who does the revealing: from Juan Deza's betrayal affecting his family, to Dick Dearlove's homicide affecting the members of the MI6 group, to the deaths of a German family affecting Valerie Wheeler, to Valerie Wheeler's suicide affecting Peter Wheeler. This cycle of cause and effect also extends to the historical context to which the novels make reference: secondhand tales of pervasive violence of the Spanish Civil War, Julián Marías's false imprisonment, and Sir Peter Russell's involvement in clandestine operations in Spain. All have wide-ranging effects on individuals and the collective to which they belong. Yet the dangers of telling do not hamper any of these characters, or Marías himself, from recounting their stories. The author fits them together under common experiences and themes, and continues to attempt to know today what will happen tomorrow.

In his 2008 speech to the Real Academia Española, Marías grapples with the inherent gaps between reality and its representation. The author is critical of the transformations subjected to historical truth when it is represented textually. Nevertheless, Marías uses this process to convert history into a form of narrative historiography in his columns and into a form of historical fiction in his novels. For Marías, "contar, narrar, relatar es imposible, sobre todo si se trata de hechos ciertos, de cosas en verdad acaecidas" ("Sobre la dificultad de contar" 10). The moment words intervene in the telling of facts or events, language irretrievably changes them, lending what happened "un principio y un fin artificiales, que quedan al siempre discutible criterio del relator, él los establece. Inevitablemente se introduce un punto de vista y por lo tanto una subjetividad" (Marías, "Sobre la dificultad de contar" 10). In essence, Marías discusses writing history into narrative historiography. The task of the historiographer is to give history a beginning and an end, to lend it narrative cohesion and subjectivity. Marías thinks these transformations distance the narrative from an ultimate truth, in that giving one witness the task of representing multiple viewpoints acts to the exclusion of a single, unified historical veracity. However, he also disparages the role of the "teller," often a writer like himself, who exacts a control over his text. This process is tantamount to the control Marías's fictional counterpart, Deza, describes in the relationship between novelist and characters. Marías concludes that it is impossible "contar nada acaecido, real, de manera absolutamente segura, veraz, objetiva, completa y definitiva" ("Sobre la dificultad de contar" 20). Historiographers and storytellers—indeed, any writer—take so-called truths that are difficult if not impossible to prove as a point of departure. They must necessarily contextualize and personalize them such that the end result is not a chronology of events nor a list of facts but rather a narrative historiography.

However, where Marías identifies an incompleteness, due to a loss of the objective truth, there is also a completeness. Those who write with history as a focal point correct, add, and revise history, incorporating other perspectives and details that were intentionally excluded or unintentionally omitted by the chroniclers who came before them. Scholars such as Herzberger, Michael Ugarte, Hayden White, and Paul Ricoeur have argued that a singular, definitive historical truth is so elusive as to perhaps not exist. History must pass through a narrative or nonnarrative filter. Narrative historiography is one of various generic results from the filtering of history. In it, the task of proving the "truth" of the historical starting point takes a back seat to the often personal, subjective, and engaging interpretation of history. Marías may read these resulting texts as "cojos, incompletos, ... [y] parciales" ("Sobre la dificultad de contar" 27), yet they can be interpreted as personalized, nuanced, detailed, and complete given the task of representing history according to the particular structure that the texts themselves identify as their organizing conceit. For Roig, that structure is the testimony of Catalan survivors of Nazi concentration camps. For Martín Gaite, it is the adolescent experiences of young Spanish women. For Blanco Aguinaga, it is the Spanish exile's lifelong navigation of his identity in Mexico. And for Marías, as we have observed through genre fusion in his columns and the *Tu rostro mañana* trilogy, that structure is a modern Spanish society that looks to its past to explain its present and predict its future.

Marías works with history in a way that differentiates him from his predecessors. His editorial columns are not, strictly speaking, historiographies. His trilogy of novels expands beyond the traditional understanding of historical fiction. Instead, he makes both of these genres into hybrids by interspersing Spanish history with opinion, suspense, fiction, theoretical musings, and criticism. His goal, nevertheless, is to make history personal, to tell the silenced stories of the past. He proves that the Spanish Civil War and postwar are relevant even in a contemporary world facing seemingly unrelated problems. Genre fusion is particularly suited to this goal because it erases boundaries. The border between history and fiction dissolves when genre fusion is applied; so do the borders between the past and the present, between the individual and the collective, between the margins and the center. Approaching these texts through genre fusion allows authors and readers to make connections that are not apparent when one observes strict divisions between genres, time periods, and individuals. A collective society expresses its history with a multitude of voices and contexts.

After decades of novels with little or no interest in Spain's past, Marías steeps the three volumes of *Tu rostro mañana* in a personalized account of his country's history, inspired by the life stories of his father and his mentor. Marías's blurring of history and fiction is bound together by the themes of deception and veracity in Spain from the Civil War to the present day. He succeeds in knitting these diverse time periods together in his fiction and nonfiction by looking beyond their temporal boundaries. He also steps back from the process of creating overlapping history and fiction to think about its risks and rewards. Genre fusion is a model for how to grasp the relevance of these innovative narrative practices in twenty-first-century Spanish literature to Spain's evolving historical memory.

Afterword

In his influential examination of the social and historical conditions that gave rise to the historical novel, Georg Lukács describes the power of a "real mass movement" to influence the way people view and lend importance to history. "The appeal to national independence and national character," Lukács writes, "is necessarily connected with a re-awakening of national history, with memories of the past, of past greatness, of moments of national dishonour, whether this results in a progressive or reactionary ideology" (25). Although Lukács's observations are trained on early nineteenth-century movements in Europe, they are equally applicable to the re-emergence of the cultural force of uncensored history in Spain after Franco's death. To Montserrat Roig, Carmen Martín Gaite, Carlos Blanco Aguinaga, and Javier Marías, the Franco dictatorship was a forty-year "moment of national dishonor." Its termination sparked a return to a past that had been publicly overlooked during the postwar years. This moment of transition and the decades that followed it inspired a re-examination of history and a progressive literary agenda, combining to form a dual gaze forward and backward in time.

The works of Roig, Martín Gaite, Blanco Aguinaga, and Marías are products of the social transformations brought about by the end of the dictatorship. They are inspired by the inequalities between the Castilian, Catholic, conservative, patriarchal institutions whose values Franco embodied and upheld, and marginalized sectors of Spanish society whose freedom of expression was curtailed by those institutions. These texts are part of a literary and historical "re-awakening" described by Lukács. But Spain's post-Franco historical revision also transformed its conception of nation and nationality. Spanish writers and readers began to welcome the varied sectors of society that have always constituted the country's population—though at any given time they may not have been viewed as integral cultural influences—back into the fold of a more united, ethnically and politically diverse nation over the course of Spain's transition to democracy. The evidence of a return to history in post-dictatorship Spain is borne out in the country's new historical novels and new narrative historiography. Both genres are concerned with the plight of those whose stories were formerly barred from the historical record. The conflict between those marginalized by the Franco dictatorship and their oppressors inspires a new way of seeing and representing the experiences of history in literature.

Roig, Martín Gaite, Blanco Aguinaga, and Marías are unconfined by traditional divisions of genre as a means of facing history. A genre fusion reading is latent in their paired texts. Until now, however, this method of reading through genre fusion has neither been identified nor articulated as a way to understand their contributions to Spain's historical memory. By looking through a lens of genre fusion at their texts, we can see that these authors combine fiction and historiography with the ultimate goal of reimagining the historical condition of marginalized Spaniards like themselves during and after Spain's postwar years. Their body of work presents untold stories and histories, open to the interpretation and personal understanding of both author and reading public. Polemical factors like historical accuracy, subjectivity, and imaginative liberties do not detract from the blending of historical fiction and narrative historiography that allows genre fusion to draw out a more inclusive representation of history from these authors' texts.

By analyzing the works of Spanish literature included in this study through the original theory of genre fusion, it becomes apparent how they contribute to the larger history/fiction debate discussed by contemporary theorists in relation to other national literatures. Genre fusion illuminates exemplary material, extracted from the seldom-mined world of contemporary Spanish letters, that seeks to understand and explain the same overarching question with which historical and narrative theorists and critics grapple: How can readers interpret the dynamic interaction between fiction and history? Roig's sagas of Catalans in Barcelona and in Nazi camps, Martín Gaite's tales of postwar adolescence and post-Franco adulthood, Blanco Aguinaga's stories of Spanish exiles in Mexico and in crisis, and Marías's epic drama and editorials of a relentlessly returning Civil War past, interpreted through genre fusion, propose fresh elucidations to this question. For one, readers and scholars are afforded a measure of interpretive control when they use genre fusion, in that this theory breaks down the traditional barrier separating these epistemological categories. Fiction and history, through the genre fusion model, work together to fill in the gaps left by either genre in isolation. The reader has the authority to decide to what extent truth and accuracy alter the historical landscape of works read through genre fusion. Nevertheless, genre fusion demonstrates the depth of historical understanding manifested when an author's historical and fictional oeuvre is examined in conjunction.

New generations of Spanish writers continue to straddle the nebulous border between history and fiction. Although the passage of time has dulled a once-urgent sense of injustice associated with the Franco regime and its treatment of those on the margins, contemporary Spanish authors maintain a committed interest in refining Spanish history through their literature. Genre fusion demonstrates the central role of Spanish literature in the formation of a non-exclusionary historical consciousness. It draws attention to the writing of an "unofficial" history of marginalized populations in Spanish fiction and historiography today, as the country enjoys a period of unadulterated democracy. Transition-era authors like Roig, Martín Gaite, and Blanco Aguinaga have influenced innovative Spanish authors such as Marías, but these twenty-first-century writers are also unique from their predecessors. Genre fusion actualizes the next transformative chapter in the literature to rise from the ashes of the Franco dictatorship and from Spain's twentieth-century democratic rebirth. The intermingling of fiction and history is now ingrained in Spanish culture at the beginning of the twenty-first century. Genre fusion recognizes these new intergeneric texts as foundational and motivating elements in a present-day Spanish historical memory renaissance.

Notes

Chapter One
Introduction: Origins of Genre Fusion in Spain

1. The public outcry over the fictional elements in James Frey's supposedly nonfiction memoir, *A Million Little Pieces,* versus the popularity of Isabel Wilkerson's *The Warmth of Other Suns,* a narrative history of African American migration that reads like a novel, are just two examples.

2. There is no universally agreed upon end date for the Transition, although the 1982 general elections mark a pivotal moment when Spain fully entered into a democratic era.

3. Many other populations resided on the periphery of a stratified dictatorship-era Spanish society by virtue of their economic standing, religious beliefs, and level of education, among other factors. These "fringe" collectives would, under a representative Spanish government, most certainly have remained contributing members of the country's social and political movements. Under Franco, they were denied these participatory powers.

4. The official title of the law is "LEY 52/2007, de 26 de diciembre, por la que se reconocen y amplían derechos y se establecen medidas en favor de quienes padecieron persecución o violencia durante la Guerra Civil y la Dictadura," but it has come to be known as the "Ley de Memoria Histórica" in Spain.

5. Translated as both the "Association for the Recuperation of Historical Memory" and the "Association for the Recovery of Historical Memory."

6. See Faber, "The Price of Peace" 1–5, and Jerez Farrán and Amago 1–6.

7. It is worth noting that our understanding of the "historical novel" is based less on notions of the nineteenth-century nation-building historical fiction—embodied by the work of Benito Pérez Galdós in Spain—than on a more inclusive category of fiction broadly related to historical reality.

8. For example, Gerald Prince's definition of *story*, which is his de facto definition of *fiction*, does not include stylistic or discursive elements of the genre. Instead, its primary description is as "the content plane of narrative" (93).

9. These broad definitions are supported by the Oxford English Dictionary, which defines *history* as "the branch of knowledge which deals with past events; the formal record or study of past events, esp. human affairs." *Historiography* is defined simply as "the writing of history."

10. *Testimony* will be further theorized in Chapter 2.

11. The distinctions I draw between narrative and non-narrative historical representation are influenced by Hayden White's discussion of this topic in "The Value of Narrativity in the Representation of Reality" in *Content* 1–25.

12. Geoffrey Roberts provides a thorough summary of "The History and Narrative Debate, 1960–2000" in *The History and Narrative Reader* 1–21, while the excerpts Keith Jenkins includes in the section on "Debates from the

Journals" is also a useful orientation to the topic in *The Postmodern History Reader* 237–383.

13. Andrew P. Norman defends White's argument while summarizing the major criticism against it in "Telling It Like It Was" 119–28.

14. This digest of the New Historicists is centered on the project's basic tenets as outlined by H. Aram Veeser in his introduction to *The New Historicism* xi and not on the many ways Gallagher and Greenblatt's original formulation has been reconfigured and redefined by subsequent theorists.

15. A non-exhaustive list of this kind of new genre-centric criticism of the post-Franco Spanish novel includes Holloway, *El posmodernismo*; Spires, *Post-Totalitarian Spanish Fiction*; Asís Garrote, *Última hora*; Brownlow and Kronik, *Intertextual Pursuits*; and Langa Pizarro, *Del franquismo a la postmodernidad: la novela española*.

16. Gonzalo Sobejano and Luís Beltrán Almería are among the few Spanish scholars to explicitly engage with the New Historicist approach in their literary criticism. See Sobejano, "The Testimonial Novel and the Novel of Memory" in Turner 172–92, and Beltrán Almería, "Hispanism and New Historicism" in Epps and Fernández Cifuentes 270–81.

17. See also Herzberger, *Narrating the Past;* and Labanyi, *Myth and History*.

18. See Vilarós, "The Novel"; Spires, *Post-Totalitarian Spanish Fiction*; and Sobejano, "The Testimonial Novel."

19. Kathryn Everly compares the two texts thematically in her chapter on "The Impossible Invention of History and the Hero in Javier Cercas's *Soldados de Salamina* and *La velocidad de la luz*" in *History, Violence, and the Hyperreal* 85–109.

Chapter Two
Montserrat Roig: Testimony of the Marginalized Catalan

1. This testimony, along with Burgos-Debray's English introduction and interpretation, is the core of Menchú, forms the backbone of Gugelberger and Jara and Vidal, and is the main focus in Beverley.

2. See Asís Garrote 24–81; and Soldevila Durante 353–68.

3. The trilogy is comprised of *Historia de una maestra, Mujeres de negro,* and *La fuerza del destino*.

4. Unless otherwise indicated, all English translations of Catalan quotations are my own.

5. In an interview with Geraldine Cleary Nichols, Roig states: "he pertenecido a una familia muy catalana en donde desde los cuatro años he leído en catalán" (147), while the author discusses her Catalan literary language in the essay "Un teló de vellut negre" in *Digues que m'estimes* 33–44.

6. The "Law of Linguistic Normalization" was passed in 1983, and was based on an earlier 1980 governmental definition of Catalan identity (Vilarós, "A Cultural Mapping" 39).

7. The nonfiction Roig published during her lifetime encompasses *Los hechiceros* (1975); *Retrats parallels* (1975); *Els catalans als camps nazis* (1977);

¿Tiempo de mujer? (1980); *Mujeres en busca de un nuevo humanismo* (1981); *Mi viaje al bloqueo: 900 días de la lucha heróica de Leningrado* (1982); and *L'agulla daurada* (1985).

8. Roig's narrative work includes the essay collections *Digues que m'estimes* (1991) and *Un pensament de sal, un pessic de pebre* (1992); the volumes of short stories *Molta roba i poc sabó... i tan neta que la volen* (1971) and *El cant de la joventut* (1989); the novelistic trilogy of the Miralpeix and Ventura-Claret families, *Ramona, adéu* (1972), *El temps de les cireres* (1977), and *L'hora violeta* (1980); and the novels *L'òpera quotidiana* (1985) and *La veu melodiosa* (1987).

9. Biruté Ciplijauskaité and Monica Szurmuk make only passing references to Roig's historiography in their studies.

10. There are many primarily feminist readings of *L'hora violeta*, for instance: Hart 107–15; Ballesteros; Davies; and Hurtley's introductory study in Roig, *La hora violeta* 7–30.

11. See, for example, Dupláa's "Testimony and Cultural Memory."

12. A number of scholars have addressed the overlapping between the two texts in these limited terms. See Nieva de la Paz; Szurmuk; Walters; Glenn, "First Person Singular;" Bellver; and Ferrán 210.

13. London also became a public face associated with *Els catalans als camps nazis* upon its publication, in an emotional unveiling of the text in Barcelona surrounded by other former deportees. See "Artur London: amor a Catalunya."

14. Though, as Dupláa notes, Roig began working on *Els catalans* in 1973 at the behest of Josep Benet, it was not until the death of Franco that the book could be published. See Dupláa, "El testimoni i la recuperació de la memoria" 142n6.

15. For a discussion of previously published accounts, see Alfaya 89–120 and Brenneis 59–60. Roig also cites many of these texts in her footnotes and in the quotes that form the epigraphs to each section of *Els catalans*.

16. The testimonial novel *K. L. Reich* by Joaquim Amat-Piniella is another work that Roig mentions as having led her to the topic, by an author to whom Roig dedicates her study.

17. Their accuracy can be judged by comparison to other historical accounts of the Spaniards in Mauthausen, including those by Le Chène, Pike, and Toran, as well as to numerous memoirs authored by Mauthausen survivors in the 1990s and early 2000s.

18. "Actual historical events" refers to those occurrences that are beyond debate: the Spanish Civil War, Spanish Republican exile in France, the Holocaust, World War II, the liberation of the Nazi concentration camps, etc. "Historiography" here is both the writing of this lowercase objective history of events and people, and the self-conscious, more subjective examination of the discursive process of transforming "history" into "historiography."

19. The majority of these documents, lists, and photographs are not included in the Castilian translation of the text, nor is the first section on the prisoners' initial deportation to French camps, suggesting the added importance of historical documentation as a means of recovering a marginalized Catalan collective memory in the original publication. See Roig, *Noche y niebla*.

20. Indeed, Picornell Belenguer calls *Els catalans* a subjective history book, but cites the difficulty of analyzing the narrative and testimonial strategies of a volume with such an emotional subject matter as a rationale for avoiding a more in-depth examination of its historical qualities: "La veritat és que es fa difícil fins i tot aproximar-se críticament a una obra d'aquestes característiques, amb la por que qualsevol explicitació dels mètodes que utilitza per autoritzar-se puqui ser malentesa com una voluntat de desconstrucció dels seus efectes documentals" ("The truth is that it becomes difficult even to approach critically a work with these characteristics, with the fear that whatever explanation of methods that one uses to authorize oneself could be misunderstood as the intention to deconstruct its documentary effects," 175).

21. White discusses the theme of historical accuracy in terms of "revisionist" historians who argue that the Holocaust never occurred in "The Politics of Historical Interpretation: Discipline and De-Sublimation," in *Content* 58–82.

22. Illustrating this point, after a talk on memory, the Latin American scholar Beatriz Sarlo responded to a question by a witness to the Argentine dictatorship as to whether her testimony was "the truth" by stating that neither she nor the witness herself knew if her testimony was the truth.

23. See Armengou and Belis; Salvadó i Valentines; Serrano i Blanquer; and Pagès and Casas.

24. See "On the Collapse of the Upper Case and Collateral Damage" in Jenkins 7–21 for a detailed discussion of the differences between "history" and "History." It is also important to note that *historia* means both "history" and "story" in Spanish. Oftentimes, writers will differentiate between the two meanings by capitalizing *Historia* in order to emphasize its significance as "history."

25. In a Borgesian spin to the doubling of Roig, later in the novel Norma will reveal that three years have passed since she published her work on Catalans in Nazi concentration camps, the same three years that have passed between Roig's publication of *Els catalans* and the novel in which Norma is a protagonist, *L'hora violeta*.

26. Evoking the criticism of New Historicism as "history without footnotes," in Thomas 187.

Chapter Three
Carmen Martín Gaite: Rewriting Spain's Memory

1. The 2011 election of Mariano Rajoy, head of the conservative Partido Popular and outspoken opponent of the Law of Historical Memory, in effect ended Spain's governmental efforts toward recuperating historical memory. Rajoy closed the Office of Victims of the Civil War and Dictatorship in February 2012. Popular organizations such as the Asociación para la Recu-

peración de la Memoria Histórica and the Federación Estatal de Foros por la Memoria have continued to operate.

2. Only Martín Gaite's work is examined explicitly in Colmeiro's study.

3. Eloy E. Merino and H. Rosi Song concur, exploring these "remnants" of Francoist ideology in contemporary Spain in *Traces of Contamination* 12. They argue that, for writers sympathetic to the left, the traces of Franco's ideology are visible in their texts through the experiences and treatment of marginalized figures.

4. Josefina Aldecoa coined the term *niños de la guerra* in her volume of the same name to describe children born between 1925 and 1928 who were from eight to eleven years of age when the Spanish Civil War began.

5. The autobiographical sketch included in Martín Gaite, *Agua pasada* 11–25, and translated in Brown, *Secrets from the Back Room* 20–34, is considered authoritative. See also Jurado Morales, *La trayectoria narrativa* 477–78 for a selection of published interviews with Martín Gaite.

6. These essays, among many others, are collected in Martín Gaite, *La búsqueda de interlocutor* (1973); *El cuento de nunca acabar: apuntes sobre la narración, el amor y la mentira* (1983); *Agua pasada: artículos, prólogos y discursos* (1993); and *Pido la palabra* (2002). Diary fragments and other writings can be found in Martín Gaite and Calvi, *Cuadernos de todo* (2002).

7. For a thorough bibliography on works by and about Martín Gaite, see Jurado Morales, *La trayectoria narrativa*. See also Jurado Morales, "La mirada ajena" for a discussion of the trajectory of critical material on the author.

8. This type of obliquely historical approach to the novel is evident in a long list of interpretative articles, such as Valverde Velasco and Álamo Felices; Chown; Nieva de la Paz; Pittarello, "Artesanías autógrafas"; Spires, "Intertextuality"; Glenn, "*El cuarto de atrás*;" and Carbayo Abengózar.

9. Although other scholars have provided nuanced readings of both of these texts, they stop short of a close analysis of them as overlapping texts. Concha Alborg aligns the two texts around their common autobiographical representation of the author, while Stephanie Anne Sieburth provides an insightful historical and cultural reading of *El cuarto de atrás* but only alludes to the novel's greater connection with *Usos amorosos de la postguerra* in the fifth chapter of *Inventing High and Low* 188–204.

10. See especially "The Politics of Historical Interpretation: Discipline and De-Sublimation" in White, *Content* 58–82.

11. And, as Brown has pointed out, live in the same apartment (*Secrets* 151n3).

12. Although she doesn't reveal C.'s first name, Martín Gaite does make one reference to the protagonist's last name: "Martín Gaite" (*El cuarto* 145).

13. Martín Gaite traveled to Coimbra, Portugal, in 1946 on a university scholarship (Brown, *Secrets* 198; Martín Gaite, *Agua pasada* 17).

14. The direct quote of the first line of *El balneario*—"Hemos llegado esta tarde, después de varias horas de autobús"—in the novel also confirms C.'s identification with Martín Gaite, much as Norma's revelation that she wrote a book on Catalans in Nazi camps directly links her to Montserrat Roig in

L'hora violeta, as discussed in Chapter 2 (Martín Gaite, *El balneario* 5; *El cuarto* 47).

15. The Sección Femenina, headed by Pilar Primo de Rivera and controlled by the Franco regime, managed young women's Social Service obligations during the postwar, with classes on domestic activities, gymnastics, and modes of comportment for girls.

16. In the autobiographical sketch included in *Agua pasada*, Martín Gaite draws the direct connection between C. and herself, when she writes: "De mi tío Joaquín... y de la influencia que tuvo en mi infancia he hablado también en '*El cuarto de atrás*'" (15), also relating her friendship with a girl whose parents were jailed teachers with whom she invented the island of Bergai, admitting that "[t]odo esto lo he contado en *El cuarto de atrás*" (16).

17. This can be attributed, in part, to the volume's blended genres. Both Robert C. Spires and Constance Sullivan, in their articles on *Usos amorosos de la postguerra* as an independent entity from *El cuarto de atrás*, highlight the difficulty of pinpointing the work's genre. Spires calls it a "hybrid text" that may qualify as "a memoir, a history, an autobiographical history, a cultural history, or some other classification" ("Embodied History" 167n2), while Sullivan argues that Martín Gaite "blurs the line between the erstwhile 'objective' historical or literary critical essay and the traditionally acceptable subjectivity of the personal essay" (42) in *Usos amorosos de la postguerra* and other essays.

18. Sullivan asserts that each of these chapters constitutes a distinct essay, following the characteristics of an essay: of a highly personal nature, with a nontraditional organization, and an attention to vernacular prose. However, basing my arguments on Graham Good's, because of the volume's length, the interrelatedness of the chapters, the use of footnotes, "its stress on accuracy of representation" (ix), and academic qualities, I argue that it is a work of scholarly nonfiction, in this case, a socio-historiographic study, and not a series of essays.

Chapter Four
Carlos Blanco Aguinaga: The Spanish Other in Mexico

1. A notable exception is the work of Mateo Gambarte, who has written extensively on second-generation Spanish exile writers in Mexico. Mateo Gambarte's critical texts generally sidestep the relationship between history and fiction in these writers' works, however.

2. See, for instance, Aznar Soler, who focuses on autobiography in exile writing; Faber's *Exile and Cultural Hegemony*, with chapters on exile literature as a political tool; Ilie, with a focus on protest literature written by those who remained in Spain; and Jato Brizuela, Ascunce Arrieta, and San Miguel Casillas, with essays on exile fiction and historiography.

3. What Ugarte calls "the concept of exile" versus "the exile of flesh and bone" (68).

4. See Rulfo; Blanco Aguinaga, *La historia y el texto literario: tres novelas de Galdós*; Blanco Aguinaga, *El Unamuno contemplativo*; Blanco Aguinaga, *Unamuno, teórico del lenguaje*; Blanco Aguinaga, *Juventud del 98*; Blanco Aguinaga, "Narrativa democrática contra la Historia"; and Blanco Aguinaga, *De restauración a restauración*.

5. The latest version of this essay appeared in 2007 as "Problemas que plantea para la historia literaria el exilio español de 1939" in Blanco Aguinaga, *De restauración a restauración* 249–94.

6. Mateo Gambarte includes Blanco Aguinaga as one of the oldest in the second-generation collective of exiles (*Diccionario del exilio español en México* 31–32).

7. Coincidentally, Blanco Aguinaga's father, who had gone to Mexico in exile in advance of the rest of the family, traveled on the ship *Normandie* along with another famous exile: Picasso's iconic painting *Guernica*, on its way to the Museum of Modern Art in New York City (Blanco Aguinaga, *Por el mundo* 91).

8. One of Blanco Aguinaga's teachers at the Instituto Luis Vives was the poet Emilio Prados, whom he would go on to study extensively (Blanco Aguinaga, *Por el mundo* 116).

9. Blanco Aguinaga delves into his life in exile in his two autobiographies: *Por el mundo* and *De mal asiento*.

10. See Prados, *Poesías completas*; Prados, *Cuerpo perseguido*; and Blanco Aguinaga, *Emilio Prados*, among others; and Blanco Aguinaga, *Historia social de la literatura española*.

11. Only Mateo Gambarte has touched briefly on Blanco Aguinaga's fiction in his critical studies of second-generation Spanish exiles in Mexico in *Literatura de los "niños de la guerra" del exilio español en México* and *Diccionario del exilio español en México*.

12. Blanco Aguinaga's works of fiction encompass *Ojos de papel volando* (1984); *Un tiempo tuyo* (1988); *Carretera de Cuernavaca* (1990); *En voz continua* (1997); *Ya no bailan los pescadores de Pismo Beach* (1998); and *Esperando la lluvia de la tarde: fábula de exilios* (2000).

13. See Chapter 2 for definitions of *testimony* and *testimonial narrative* as they operate in contemporary Spanish literature.

14. Many of Blanco Aguinaga's essays on exile are collected in *De restauración a restauración*, published in Spain, and *Ensayos sobre la literatura del exilio español*, published in Mexico. The author also writes about second-generation exile poets in the article "Aquí y allá."

15. *Transterrado* (transliterated by Blanco Aguinaga as *trasterrado*) is a neologism coined by José Gaos, a Spanish philosopher who taught at the Universidad Nacional de México, in the mid-1950s. According to Ugarte, for Gaos the term represents an "ability to continue where he left off" (58).

16. In "A modo de prólogo: sobre la especificidad del exilio español en México," Blanco Aguinaga reveals that the word *exile* did not even appear in the 1950 edition of the *Diccionario de la Real Academia Española*, making

its return in the 1970 edition, five years before Franco died. In this essay, Blanco Aguinaga defines exile as "un concepto político que indica des-tierro obligado por decreto de los poderes establecidos en la tierra de uno o por la fuerza de circunstancias tales como una guerra en la que los vencedores persiguen a los vencidos" (*Ensayos sobre la literatura del exilio español* 13).

17. By the second generation of exiles, this publishing system had changed: all of Blanco Aguinaga's works of fiction were published by Spanish publishing houses. However, they garnered almost no attention from Mexican or Spanish literary scholars.

18. Unión General de Trabajadores, Confederación Nacional del Trabajo, and Uníos Hermanos/Hijos Proletarios.

19. *Castellano* refers to the Spanish spoken in Spain.

20. Blanco Aguinaga mentions *Rayuela* specifically in "Otros tiempos," in which he presents Cortázar as an example of an author's complex relationship to his own displacement, as witnessed in the international melding in *Rayuela*. Blanco Aguinaga argues that, despite the novel's strong sense of place in Paris, "el meollo de su obra escrita en el exilio parisino (*Rayuela*, … por ejemplo) es radicalmente argentino y latinoamericano" (253).

21. Among the many other ways in which Antonio mirrors Blanco Aguinaga is the fact that the author married a Mexican woman, presenting a similar quandary of pertinence through association for author and character.

22. Blanco Aguinaga mentions both ships in his first autobiography, revealing that he also learned details about the ships from his neighbor in Mexico, Mariano Manresa, who was the captain of the *Vita* (*Por el mundo* 146–47).

23. Blanco Aguinaga makes the same point in a rhetorical question in "Sobre el exilio": "¿Concluye así, en hermoso *happy ending*, la extraordinaria historia de los españoles que, huyendo del fascismo llegaron a México pensando que, con un poco de suerte (y la ayuda de las nada fiables democracias de Occidente), no serían *refugiados* sino por unos pocos años?" (30).

Chapter Five
Javier Marías: Genre Fusion in the New Millennium

1. I discuss the extensive scholarship on historical memory in late twentieth-century and early twenty-first-century Spanish cultural production that has accompanied this popular boom in Chapter 1.

2. Silva has said that Garzón practiced "silencio judicial" by withholding commentary on the parallels between his own prosecution of Pinochet for the disappeared in Chile and Argentina and the growing drive in Spain to gather information on its own group of Civil War "desaparecidos" (85).

3. A brief fake news article originally appearing in the satirical newspaper *The Onion* in the mid-1990s anecdotally reflects this attitude in the United States, declaring in its headline "Spain Not Important." This article includes a simulated interview with King Juan Carlos I, who admits that:

> his nation is of no importance. … "In terms of recent culture, politics, industry or any other real measure, we truly are a people

of little significance," the King said. "We played a part in neither WWI nor WWII, we have never produced an automobile, and we have almost no famous citizens to speak of. We truly do not deserve to be on a successful, modernized continent like Europe." ("Spain Not Important")

4. Javier Marías's prodigious literary career continued with the novels *Travesía del horizonte* (1972); *El monarca del tiempo* (1978); *El siglo* (1983); *El hombre sentimental* (1986); *Todas las almas* (1989); *Corazón tan blanco* (1992); *Mañana en la batalla piensa en mí* (1994); *Negra espalda del tiempo* (1998); *Tu rostro mañana. 1 Fiebre y lanza* (2002); *Tu rostro mañana. 2 Baile y sueño* (2004); *Tu rostro mañana. 3 Veneno y sombra y adiós* (2007); and *Los enamoramientos* (2011).

5. Marías's father, Julián Marías, also belonged to the Real Academia Española until his death in 2005.

6. Marías has published these columns in the following collections: *Mano de sombra* (1997); *Seré amado cuando falte* (1999); *A veces un caballero* (2001); *Harán de mí un criminal* (2003); *El oficio de oír llover* (2005); *Demasiada nieve alrededor* (2007); *Lo que no vengo a decir* (2009); and *Ni se les ocurra disparar* (2011).

7. Rosa Montero, Almudena Grandes, and Javier Cercas, among others, have written for *El País* while continuing to publish novels.

8. Alexis Grohmann and Maarten Steenmeijer's edited volume of literary studies of the *Tu rostro mañana* trilogy includes a number of articles that address Marías's intertexts with his other novels or other works of literature, but none that addresses the relationship of his *El País Semanal* columns to the trilogy.

9. Widespread demonstrations against the war in Iraq occurred in Spain in 2003 and 2004. A survey conducted by the Centro de Investigaciones Sociológicas in February 2003 put Spanish opposition to the war with Iraq at 90.8% (Centro 8).

10. Deza's name changes depending on the country and the people around him: from Jaime, to Jack, to Iago, to Jacobo, to Jacques. Throughout the trilogy, he ruminates about having to answer to a name that is not his own. The identity crises associated with inconsistent naming is a difficulty about which Blanco Aguinaga theorizes in his essays on exile, as discussed in Chapter 4.

11. The fact that the majority of the historians Deza uses in his nocturnal investigations are not Spanish is also significant since, as Faber has pointed out, foreign historians took up an influential mantle of historical research into the Spanish Civil War at a time when Spanish historians were often limited in their sources, censored, or lacking in the objectivity necessary to revisit this period ("Entre el respeto y la crítica" 47–48).

12. Bond and Deza share career paths, as both are (fictional) members of the British Secret Intelligence MI6 group.

13. The original quote appears as: "Una noche oscura, probablemente la del 22 o 23 de junio, diez individuos alemanes pertenecientes a las Brigadas Internacionales asaltaron el local en que se hallaba recluido Nin" (Thomas 760–61).

14. Published in 2007, the third volume of *Tu rostro mañana* was the fifth of Marías's novels to include Russell as a lead character, after *Todas las almas*, *Negra espalda del tiempo*, and the first two volumes of the trilogy.

15. The deaths of both Julián Marías and Sir Peter Russell occurred while Marías was writing *Tu rostro mañana. 3*, in which the characters based on them also die. Marías acknowledges both men's contributions to the trilogy in this final volume: "Mención aparte merecen mi padre, Julián Marías, y Sir Peter Russell, que nació Peter Wheeler, sin cuyas vidas prestadas este libro no habría existido. Descansen ambos ahora, también en la ficción de estas páginas" (*Tu rostro mañana. 3* after the last numbered page).

16. I discuss Hayden White's and Paul Ricoeur's theories of historiographic emplotment in Chapter 1.

17. The name "Custardoy" appears elsewhere in the Marías body of work, as a self-admitted foil for the author himself and another point of convergence between fiction and reality. Marías says he uses secondary last names from the annals of his family—Custardoy is one of them—purposefully for some of his secondary characters, especially "gentes con pocos escrúpulos, gente inquietante, preocupante. ... Y hay una especie también de guiño, no respeto al lector, que no tiene por qué saber cuáles son mis apellidos secundarios, sino respeto a mí mismo, es decir: 'Yo también soy éste, también soy estos individuos sin escrúpulos'" (Pittarello, *Una entrevista* 28–29). The author, admittedly, is the implied reader of his own novels. His knowledge activates the meaning behind the repeated use of family names.

18. Sir Peter Russell's adventures with British intelligence and as a Hispanist at Oxford are discussed in great detail in his obituaries. A comparison with the stories Wheeler relates to Deza in *Tu rostro mañana. 3* highlights numerous overlaps (587–602). See "Professor Sir Peter Russell"; and Deyermond and Martin.

Works Cited

Aguilar, Paloma. *Memory and Amnesia: The Role of the Spanish Civil War in the Transition to Democracy.* Trans. Mark Oakley. New York: Berghahn, 2002.

Alberca, Manuel. *El pacto ambiguo: de la novela auobiográfica a la autoficción.* Madrid: Biblioteca Nueva, 2007.

———. "Las vueltas autobiográficas de Javier Marías." *Javier Marías.* Ed. Irene Andres-Suárez and Ana Casas. Neuchâtel, Switz.: U of Neuchâtel, 2005. 49–72.

Alborg, Concha. "A Never-Ending Autobiography: The Fiction of Carmen Martín Gaite." *Redefining Autobiography in Twentieth-Century Women's Fiction: An Essay Collection.* Ed. Janice Morgan and Colette Trout Hall. New York: Garland, 1991. 243–60.

Aldecoa, Josefina R. *La fuerza del destino.* Barcelona: Anagrama, 1997.

———. *Historia de una maestra.* Barcelona: Anagrama, 1990.

———. *Mujeres de negro.* Barcelona: Anagrama, 1994.

———. *Los niños de la guerra.* Madrid: Anaya, 1983.

———. "Nosotros, los de entonces." *Cinco voces ante el arte de narrar.* Ed. Miguel García-Posada. Madrid: Comunidad de Madrid, Consejería de Educación, 2002. 11–19.

Alfaya, Javier. "Españoles en los campos de concentración nazis." *El exilio español de 1939.* Ed. José Luis Abellán. Madrid: Taurus, 1976. 89–120.

Amago, Samuel. *True Lies: Narrative Self-consciousness in the Contemporary Spanish Novel.* Lewisburg, KY: Bucknell UP, 2006.

Amat-Piniella, J. *K. L. Reich.* Barcelona: Club Editor, 1963.

Ankersmit, Frank. "Truth in History and Literature." *Narrative* 18.1 (2012): 29–50.

Aristotle. *Poetics.* 1961. Trans. S. H. Butcher. New York: Hill and Wang, 1998.

Armengou, Montse, and Richard Belis. *El comboi dels 927.* Spain, Televisió de Catalunya, 2005.

"Artur London: amor a Catalunya; Presentà el llibre de M Roig entre altres deportats." *Avuí* [Barcelona] 21 Apr. 1977: 6.

Asís Garrote, María Dolores de. *Última hora de la novela en España.* Madrid: Pirámide, 1996.

Aznar Soler, Manuel, ed. *El exilio literario español de 1939: actas del primer congreso internacional: Bellaterra, 27 de noviembre–1 de diciembre de*

Works Cited

    1995. Vol. 1. San Cugat del Vallès, Spain: Seminari de Literatura Espanyola Contemporània, 1998.

Balibrea, Mari Paz, ed. *Encuentros en la diáspora: Ensayos en honor de Carlos Blanco Aguinaga*. Barcelona: GEXEL, 2002.

Ballesteros, Isolina. "The Feminism (Anti-Feminism) according to Montserrat Roig." *Catalan Review: International Journal of Catalan Culture* 7.2 (1993): 117–28.

Barnet, Miguel. "La novela testimonio. Socio-literatura." *Testimonio y literatura*. Ed. René Jara and Hernán Vidal. Edina, MN: Society for the Study of Contemporary Hispanic and Lusophone Revolutionary Literatures, 1986. 280–302.

Barral, Carlos. *Años de penitencia*. Madrid: Alianza, 1975.

Barthes, Roland. "The Death of the Author." Trans. Stephen Heath. *Image, Music, Text*. New York: Hill and Wang, 1977. 142–48.

Bellver, Catherine G. "Montserrat Roig: A Feminine Perspective and a Journalistic Slant." *Feminine Concerns in Contemporary Spanish Fiction by Women*. Ed. Robert C. Manteiga, Carolyn L. Galerstein, and Kathleen McNerney. Potomac, MD: Scripta Humanistica, 1988. 152–68.

Beltrán Almería, Luís. "Hispanism and New Historicism." *Spain beyond Spain: Modernity, Literary History, and National Identity*. Ed. Bradley S. Epps and Luis Fernández Cifuentes. Lewisburg, PA: Bucknell UP, 2005. 270–81.

Beverley, John. *Testimonio: On the Politics of Truth*. Minneapolis: U of Minnesota P, 2004.

Bhabha, Homi K. *The Location of Culture*. Abingdon, Eng.: Routledge, 1994.

Blanco Aguinaga, Carlos. "Aquí y allá: sobre la poesía de quienes eran niños españoles durante la Guerra Civil." *España en la encrucijada de 1939: exilio, cultura e identidades*. Ed. Mónica Jato Brizuela, José Ángel Ascunce Arrieta and María Luisa San Miguel Casillas. Bilbao: Universidad de Deusto, 2007. 315–26.

———. *Carretera de Cuernavaca*. Madrid: Alfaguara, 1990.

———. "La cuestión de la vuelta en los poetas del exilio mexicano." *Sesenta años después. Las literaturas del exilio republicano de 1939*. Ed. Manuel Aznar Soler. 2 vols. Vol. 1. Sant Cugat del Vallès, Spain: GEXEL, 2000. 439–58.

———. *De mal asiento*. Barcelona: Caballo de Troya, 2010.

———. *De mitólogos y novelistas*. Madrid: Turner, 1975.

———. *De restauración a restauración (Ensayos sobre literatura, historia e ideología)*. Seville: Renacimiento, 2007.

Works Cited

———. *Emilio Prados; vida y obra; bibliografía; antología.* New York: Hispanic Institute in the United States, 1960.

———. *En voz continua.* Madrid: Alfaguara, 1997.

———. *Ensayos sobre la literatura del exilio español.* Mexico, DF: El Colégio de México, Centro de Estudios Lingüísticos y Literarios, 2006.

———. *Esperando la lluvia de la tarde: fábula de exilios.* Madrid: Brand, 2000.

———. *Historia social de la literatura española.* 3 vols. Madrid: Akal, 2000.

———. *La historia y el texto literario: tres novelas de Galdós.* Madrid: Nuestra Cultura, 1978.

———. *Juventud del 98.* Madrid: Taurus, 1998.

———. "Narrativa democrática contra la Historia." *Del franquismo a la posmodernidad: cultura española 1975–1990.* Ed. José B. Monleón. Madrid: Akal, 1995. 251–63.

———. *Ojos de papel volando.* Barcelona: Grijalbo, 1984.

———. "Otros tiempos, otros espacios en la narrativa española del exilio en América." *Critica: A Journal of Critical Essays (University of California, San Diego)* 2.2 (1990): 249–57.

———. *Por el mundo: infancia, guerra y principio de un exilio afortunado.* Irún: Alberdania, 2007.

———. "Sobre el exilio español en México." *Memoria viva de los exilios.* Ed. Carlos Blanco Aguinaga, Manuel Ballesteros, and Julia Vigre. Madrid: Entinema, 2001. 13–40.

———. *Un tiempo tuyo.* Madrid: Alfaguara, 1988.

———. *El Unamuno contemplativo.* Barcelona: Laia, 1975.

———. *Unamuno, teórico del lenguaje.* Madrid: El Colegio de México, 1954.

———. *Ya no bailan los pescadores de Pismo Beach.* Zaragoza: Prames, 1998.

Brenneis, Sara J. "Carlos Rodríguez del Risco: The First Spanish Voice from the Holocaust." *History & Memory* 25.1 (2013): 51–76.

Brown, Joan Lipman. "Carmen Martín Gaite: Reaffirming the Pact between Reader and Writer." *Women Writers of Contemporary Spain: Exiles in the Homeland.* Ed. Joan L. Brown. Newark: U of Delaware P, 1991. 72–92.

———. *Secrets from the Back Room: The Fiction of Carmen Martín Gaite.* University, MS: Romance Monographs, 1987.

Brownlow, Jeanne P., and John W. Kronik. *Intertextual Pursuits: Literary Mediations in Modern Spanish Narrative.* Lewisburg, PA: Bucknell UP, 1998.

Works Cited

Carbayo Abengózar, Mercedes. "De la intra-historia a la propia-historia. Lidiando con la historia y la literatura en María Zambrano y Carmen Martín Gaite." *Escribir mujer. Narradoras españolas hoy.* Ed. Cristóbal Cuevas García. Málaga: Congreso de Literatura Española Contemporánea, 2000. 305–13.

Carulla, Jordi, and Arnau Carulla. *La Guerra Civil en 2000 carteles: República-Guerra civil-Posguerra.* 2 vols. Barcelona: Postermil, 1997.

Carvajal, Pedro. *Exilio.* Spain, Televisión Española, 2002.

Castillo, Debra A. "Never-Ending Story: Carmen Martín Gaite's *The Back Room.*" *PMLA: Publications of the Modern Language Association of America* 102.4 (1987): 814–28.

Centro de Investigaciones Sociológicos. *Barómetro de febrero, Estudio no. 2481.* Madrid: CIS, Feb. 2003. Web. 23 Aug. 2012.

Cercas, Javier. *Anatomía de un instante.* Barcelona: Mondadori, 2009.

———. *Soldados de Salamina.* Barcelona: Tusquets, 2001.

Certeau, Michel de. *The Practice of Everyday Life.* Trans. Steven Rendall. Berkeley: U of California P, 1984.

Chown, Linda. "Palimpsestic Biography: *The Back Room.*" *Critical Essays on the Literatures of Spain and Spanish-America.* Ed. Luis González del Valle and Julio Baena. Boulder, CO: Society of Spanish and Spanish American Studies, 1991. 57–64.

Cipllijauskaité, Biruté. *La novela femenina contemporánea (1970–1985): hacia una tipología de la narración en primera persona.* Barcelona: Anthropos, 1988.

Cohn, Dorrit. *The Distinction of Fiction.* Baltimore: Johns Hopkins UP, 1999.

Colmeiro, José F. *Memoria histórica e identidad cultural: de la postguerra a la postmodernidad.* Barcelona: Anthropos, 2005.

Crameri, Kathryn. *Language, the Novelist and National Identity in Post-Franco Catalonia.* Oxford: Legenda, 2000.

Culler, Jonathan. "Towards a Theory of Non-Genre Literature." *Surfiction: Fiction Now—and Tomorrow.* Ed. Raymond Federman. Chicago: Swallow, 1981. 255–62.

Cuñado, Isabel. *El espectro de la herencia: la narrativa de Javier Marías.* Amsterdam: Rodopi, 2004.

Davies, Catherine. *Contemporary Feminist Fiction in Spain: The Work of Montserrat Roig and Rosa Montero.* Oxford: Berg, 1994.

Delibes, Miguel. *Cinco horas con Mario.* Barcelona: Destino, 1966.

de Lucas, Javier. *Puertas que se cierran: Europa como fortaleza.* Barcelona: Icaria, 1996.

Works Cited

Del Villar, Arturo. "Carmen Martín Gaite." *Estafeta Literaria* 1–15 Oct. 1978: 8–11.

Deyermond, Alan, and Ian Michael. "Professor Sir Peter Russell." *The Independent*. The Independent, 5 July 2006. Web. 21 Aug. 2012.

Diccionario de la Lengua Española. Real Academia Española. Web. 21 Aug. 2012.

Dupláa, Christina. "Essay, Memory, and Testimony in Montserrat Roig." *Spanish Women Writers and the Essay: Gender, Politics, and the Self*. Ed. Kathleen Mary Glenn and Mercedes Mazquiarán de Rodríguez. Columbia: U of Missouri P, 1998. 212–30.

———. "El testimoni i la recuperació de la memoria." *Catalan Review: International Journal of Catalan Culture* 7.2 (1993): 137–49.

———. "Testimony and Cultural Memory in Hispanic Narratives: The Case of Montserrat Roig's *Els catalans als camps nazis*." *Bulletin of Hispanic Studies* 76.2 (1999): 235–43.

———. *La voz testimonial en Montserrat Roig: estudio cultural de los textos*. Barcelona: Icaria, 1996.

Encarnación, Omar G. "Reconciliation after Democratization: Coping with the Past in Spain." *Political Science Quarterly* 123.3 (2008): 435–59.

Everly, Kathryn. *Catalan Women Writers and Artists: Revisionist Views from a Feminist Space*. Lewisburg, PA: Bucknell UP, 2003.

———. *History, Violence, and the Hyperreal: Representing Culture in the Contemporary Spanish Novel*. West Lafayette, IN: Purdue UP, 2010.

Faber, Sebastiaan. "Entre el respeto y la crítica. Reflexiones sobre la memoria histórica en España." *Migraciones y Exilios* 5 (2004): 37–50.

———. *Exile and Cultural Hegemony: Spanish Intellectuals in Mexico, 1939–1975*. Nashville: Vanderbilt UP, 2002.

———. "The Price of Peace: Historical Memory in Post-Franco Spain, A Review-Article." *Revista Hispánica Moderna* 58.1–2 (2005): 205–19.

Fanjul, Enrique. "Una guerra no tan lejana de Canadá." *El País* [Madrid] 27 July 2008: 20.

Felman, Shoshana, and Dori Laub. *Testimony: Crises of Witnessing in Literature, Psychoanalysis and History*. New York: Routledge, 1992.

Ferrán, Ofelia. *Working through Memory: Writing and Remembrance in Contemporary Spanish Narrative*. Lewisburg, PA: Bucknell UP, 2007.

Fish, Stanley Eugene. *Is There a Text in This Class?: The Authority of Interpretive Communities*. Cambridge, MA: Harvard UP, 1980.

Works Cited

Frey, James. *A Million Little Pieces*. New York: N.A. Talese/Doubleday, 2003.

Gallagher, Catherine, and Stephen Greenblatt. *Practicing New Historicism*. Chicago: U of Chicago P, 2000.

Genette, Gérard. "Fictional Narrative, Factual Narrative." *Poetics Today* 11.4 (1990): 755–74.

Gies, David T. *The Cambridge Companion to Modern Spanish Culture*. Cambridge, Eng.: Cambridge UP, 1999.

Glenn, Kathleen M. "*El cuarto de atrás*: Literature as *juego* and the Self-Reflexive Text." *From Fiction to Metafiction: Essays in Honor of Carmen Martín-Gaite*. Ed. Mirella D'Ambrosio Servodidio and Marcia L. Welles. Lincoln, NE: Society of Spanish and Spanish-American Studies, 1983. 149–59.

———. "First Person Singular: Montserrat Roig and the Essay." *Catalan Review: International Journal of Catalan Culture* 9.1 (1995): 81–90.

González, Miguel. "Carme Chacón, Ministra de Defensa." *El País* [Madrid] 27 July 2008: 16–17.

Good, Graham. *The Observing Self: Rediscovering the Essay*. London: Routledge, 1988.

Graham, Helen, and Jo Labanyi. *Spanish Cultural Studies: An Introduction: The Struggle for Modernity*. Oxford: Oxford UP, 1995.

Grandes, Almudena. *El corazón helado*. Barcelona: Tusquets, 2007.

Grohmann, Alexis, and Maarten Steenmeijer, eds. *Allí donde uno diría que ya no puede haber nada: Tu rostro mañana de Javier Marías*. Amsterdam: Rodopoli, 2009.

Gugelberger, Georg M., ed. *The Real Thing: Testimonial Discourse and Latin America*. Durham, NC: Duke UP, 1996.

Guillén, Claudio. *Literature as System: Essays toward the Theory of Literary History*. Princeton, NJ: Princeton UP, 1971.

Halbwachs, Maurice. *The Collective Memory*. 1950. Trans. Francis J. Ditter Jr. and Vida Yazdi Ditter. New York: Harper & Row, 1980.

Hart, Stephen M. *White Ink: Essays on Twentieth-Century Feminine Fiction in Spain and Latin America*. London: Tamesis, 1993.

Hegel, Georg Wilhelm Friedrich. *The Philosophy of History*. Kitchener, ONT: Batoche, 2001.

Hermoso, Miguel, dir. *La luz prodigiosa*. Azalea Films, 2002.

Herzberger, David K. "Javier Marías's *Tu rostro mañana*: The Search for a Usable Future." *Anales de la Literatura Española Contemporánea* 30.1–2 (2005): 205–19.

———. *Narrating the Past: Fiction and Historiography in Postwar Spain*. Durham, NC: Duke UP, 1995.

Holloway, Vance R. *El posmodernismo y otras tendencias de la novela española (1967–1995)*. Madrid: Fundamentos, 1999.

Hutcheon, Linda. *A Poetics of Postmodernism: History, Theory, Fiction*. New York: Routledge, 1988.

Ilie, Paul. *Literature and Inner Exile: Authoritarian Spain, 1939–1975*. Baltimore: Johns Hopkins UP, 1980.

Iser, Wolfgang. *The Act of Reading: A Theory of Aesthetic Response*. Baltimore: Johns Hopkins UP, 1978.

Izquierdo, Soledad. "Carmen Martín Gaite: la literatura como placer." *Crítica* Feb. 1979: 16–19.

Jara, René, and Hernán Vidal, eds. *Testimonio y literatura*. Edina, MN: Society for the Study of Contemporary Hispanic and Lusophone Revolutionary Literatures, 1986.

Jato Brizuela, Mónica, José Ángel Ascunce Arrieta, and María Luisa San Miguel Casillas. *España en la encrucijada de 1939: exilio, cultura e identidades*. Bilbao: Universidad de Deusto, 2007.

Jenkins, Keith. *The Postmodern History Reader*. London: Routledge, 1997.

Jerez Farrán, Carlos, and Samuel Amago, eds. *Unearthing Franco's Legacy: Mass Graves and the Recovery of Historical Memory in Spain*. Notre Dame, IN: U of Notre Dame P, 2010.

Juliá, Santos. "Echar al olvido: memoria y amnistía en la transición." *Claves de razón práctica* Jan./Feb. 2003: 14–24.

———. *Historias de las dos Españas*. Madrid: Taurus, 2004.

Jurado Morales, José. "La mirada ajena: medio siglo de bibliografía sobre la obra de Carmen Martín Gaite." *Anales de la Literatura Espanola Contemporánea* 29.1 (2004): 135–65.

———. *La trayectoria narrativa de Carmen Martín Gaite (1925–2000)*. Madrid: Gredos, 2003.

Klein, Kerwin Lee. *Frontiers of Historical Imagination: Narrating the European Conquest of Native America, 1890–1990*. Berkeley: U of California P, 1997.

———. "In Search of Narrative Mastery: Postmodernism and the People without History." *History and Theory* 34.4 (1995): 275–98.

Labanyi, Jo, ed. *Constructing Identity in Contemporary Spain: Theoretical Debates and Cultural Practice*. Oxford: Oxford UP, 2002.

———. "The Languages of Silence: Historical Memory, Generational Transmission and Witnessing in Contemporary Spain." *Journal of Romance Studies* 9.3 (2009): 23–35.

———. *Myth and History in the Contemporary Spanish Novel*. Cambridge, Eng.: Cambridge UP, 1989.

Labanyi, Jo "The Politics of Memory in Contemporary Spain." *Journal of Spanish Cultural Studies* 9.2 (2008): 119–25.

———. "Testimonies of Repression: Methodological and Political Issues." *Unearthing Franco's Legacy: Mass Graves and the Recovery of Historical Memory in Spain*. Ed. Carlos Jerez Farrán and Samuel Amago. Notre Dame, IN: U of Notre Dame P, 2010. 192–205.

Lacruz Pardo, Javier. "Carmen Martín Gaite: 'En "El cuarto de atrás" se va viendo mi concepción del amor.'" *Nueva* Aug. 1978: 16.

Laforet, Carmen. *Nada*. Barcelona: Destino, 1945.

Langa Pizarro, M. Mar. *Del franquismo a la posmodernidad: la novela española (1975–1999): análisis y diccionario de autores*. Alicante, Spain: Universidad de Alicante, 2000.

Le Chène, Evelyn. *Mauthausen: The History of a Death Camp*. London: Methuen, 1971.

"LEY 52/2007, de 26 de diciembre, por la que se reconocen y amplían derechos y se establecen medidas en favor de quienes padecieron persecución o violencia durante la guerra civil y la dictadura." *Boletín Oficial del Estado* 310. Madrid: Jefatura del estado, 27 Dec. 2007. 53410–16.

López-Quiñones, Antonio Gómez. *La guerra persistente: memoria, violencia y utopía: representaciones contemporáneas de la Guerra Civil Española*. Madrid: Iberoamericana, 2006.

Lukács, Georg. *The Historical Novel*. Trans. Hannah and Stanley Mitchell. London: Merlin, 1962.

"Madrid acoge el congreso más ambicioso sobre la Guerra Civil." *El País*. El País, 27 Nov. 2006. Web. 21 Aug. 2012.

Marcos, Pilar. "Rajoy: 'España acabará con la lacra asesina del terrorismo.'" *El País* [Madrid] 12 Mar. 2004: 1.

Marías, Javier. "Another Silent Noon in Madrid." *New York Times* 12 Mar. 2004: op-ed.

———. *A veces un caballero*. Madrid: Alfaguara, 2001.

———. *Corazón tan blanco*. Barcelona: Anagrama, 1992.

———. "De buena mañana." *El País* [Madrid] 12 Mar. 2004: 45.

———. *Demasiada nieve alrededor*. Madrid: Alfaguara, 2007.

———. *Los enamoramientos*. Madrid: Alfaguara, 2011.

———. *Harán de mí un criminal*. Madrid: Alfaguara, 2003.

———. *El hombre sentimental*. Barcelona: Anagrama, 1986.

———. "How to Remember, How to Forget." *New York Times* 11 Sept. 2004: op-ed.

———. *Literatura y fantasma*. Barcelona: Random House Mondadori, 2007.

———. *Lo que no vengo a decir*. Madrid: Alfaguara, 2009.

———. *Mañana en la batalla piensa en mí*. Barcelona: Anagrama, 1994.

———. *Mano de sombra*. Madrid: Santillana, 1997.

———. *El monarca del tiempo*, Literatura Alfaguara. Madrid: Alfaguara, 1978.

———. *Negra espalda del tiempo*. Madrid: Alfaguara, 1998.

———. *Ni se les ocurra disparar*. Madrid: Alfaguara, 2011.

———. *El oficio de oír llover*. Madrid: Alfaguara, 2005.

———. "El padre." *El País*. El País, 16 June 1994. Web. 21 Aug. 2012.

———. *Seré amado cuando falte*. Madrid: Alfaguara, 1999.

———. *El siglo*. Barcelona: Seix Barral, 1983.

———. "Siglos de desperdicio." *El País Semanal* 27 July 2008: 102.

———. "Sobre la dificultad de contar. Discurso leído el día 27 de abril de 2008 en su recepción pública por el Excmo. Sr. D. Javier Marías y contestación del Excmo. Sr. D. Francisco Rico." *Real Academia Española*. Real Academia Española, 2008. Web. 21 Aug. 2012.

———. *Todas las almas*. Barcelona: Anagrama, 1989.

———. *Travesía del horizonte*. Barcelona: La Gaya Ciencia, 1972.

———. *Tu rostro mañana. 1 Fiebre y lanza*. Madrid: Alfaguara, 2002.

———. *Tu rostro mañana. 2 Baile y sueño*. Madrid: Alfaguara, 2004.

———. *Tu rostro mañana. 3 Veneno y sombra y adiós*. Madrid: Alfaguara, 2007.

Marsé, Juan. *Últimas tardes con Teresa*. Barcelona: Seix Barral, 1966.

Martín Gaite, Carmen. *Agua pasada: artículos, prólogos y discursos*. Barcelona: Anagrama, 1993.

———. *El balneario*. Madrid: Artes Gráficas Clavileño, 1955.

———. *La búsqueda de interlocutor*. Madrid: Nostromo, 1973.

———. *El cuarto de atrás*. Barcelona: Destino, 1992.

———. *El cuento de nunca acabar: apuntes sobre la narración, el amor y la mentira*. Madrid: Trieste, 1983.

———. *Desde la ventana*. Madrid: Espasa-Calpe, 1987.

———. *Entre visillos*. Barcelona: Destino, 1958.

———. *Pido la palabra*. Barcelona: Anagrama, 2002.

Works Cited

Martín Gaite, Carmen. *El proceso de Macanaz. Historia de un empapelamiento*. Madrid: Moneda y Crédito, 1970.

———. *Retahílas*. Barcelona: Destino, 1974.

———. *Ritmo lento*. Barcelona: Seix Barral, 1963.

———. *Usos amorosos de la postguerra española*. Barcelona: Anagrama, 1996.

———. *Usos amorosos del dieciocho en España*. Madrid: Siglo XXI de España, 1972.

Martín Gaite, Carmen, and Maria Vittoria Calvi. *Cuadernos de todo*. Barcelona: Areté, 2002.

Mate, Reyes. *Justicia de las víctimas: Terrorismo, memoria, reconciliación*. Barcelona: Anthropos, 2008.

Mateo Gambarte, Eduardo. *Diccionario del exilio español en México: de Carlos Blanco Aguinaga a Ramón Xirau*. Pamplona: Eunate, 1997.

———. *Literatura de los "niños de la guerra" del exilio español en México*. Lérida, Spain: Universitat de Lleida: Pagès, 1996.

———. "La segunda generación del exilio español en México: ¿Españoles o mexicanos?" *Eurídice* 1 (1991): 173–94.

Medina Domínguez, Alberto. *Exorcismos de la memoria: políticas y poéticas de la melancolía en la España de la transición*. Madrid: Libertarias, 2001.

Melenchón i Xamena, Joanna María. *Mauthausen, des de l'oblit*. Barcelona: Amicron, 2008.

Menchú, Rigoberta. *I, Rigoberta Menchú: An Indian Woman in Guatemala*. Trans. Ann Wright. Ed. Elisabeth Burgos-Debray. London: Verso, 1984.

Merino, Eloy E., and H. Rosi Song. *Traces of Contamination: Unearthing the Francoist Legacy in Contemporary Spanish Discourse*. Lewisburg, KY: Bucknell UP, 2005.

Mesquida, Evelyn. "Españoles contra Hitler." *El País* [Madrid] 27 July 2008: sec. Domingo.

Moa, Pío. *Los mitos de la Guerra Civil*. Madrid: La Esfera de los Libros, 2004.

Montero, Rosa. "Carmen Martín Gaite, premio Anagrama de Ensayo: El triunfo de la supervivencia." *El País* [Madrid] 31 Mar. 1987: 34.

Moreno-Nuño, Carmen. *Las huellas de la guerra civil: mito y trauma en la narrativa de la España democrática*. Madrid: Libertarias, 2006.

Nichols, Geraldine Cleary. *Escribir, espacio propio: Laforet, Matute, Moix, Tusquets, Riera y Roig por sí mismas*. Minneapolis: Institute for the Study of Ideologies and Literature, 1989.

Nieva de la Paz, Pilar. "La memoria de un tiempo: tres acercamientos narrativos de escritoras durante la transicion politica." *Estudios de literatura española de los siglos XIX y XX. Homenaje a Juan María Díez Taboada.* Ed. Angel Garrido Gallardo. Madrid: Consejo Superior de Investigaciones Científicas, 1998. 648–54.

Nora, Pierre. "Between Memory and History: *Les Lieux de Mémoire*." *Representations* 26 (1989): 7–24.

———. "Reasons for the Current Upsurge in Memory." *The Collective Memory Reader.* Ed. Jeffrey K. Olick, Vered Vinitzky-Seroussi, and Daniel Levy. New York: Oxford UP, 2011. 437–41.

Norman, Andrew P. "Telling It Like It Was: Historical Narratives on Their Own Terms." *History and Theory* 30.2 (1991): 119–35.

Ortiz, Christopher. "The Politics of Genre in Carmen Martín Gaite's *Back Room*." *Autobiography & Postmodernism.* Ed. Kathleen M. Ashley, Leigh Gilmore, and Gerald Peters. Amherst: U of Massachusetts P, 1994. 33–53.

Oxford English Dictionary. Oxford: Oxford UP, 2012. Web. 21 Aug. 2012.

Pagès, Joan, and Montserrat Casas. *Republicans i republicanes als camps de concentració nazis: testimonis i recursos didàctics per a l'ensenyamente secundari.* Barcelona: Ajuntament de Barcelona, 2005.

Payne, Stanley G. "Mitos y tópicos de la Guerra Civil." *Revista de Libros* 79–80. Revista de Libros, July–Aug. 2003. Web. 21 Aug. 2012.

Picornell Belenguer, Mercè. *Discursos testimonials en la literatura catalana recent (Montserrat Roig i Teresa Pàmies).* Palma de Mallorca, Spain: Biblioteca Miquel dels Sants Oliver, 2002.

Pike, David Wingeate. *Spaniards in the Holocaust: Mauthausen, the Horror on the Danube.* London: Routledge, 2000.

Pittarello, Elide. "Artesanías autógrafas de Carmen Martín Gaite." *Journal of Interdisciplinary Literary Studies* 5.1 (1993): 101–18.

———. *Una entrevista con Javier Marías.* Barcelona: Debolsillo, 2006.

———. "Haciendo tiempo con las cosas." *Javier Marías.* Ed. Irene Andres-Suárez and Ana Casas. Neuchâtel, Switz.: U of Neuchâtel, 2005. 19–48.

Pope, Randolph D. "Historia y novela en la posguerra espanola." *Siglo XX/20th Century* 5.1–2 (1987): 16–24.

Porter, Carolyn. "History and Literature: 'After the New Historicism.'" *New Literary History* 21.2 (1990): 253–72.

Prados, Emilio. *Cuerpo perseguido.* Ed. Carlos Blanco Aguinaga and Antonio Carreira. Barcelona: Labor, 1971.

Works Cited

Prados, Emilio. *Jardín cerrado (Nostalgias, sueños y presencias): poema*. Buenos Aires: Losada, 1960.

———. *Poesías completas*. Ed. Carlos Blanco Aguinaga and Antonio Carreira. Madrid: Visor Libros, 1999.

Preston, Paul. *Franco: A Biography*. London: HarperCollins, 1993.

Prince, Gerald. *A Dictionary of Narratology*. Lincoln, NE: U of Nebraska P, 2003.

"Professor Sir Peter Russell." *The Times*. Times Newspapers Ltd., 14 July 2006. Web. 2 June 2011.

Resina, Joan Ramon, and Ulrich Winter. *Casa encantada: lugares de memoria en la España constitucional (1978–2004)*. Madrid: Iberoamericana, 2005.

Ricoeur, Paul. *Memory, History, Forgetting*. Trans. Kathleen Blamey and David Pellauer. Chicago: U of Chicago P, 2004.

———. *Time and Narrative*. Trans. Kathleen McLaughlin and David Pellauer. 3 vols. Vol. 1. Chicago: U of Chicago P, 1984.

———. *Time and Narrative*. Trans. Kathleen McLaughlin and David Pellauer. 3 vols. Vol. 3. Chicago: U of Chicago P, 1988.

Roberts, Geoffrey, ed. *The History and Narrative Reader*. London: Routledge, 2001.

Robinson, Alan. *Narrating the Past: Historiography, Memory and the Contemporary Novel*. New York: Palgrave Macmillan, 2011.

Roig, Montserrat. *L'agulla daurada*. Barcelona: Edicions 62, 1985

———. *El cant de la joventut*. Barcelona: Edicions 62, 1989.

———. *Els catalans als camps nazis*. Barcelona: Edicions 62, 1977.

———. *Digues que m'estimes encara que sigui mentida: sobre el plaer solitari d'escriure i el vici compartit de llegir*. Barcelona: Edicions 62, 1991.

———. *Los hechiceros de la palabra*. Barcelona: Martínez Roca, 1975.

———. *L'hora violeta*. Barcelona: Edicions 62, 1980.

———. *La hora violeta*. Trans. Enrique Sordo. Ed. Jacqueline A. Hurtley. Madrid: Castalia, 2000.

———. *Mi viaje al bloqueo: 900 días de la lucha heróica de Leningrado*. Moscow: Progreso, 1982.

———. *Molta roba i poc sabó... i tan neta que la volen*. Barcelona: Selecta, 1971.

———. *Mujeres en busca de un nuevo humanismo*. Barcelona: Salvat, 1981.

———. *Noche y niebla: los catalanes en los campos nazis.* Barcelona: Península, 1978.

———. *L'òpera quotidiana.* Barcelona: Planeta, 1985.

———. *Un pensament de sal, un pessic de pebre: dietari obert 1990–1991.* Barcelona: Edicions 62, 1992.

———. *Ramona, adéu.* Barcelona: Edicions 62, 1972.

———. *Retrats parallels.* Barcelona: Publicacions de l'Abadia de Montserrat, 1975.

———. *El temps de les cireres.* Barcelona: Edicions 62, 1977.

———. *¿Tiempo de mujer?* Esplugues de Llobregat, Spain: Plaza & Janés, 1980.

———. *La veu melodiosa.* Barcelona: Edicions 62, 1987.

Ruiz Funes, Concepción, and Enriqueta Tuñón. *Palabras del exilio 2. Final y comienzo: el Sinaia.* Mexico, DF: Instituto Nacional de Antropología e Historia, 1982. *Biblioteca Virtual Miguel de Cervantes.* Fundación Biblioteca Virtual Miguel de Cervantes, 2012. Web. 21 Aug. 2012.

Rulfo, Juan. *El llano en llamas.* Ed. Carlos Blanco Aguinaga. Madrid: Cátedra, 1997.

Said, Edward W. *Orientalism.* New York: Vintage, 1979.

Salvadó i Valentines, Ramon. *Un clam de llibertat: vivències de Josep Simon i Mill, exdeportat de Mauthausen (4.929).* Saldes, Spain: Abadia, 2003.

Sarlo, Beatriz, "On Memory: A Critical Reading." Townsend Center for the Arts Lecture Series. U of California, Berkeley, 5 Apr. 2005.

Serrano i Blanquer, David. *Un català a Mauthausen: el testimoni de Francesc Comellas.* Barcelona: Pòrtic, 2001.

Sieburth, Stephanie Anne. *Inventing High and Low: Literature, Mass Culture, and Uneven Modernity in Spain.* Durham, NC: Duke UP, 1994.

Silva, Emilio. *Las fosas de Franco: crónica de un desagravio.* Madrid: Temas de hoy, 2006.

Sklodowska, Elzbieta. "Spanish American Testimonial Novel: Some Afterthoughts." *The Real Thing: Testimonial Discourse and Latin America.* Ed. Georg M. Gugelberger. Durham, NC: Duke UP, 1996. 84–100.

Sobejano, Gonzalo. "The Testimonial Novel and the Novel of Memory." *The Cambridge Companion to the Spanish Novel: From 1600 to the Present.* Ed. Harriet S. Turner and Adelaida López de Martínez. Cambridge, Eng.: Cambridge UP, 2003. 172–92.

Soldevila Durante, Ignacio. *Historia de la novela española, 1936–2000*. Madrid: Cátedra, 2001.

"Spain Not Important." *The Onion Radio News. 2004: The Premium Collection*, disc 1. The Onion, 2007.

Spires, Robert C. *Beyond the Metafictional Mode: Directions in the Modern Spanish Novel*. Lexington, KY: UP of Kentucky, 1984.

———. "Embodied History: *Usos amorosos de la postguerra española* and *La Codorniz*." *Carmen Martín Gaite: Cuento de nunca acabar / Never-ending story*. Ed. Kathleen Mary Glenn and Lissette Rolón-Collazo. Boulder, CO: Society of Spanish and Spanish-American Studies, 2003. 141–68.

———. "Intertextuality in *El cuarto de atrás*." *From Fiction to Metafiction: Essays in Honor of Carmen Martín-Gaite*. Ed. Mirella D'Ambrosio Servodidio and Marcia L. Welles. Lincoln, NE: Society of Spanish and Spanish-American Studies, 1983. 139–48.

———. *Post-Totalitarian Spanish Fiction*. Columbia: U of Missouri P, 1996.

Steenmeijer, Maarten. "Javier Marías, columnista: el otro, el mismo." *Javier Marías*. Ed. Irene Andres-Suárez and Ana Casas. Neuchâtel, Switz.: U of Neuchâtel, 2005. 255–73.

Sullivan, Constance A. "The Boundary-Crossing Essays of Carmen Martín Gaite." *The Politics of the Essay: Feminist Perspectives*. Ed. Ruth-Ellen B. Joeres and Elizabeth Mittman. Bloomington, IN: Indiana UP, 1993. 41–56.

Szurmuk, Monica. "Intersecciones ideológicas en la obra de Montserrat Roig." *Escritos: Revista del Centro de Ciencias del Lenguaje* 25 (2002): 157–74.

Thomas, Brook. "The New Historicism and Other Old-fashioned Topics." *The New Historicism*. Ed. H. Aram Veeser. New York: Routledge, 1989. 182–203.

Thomas, Hugh. *La guerra civil española: 1936–1939*. Vol. 2. Trans. Neri Daurella. Barcelona: Gribaljo, 1976.

Todorov, Tzvetan. *The Fantastic: A Structural Approach to a Literary Genre*. Trans. Richard Howard. Cleveland: The Press of Case Western Reserve, 1973.

Toran, Rosa. *Vida i mort dels republicans als camps nazis*. Barcelona: Proa, 2002.

Torres, Francesc. *Dark Is the Room Where We Sleep = Oscura es la habitación donde dormimos*. Barcelona: Actar-D, 2007.

"Trial Testimony against Albert Speer." Jan. 1946. *United States Holocaust Memorial Museum*. Web. 21 Aug. 2012.

Tsuchiya, Akiko. "Reflections on Historiography in Montserrat Roig's *L'hora violeta*." *Arizona Journal of Hispanic Cultural Studies* 2 (1998): 163–74.

Ugarte, Michael. *Shifting Ground: Spanish Civil War Exile Literature*. Durham, NC: Duke UP, 1989.

Valverde Velasco, Alicia, and Francisco Álamo Felices. "La novela como historia, realidad y metáfora de la dictadura: La narrativa española de la transición (1975–1990)." *La palabra del poder y el poder de la palabra: aproximaciones a las relaciones entre el discurso político y el narrativo*. Ed. Rubén D. Medina and José R. Valles Calartava. Acatlan, Mex.: Seminario de Semiología del Poder, UNAM, 1999. 23–44.

Vargas Llosa, Mario. *La verdad de las mentiras*. Madrid: Punto de lectura, 2003.

Veeser, H. Aram. *The New Historicism*. New York: Routledge, 1989.

Vilarós, Teresa. "A Cultural Mapping of Catalonia." *The Cambridge Companion to Modern Spanish Culture*. Ed. David T. Gies. Cambridge, Eng.: Cambridge UP, 1999. 37–53.

———. "The Novel beyond Modernity." *The Cambridge Companion to the Spanish Novel: From 1600 to the Present*. Ed. Harriet S. Turner and Adelaida López de Martínez. Cambridge, Eng.: Cambridge UP, 2003. 251–63.

Villanueva, Darío. *Theories of Literary Realism*. Albany: State U of New York P, 1997.

Vives i Clavé, Pere. *Cartes des dels camps de concentració*. Barcelona: Edicions 62, 1972.

Walters, D. Gareth. "Silences and Voices: Salvador Espriu, Montserrat Roig and the Experience of the Franco Years." *Tesserae: Journal of Iberian and Latin American Studies* 6.2 (2000): 181–94.

White, Hayden V. *The Content of the Form: Narrative Discourse and Historical Representation*. Baltimore: Johns Hopkins UP, 1987.

———. *Figural Realism: Studies in the Mimesis Effect*. Baltimore: Johns Hopkins UP, 1999.

———. "New Historicism: A Comment." *The New Historicism*. Ed. H. Aram Veeser. New York: Routledge, 1989. 293–302.

———. *Tropics of Discourse: Essays in Cultural Criticism*. Baltimore: Johns Hopkins UP, 1978.

Wilkerson, Isabel. *The Warmth of Other Suns*. New York: Random House, 2010.

Works Cited

Wing, Helen. "Deviance and Legitimation: Archetypal Traps in Roig's *La hora violeta*." *Bulletin of Hispanic Studies* 72.1 (1995): 87–96.

Woolf, Virginia. *A Room of One's Own*. 1929. Orlando: Harcourt, 1989.

Yoldi, José. "La fiscalía apoya que se persiga a los nazis." *El País* [Madrid] 15 July 2008: 12.

Yúdice, George. "*Testimonio* and Postmodernism." *The Real Thing: Testimonial Discourse and Latin America*. Ed. Georg M. Gugelberger. Durham, NC: Duke UP, 1996. 42–57.

Index

Afghanistan war, 173, 175
Aldecoa, Josefina, 32, 43, 96, 176
Al Qaeda, 172, 183
Amat-Piniella, Joaquim, 59–60, 82–83
Amnesty Law, 1977, 13, 64
Asociación para la Recuperación de la Memoria Histórica, 12, 175
assimilation, resistance of exiles to, 158–61, 163–64
Atocha train station terrorist attack, 171–72, 173, 176, 183–84
autobiography, 132–35, 190–91
Aznar, José María, 180, 182–83

Basques, 5–6, 33
    ETA, 171–72, 175–76
Beverley, John, 25, 40, 45–46, 62
Bhabha, Homi, 8, 145–46
Blanco Aguinaga, Carlos, 4, 7–8, 21, 30, 32, 33, 37–38, 94, 173, 177, 183, 184, 205–07. *See also Carretera de Cuernavaca*; "Otros tiempos"; "Sobre el exilio"
    autobiographical writing by, 133–34
    childhood of, 33–34, 138–39, 156–58
    on children's view of Spanish Civil War, 155–56
    exile identity and, 132–33, 144–47
    genre fusion and, 136–38, 140, 142, 153, 161, 163, 167, 206–07
    on language and literature of exiles, 164–66
    on nationality and personal identity, 149–50
    otherness and, 145–47
    postwar experiences and writing of, 35–36
    problems of second-generation exiles and, 153–69

    on resistance to assimilation, 158–61, 163–64
    writing style of, 139–40, 147–48

Carretera de Cuernavaca (Blanco Aguinaga), 37–38, 139–40, 145, 151, 153–69
    challenges of second-generation exiles portrayed in, 153–69
    on children's view of Spanish Civil War, 155–56
    exile identity portrayed in, 145
    genre fusion joining "Otros tiempos," "Sobre el exilio," and, 136–38, 140, 142, 153, 161, 163, 167, 206–07
    on language and literature of exiles, 164–66
    protagonist modeled on Blanco Aguinaga, 162–63
Catalans, 44, 49–50
    deported after the Spanish Civil War, 48–49, 82–84
    female, 50–51
    nationalism, 54–55
    in Nazi concentration camps, 47–48 (*See also catalans als camps nazi, Els*)
    postwar life of, 76–78
    subjugated under Franco, 5–6
    testimonial writing by, 43–44
catalans als camps nazi, Els (Roig), 14, 64, 69, 70, 73, 79, 80, 191, 212n20
    collective memory and, 64–65, 68–69
    genre fusion joining *L'hora violeta* and, 51–52, 62–63, 69–70, 81, 85–86
    individual testimonies in, 57–58
    publication of, 54–55
    relationship to reality, 66–67
    Roig's authoritative presence in, 56–57, 60–65
    as testimonial literature, 48, 51, 52–69

Index

Cercas, Javier, 16–17, 32, 176
Civil War, 1936–39. *See* Spanish Civil War, 1936–39
Cohn, Dorrit, 23–24, 27–28
collective memory, 9–10, 15–16
  José F. Colmeiro on, 92–93
  Maurice Halbwachs on, 9–10
  through *El cuarto de atrás*, 113–15
  through *Els catalans als camps nazi*, 64–65, 68–69
Colmeiro, José F., 15–16, 92–95
courtship customs, 110, 116–25
cuarto de atrás, El (Martín Gaite), 34, 37, 88, 90, 93, 94, 97, 116, 118, 120, 123, 179, 196
  accolades for, 98
  blending of genres, 100–02
  collective memory through, 113–15
  as fantastic interruption of history, 102–15
  as fantastic novel, 100, 101–02, 128–30
  genre fusion joining *Usos amorosos de la postguerra española* and, 95–97, 101–03, 109–10, 117, 120, 129–30
  structure of, 104–05

destape, 5
diaspora. *See* exiled Spaniards
Dupláa, Christina, 45–46, 55, 60, 62

El País, 10–12, 35, 171–72, 178–79
ETA, 171–72, 175–76
exiled Spaniards, 12, 34, 48–49, 82–84. *See also* Blanco Aguinaga, Carlos; *Carretera de Cuernavaca*; *catalans als camps nazi, Els*; *hora violeta, L'*; Spanish Civil War, 1936–39
  autobiographical accounts of, 132–35
  Carlos Blanco Aguinaga as, 132–33
  critical reception of writing by, 144–45
  critical study of writing by, 132–33
  education of, 164
  generational definitions of, 131–32
  genre fusion in writing of, 136–38, 142
  identity, 131–40, 144–47, 149–50
  language and, 164–66
  narratives of, 147–48
  nationality of, 149–50
  otherness of, 145–47
  problems of second-generation, 153–69
  resistance to assimilation, 158–61, 163–64
  restrictions on participation in Mexican life, 143–44
  self-doubt of, 152–53

fiction. *See also* Spanish literature
  conflict between history and, 99–100
  defined, 18–19
  fusion with history, 1–4, 15, 72–74, 177
  historical (*See* historical fiction)
  inclusion of representations of the real in, 197–203
  primacy of historiography over historical, 21–22
  revaluation of marginalized voice in historiography and, 25–26
  self-referentiality of postmodern Spanish, 16–17, 36
  strict boundaries separating history from, 23–24
Franco, Carmen, 87–89, 109

Index

Franco, Francisco, 5, 6, 11, 18
  Catalan exiles under, 48–49
  death and funeral of, 54–55, 87–89, 112
  Javier Marías on, 181–82
  postwar Spanish society embodied by, 120–22
  women subjugated under, 12, 33–34, 106–07

genre fusion, 1–4, 15, 16, 17–18, 26–27
  democratization of history and, 26
  divergent experiences of authors in, 32–38
  exile writing and, 136–38, 142
  the fantastic in, 128–30
  goal of, 20–21
  history, fiction, and narrative in, 18–22
  joining *Carretera de Cuernavaca*, "Otros tiempos," and "Sobre el exilio," 136–38, 140, 142, 153, 161, 163, 167, 206–07
  joining *Els catalans* and *L'hora violeta*, 51–52, 62–63, 69–70, 81, 85–86
  joining *Tu rostro mañana* and *El oficio*, 184–86, 191, 202–03
  joining *Usos amorosos de la postguerra española* and *El cuarto de atrás*, 95–97, 101–03, 109–10, 117, 120, 129–30
  New Historicism and, 25–26
  as part of literary and historical "re-awakening," 206–07
  primacy of historiography over historical fiction and, 21–22
  truth and, 202–03

Halbwachs, Maurice, 9
Herzberger, David, 15, 31, 89, 90, 202

historical fiction, 19
  borrowing from historical narratives, 24–25
  truth value and, 27–29
historical memory, 9–18
  José F. Colmeiro on, 92–93
  Pact of Silence and, 13–14
  recuperation of, 15–16
historiography, 19, 211n18
  autobiography and, 132–35
  Carlos Blanco Aguinaga and, 137–38, 153
  Carmen Martín Gaite and, 98–100, 117–18
  democratization of history and, 26
  exile writing and, 135–38
  the fantastic in, 128–30
  Francoist, 89–90
  Montserrat Roig and, 51–52
  narrative, 20, 35, 51–52, 114–15, 117–18, 174–75, 185–86
  primacy over historical fiction, 21–22
  revaluation of marginalized voice in fiction and, 25–26
  truth value and, 27–29
history, 16, 19–20
  Carmen Martín Gaite and the uses of, 96–102
  collective memory and, 9–10, 64–65, 68–69, 92–93, 113–15
  conflict between fiction and, 99–100
  as dynamic confluence of public and private lives, 97–98
  editorializing of, 178–85
  effect of the novel on, 6–7
  fusion with fiction, 1–4, 72–74, 177
  literature at the margins of postwar Spain and, 4–9
  postmodern collapse of traditional generic boundaries and, 15

237

Index

historiography *(continued)*
  revisionist, 30–31
  strict boundaries separating fiction from, 23–24
  truth and subjective interpretation of, 202
  truth value of, 27–29
Hitler, Adolf, 48, 125
hora violeta, L' (Roig), 14, 37, 47–48, 51, 57, 67–68, 187, 191
  as fictional framing of historiography, 69–86
  genre fusion joining *Els catalans* and, 51–52, 62–63, 69–70, 81, 85–86
  history and fiction as discrete entities in, 73–74
  interactions between literature and history in, 70
  Norma, as double of Montserrat Roig in, 70–71, 84–85
  "La novel-la de l'hora violeta" within, 74–78
  untrustworthy memory in, 72–73
Hutcheon, Linda, 2, 23, 26–27

identity, exile, 131–40, 144–47
  nationality and, 149–50
  self-doubt and, 152–53
intentionality in historical fiction and narrative historiography, 24–25
Iraq war, 173, 180–81, 183, 190

Juan Carlos I, King of Spain, 68–69, 216n3

Labanyi, Jo, 9, 12, 16, 31, 44–45, 93
Law of Historical Memory, 2007, 11, 12, 13, 93, 176, 209n4

Marías, Javier, 4, 7–8, 21, 30, 32, 33, 38, 94, 133, 163, 197, 205–07. *See also oficio de oír llover, El; Tu rostro mañana*
  autobiography and, 190–91
  comparison of contemporary Spain with Spanish Civil War era, 181–85
  early writing career of, 34–35
  editorializing history, 178–85
  El País Semanal column, 11–12, 172, 179
  father of, 190, 196, 218n15. *See also* Marías, Julián
  on fictionalized representation of the real, 197–203
  genre fusion and, 184–06, 191, 202–03
  on intermingling of fiction and history, 177
  narrative historiography by, 174–75, 185–86
  postwar experiences and writing of, 35–36
  on the Spanish Civil War, 181–85
  on terrorism, 171–73, 179
  on the Transition period, 177–78
Marías, Julián, 190, 196, 218n15
Martín Gaite, Carmen, 4, 7–8, 21, 30, 32, 33, 37, 133, 141, 163, 173, 177, 179, 183, 184, 196, 205–07. *See also cuarto de atrás, El; Usos amorosos de la postguerra española*
  accolades for writing of, 98
  genre fusion and, 95–97, 101–03, 109–10, 117, 120, 129–30
  childhood of, 33–34, 96, 106–08, 112
  collective memory and, 113–15
  as correction to Colmeiro's view of historical memory, 95
  on courtship customs, 110, 116–25
  education of, 96, 106

the fantastic in writings by, 128–30
funeral of Francisco Franco and, 87–88
historiography and, 98–100, 117–18
history as subjective and writing of, 91–93
nonconformity of, 106–07, 123–24
postwar experiences and writing of, 35–36
as social realist, 90–91
stream-of-consciousness used by, 110
uses of history and, 96–102
view of history as dynamic confluence of public and private, 97–98
memory
collective, 9–10, 15–16, 64–65, 92–93, 113–15
democratization of history and minority, 26
efforts to forget and, 80–81
historical, 9–18
untrustworthy, 72–73
Mexico, 132–34
exile identity in, 144–47, 149–50
exiles restrictions on participation in life in, 143–44
interactions between Mexicans and Spanish exiles in, 149–50
otherness in, 145–47
problems of second-generation exiles in, 153–69
resistance to assimilation in, 158–61
Spanish Republican party in, 149

narrative, 20, 22–23
nonreferential, 23
testimonial literature and, 39–47

narrative historiography, 20, 35
borrowings from historical fiction, 24–25
Carlos Blanco Aguinaga and, 141, 148, 167
Carmen Martín Gaite and, 114–15, 117–18
Javier Marías and, 174–75, 177–78, 185–86
Montserrat Roig and, 51–52, 57, 69
nationalism, Catalan, 54–55
nationality and personal identity, 149–50
Nazi concentration camps, 12, 14, 28, 34–35, 39. *See also catalans als camps nazi, Els; hora violeta, L'*
New Historicism, 25–26, 31, 210n14
New York Times, The, 172, 183
novel, the, 6–7. *See also* Spanish literature
conflict with history, 100–02
fictionalized representation of the real in, 197–203
testimonial literature and, 39–40
novela rosa, 113, 120, 124, 126–27

oficio de oír llover, El (Javier Marías), 180–81, 183, 184–85, 190
genre fusion joining *Tu rostro mañana* and, 184–06, 191, 202–03
Orinoco (ship), 138
otherness, 145–47
"Otros tiempos, otros espacios en la narrativa española del exilio en América" (Blanco Aguinaga), 140–47, 151–52, 163, 167, 216n20
genre fusion joining *Carretera de Cuernavaca,* "Sobre el exilio" and, 136–38, 140, 142, 153, 161, 163, 167, 206–07

239

Index

Pact of Silence, 13–14, 64, 175–76
País, El. See *El País*
Popular Party (Partido Popular) (PP), 171–72, 176, 212n1
Prados, Emilio, 139, 141, 142

Rajoy, Mariano, 171–72, 212n1
Real Academia Española, 173, 178, 197, 201
revisionist history, 30–31
Ricoeur, Paul, 13, 23, 24–25, 100, 137, 202
Roig, Montserrat, 4, 7–8, 14–15, 21, 30, 32, 33, 37, 93, 133, 163, 173, 177, 183, 184, 191, 205–07. *See also catalans als camps nazi, Els; hora violeta, L'*
    Catalan exiles and, 48–49
    on Catalan identity, 49–50
    dual role as journalist and novelist, 47–52
    genre fusion and, 51–52, 62–63, 69–70, 81, 85–86
    as historian, 65–66
    on interactions between literature and history, 70
    politics of feeling and, 45
    postwar experiences and writing of, 35–36
    reality-based topics addressed by, 50–51
    on relationship of her work to reality, 66–67
    testimonial writing by, 43–47
    testimony as representation of history texts by, 45–46
    use of narrative historiography, 51–52, 57, 69
Russell, Peter, 188–89, 191, 200–01, 218n15, 218n18

self-referentiality of postmodern Spanish fiction, 16–17, 36
Sinaia (ship), 131, 148

"Sobre el exilio español en México" (Blanco Aguinaga), 147–53, 163, 216n23
    genre fusion joining *Carretera de Cuernavaca*, "Otros tiempos," and, 136–38, 140, 142, 153, 161, 163, 167, 206–07
Soldados de Salamina (Cercas), 16–17, 32, 176
Spain. *See also* Catalans; exiled Spaniards; Spanish Civil War, 1936–39; Transition, 1975–82
    Amnesty Law, 1977, 13, 64
    collective memory in, 9–10, 92–93
    courtship customs, 110, 116–25
    ETA and, 171–72, 175–76
    feminism in, 50, 95
    fiction/history debate beyond, 22–32
    global, 178–85
    historiography of Francoist, 89–90
    Law of Historical Memory, 2007, 11, 12, 13, 93, 176, 209n4
    memory renaissance in, 4
    postwar, transition, and democracy in, 4–9
    terrorism and, 171–73
    World War II and, 12, 14
Spanish Civil War, 1936–39, 4–6, 32, 91, 112. *See also* exiled Spaniards
    authors' experiences and, 32–38
    Catalans' experiences during, 74–75
    children's view of, 155–56
    collective memory and, 11
    investigations into, 175
    mass exile after, 12
    Nationalist victory, 131–32
    vencidos of, 173–74, 175

Spanish literature, 205–07. *See also* genre fusion
  autobiographical, 132–35, 190–91
  enjoyed by women and girls, 126–27
  fictionalized representation of the real in, 197–203
  fusion of history and fiction in, 1–4
  historical memory and, 9–18
  historical understanding through, 7–9
  the novel in, 6–7
  self-referentiality of postmodern, 16–17, 36
  social realism in, 90–91
  testimonial, 39–47, 135–36 (*See also catalans als camps nazi, Els*)
  transition period, 30–32

terrorism
  by Al Qaeda, 172, 183
  Atocha train station, 171–72, 183
  by ETA, 171–72, 175–76
  Iraq war and, 180–81
  Javier Marías on, 171–73, 179
  World Trade Center attack, 172, 175
testimonial literature, 39–47
  defined, 39–41
  Els catalans als camps nazi as, 52–69
  exile experience and, 135–36
  insight through, 44–45
  by Montserrat Roig, 43–47
  personal authorial "I" in, 43
  as representation of history in Roig's texts, 45–46
  truthfulness of, 41–42
  voices of marginalized authors in, 44
Todorov, Tzvetan, 2, 100, 105–06

Transition, 1975–82, 5–7, 49, 177–78
  collective memory during, 93
  destape, 5
  Spanish literature during, 30–32
truth value, 27–29
Tu rostro mañana (Javier Marías), 38, 173, 174, 179–80, 184, 185–203
  fictionalized representations of the real in, 198–202
  genre fusion joining *El oficio* and, 184–06, 191, 202–03
  interpretation of Juan Deza's past in, 192–94
  investigation into the Civil War in, 185–91

Ugarte, Michael, 134–37, 168, 202
Usos amorosos de la postguerra española (Martín Gaite), 37, 88–89, 97, 104–05, 110, 111, 214n17
  accolades for, 98
  the fantastic in, 128–30
  genre fusion joining *El cuarto de atrás* and, 95–97, 101–03, 109–10, 117, 120, 129–30
  as narrative historiography, 114–15
  postwar society reinterpreted in, 115–30
  as sociological study, 115–16
  structure of, 119–20

vencidos, 173–74, 175

White, Hayden, 2, 22–24, 100, 202
  on exile writing, 136
  on historical content in narrative, 167
  on truth, 41
women and girls
  courtship customs and, 110, 116–25

women and girls *(continued)*
   exiled, 158–59
   fantasy life and, 124–28
   feminism and, 50, 95
   marginalization of Catalan, 50–51
   marriage and, 121–22, 126
   physical appearance of, 121, 122
   rebellion by, 123–24
   Spanish literature favored by, 126–27
   subjugated under Franco, 5–6, 12, 33–34, 106–07
World War II, 12, 14, 28, 35–36, 149. *See also catalans als camps nazi, Els*
World Trade Center attack, 172, 175

About the Book

Genre Fusion: A New Approach to History, Fiction, and Memory in Contemporary Spain
Sara J. Brenneis
PSRL 60

Although the boom in historical fiction and historiography about Spain's recent past has found an eager readership, these texts are rarely studied as two halves of the same story. With *Genre Fusion: A New Approach to History, Fiction, and Memory in Contemporary Spain*, Sara J. Brenneis argues that fiction and nonfiction written by a single author and focused on the same historical moment deserve to be read side-by-side. By proposing a literary model that examines these genres together, *Genre Fusion* gives equal importance to fiction and historiography in Spain. In her book, Brenneis develops a new theory of "genre fusion" to show how authors who write both historiography and fiction produce a more accurate representation of the lived experience of Spanish history than would be possible in a single genre.

Genre Fusion opens with a straightforward overview of the relationships among history, fiction, and memory in contemporary culture. While providing an up-to-date context for scholarly debates about Spain's historical memory, *Genre Fusion* also expands the contours of the discussion beyond the specialized territory of Hispanic studies. To demonstrate the theoretical necessity of genre fusion, Brenneis analyzes pairs of interconnected texts—one a work of literature, the other a work of historiography—written by a single author. She explores how fictional and nonfictional works by Montserrat Roig, Carmen Martín Gaite, Carlos Blanco Aguinaga, and Javier Marías unearth the collective memories of Spain's past. Through these four authors, *Genre Fusion* traces the transformation of a country once enveloped in a postwar silence to one currently consumed by its own history and memory. Brenneis demonstrates that when read through the lens of genre fusion, these Spanish authors shelve the country's stagnant official record of its past and unlock the collective and personal accounts of the people who constitute Spanish history.

About the Author

Sara J. Brenneis, Amherst College, teaches a diverse array of courses on contemporary Spanish culture. She has published scholarly articles in journals such as the *Bulletin of Hispanic Studies*, *Letras Femeninas* and *History & Memory* on the overlapping of history and fiction in Spanish literature. Dr. Brenneis's current work focuses on issues of historical memory in Spanish representations of the Holocaust.